SANCTUARY

KARI DUMOUCHEL PARKER

Grace and Mercy
727-543-9860
kari.dumouchel@gmail.com

Table of Contents

Sam was a sarcophagus and all I could see was
a dark abyss in his black eyes. His rapacious
appetite did not see me as human.

There was nothing to appeal to.

Foreward

The joy of reading has always been two-fold for me, escaping and learning. It's hard to separate the two because if a story is in the hands of a talented wordsmith, I learn from fully escaping into the experience of places I may never have been, situations I may never have encountered and people engaging in daily lives unlike those I may be familiar with. In that escape I can gain perspectives and "coattail" in decision making moments new to my own experience. Would I have done this or that, can I understand why a character made this decision, took these actions, etc? These are all questions that, whether consciously or subconsciously considered, I learn as much about myself as I do about the characters. Sanctuary took me deep into another world and I found myself slowing down my normal reading pace to actually savor this world.

At times I thought things progressed in ways that were typical for romance novels; the trials, good guys, bad guys, redemption … but while I had that reaction, I also realized that I didn't miss the filler so often used in storytelling. Books offer elements for escapism, but what I found that was really important to all these elements; life's struggles, romance, drama, horror, was the internal dialogue Tess maintained throughout. I walked in her shoes because the author created such a layered and fully realized character that even though I am nothing like Tess, for the time I spent immersed in the reading I understood her … and that brings me back to the learning.

As simplistic as it sounds, I learned about living a Christ-centered daily life while experiencing deeply sensual and thoughtful feelings about attraction and love. Tess is a fully realized woman with goals, friendships and challenges while constantly turning to God for direction and understanding. I would like to emulate her faith. I would like to *feel in love with Christ* … I confess I had never thought of my faith in those terms, just more in terms of thankfulness and forgiveness. Being *in love* goes beyond that. The author isn't preachy or judgmental … she is obviously like Tess herself. A real person pouring her faith and passions into a character in a somewhat fairytale existence. Again, I was able to escape and learn at the same time.

I highly recommend Sanctuary if you like action, romance and world-building … and are open to experiencing a truly Christian perspective that seems so much more relatable and realistic in emotion that so many of this genre lack. Plus, it was just an enjoyable and entertaining read.

Darla James

Chapter One

The Call

For I know the plans I have for you, plans for good
And not evil, to give you a future with hope..(*)

Salt Lake City lay below, a sprawling city that stretched out under the protective and watchful presence of the Wasatch Mountain range. I had come here looking for a new life.

As my plane landed and I collected my things preparing to de-plane, I mentally checked off my itinerary. First was luggage and then locate the car rental booth. I wasn't frightened. The plane trip had allowed me time to locate what I was feeling.

Years earlier I had felt a call to a ministry involving Native Americans 'somewhere' out West. But I had no clue as to where or what that meant. I wasn't a missionary. I was ready to begin a completely different chapter. I had recently divorced and something new was calling me. There was no longer any real obligation that held me to my life in Florida. If I was going to make a change, this was the time.

I had grown up in Florida. But I'd had an epiphany, a close encounter of the highest kind a few years earlier and experienced this 'call'. Inexplicably I felt drawn to the West. My vision was filled with images of red-brown mesas and valleys that rested against an evening outline; and for reasons not yet clear, I felt joy at this image ... the purpose of this vision and my future life here, however, was vague; there was nothing defined about it.

Familiarizing myself with the vehicle, I plotted a path heading north and made a left out of the airport in my rented SUV. My thought was to search for this 'call' in western Wyoming. With no clear direction in mind, I did have this sense that I would 'know' when I found the location for this next life. I believed there would be an inner connection to the place. As a child from a military family, I understood that some places became home while others always stayed unfamiliar. I also believed that there was a sovereign influence about our life's purpose and plan; I trusted that He would reveal, if not the whole picture, at least the next step.

When I thought of what might lie ahead, it was nondescript; a house maybe with a barn that leant itself to ministry opportunities. I was totally open for the adventure that lay ahead ... the possibilities. I considered a ranch. Even though, as a Floridian, I had no clear idea of how to run a ranch, or what that even involved, I had some confidence that I could learn. I believed that I was going to start a homestead that would become a safe harbor for the people I wanted to minister too, a sanctuary.

I felt energized with excitement and anticipation.

The open road always thrilled me. I loved an adventure and traveling by vehicle. There was an exhilarating freedom being able to go where I choose, stop when I wanted… no bosses or schedules that controlled time. It presented the prospect of mystery and challenge, testing, independence, and courage; new discoveries just ahead, around a bend in the road, over an ancient bridge, down a trail that sat timeless and quiet waiting for me to find and explore. Places where people unknown and foreign had and were living out their lives. We're all part of the human family where, irrespective of lifestyles and cultures, geography, and climate, we share inner hopes and wonderment about what life might hold ahead for us, expectant with our blank slates ready to be etched and painted, with developing hopes, desires, and the fulfillment of dreams. This trip spoke to my personal elemental and primal composition, those things that make me ME. I felt whatever lay ahead, it was a road I was intended to follow, the purpose for my life.

Soon I was out of the sprawling Salt Lake City limits and headed toward hills and mountains that loomed majestically ahead in the near distance. Looking through the windshield at these mountains, as darkness started to settle in, I was overwhelmed with their beauty. There was nothing like this in sunny Florida. My only real comparison to the greatness of these mountains in Florida would be the vast expanse of the oceans, stretching out towards the horizon, with their wide openness that raced eastward in the Atlantic and westward in the Gulf. But these mountains. Looking at them, I could feel their formidable strength, immovable and intimidating. They defined their horizons, and I felt a heartless indifference in them towards my frail endeavors. I knew their grounded granite that pinnacled toward the heavens would survive long after I was dust; and they reminded me I was in the Wild West, not the sunny tropics.

The road wound, dipped and climbed. As I passed homesteads and farms and wild white-water rivers surrounded by towering bluffs and wilderness, evening approached with darkness chasing a lit amber sky. Leaving Utah behind, I ventured into rural Wyoming. Communities started cropping up. Small towns and structures hiding lives behind their warm lights, worlds and lives unknown to me. I was fascinated by the local color and struck by the realization of the separation in my life experiences and theirs. The mountains made me feel small and these communities punctuated the fact that I was an outsider.

I decided to take 351 and head east catching 191 towards Bondurant. I chose a wayside Inn and settled in for the night.

Staying in hotels alone has always made me feel well *alone*. Families and couples populate these establishments, heightening my awareness of the distance of my own family and my aloneness. Oddly, sadness tugged at my heart. While I was filled with exhilaration about this new path, there was a counter emotion that harbored at the edges of my heart and wanted to bury me in grief and fear. I knew thoughts about the distance of my family and my world, if allowed, could reach out and overwhelm me and cripple this adventure.

After showering, I decided to find a local restaurant. Taking off on foot I soon found a mom-and-pop restaurant that offered home cooked food. I ordered food, wrote in my journal, and consulted maps for tomorrow's heading. As I sat there, portions of the community came and went, offering an opportunity to engage in a favorite pastime of mine, people watching.

I paused as I walked back to my hotel, staring up at the night Wyoming sky, this is a different world out here. Does my future lie out here?

After rising early at 6:00, I found myself standing in the hotel parking lot in the predawn fog, surveying the land. The morning was quiet; the air charged with prospects for the unfolding day. Watching the day wake, I felt a hushed reverence, this idea that I needed to respect its quiet, having no rights here, yet. I was alone. I liked being alone to some extent. I felt small yet exhilarated at the same time, like a child who has been released from parental control. Free to do whatever I wanted with the day. I owned the day.

As I travelled still north on a road taking me to Hoback Junction and the Grand Tetons, my thoughts mused over this aloneness and my life back home.

Traveling on a road that borders the Rocky Mountains, not far from the Wind River Indian Reservation seemed like a good place to look for the next chapter in my life. I planned to take the day to drive around. I passed through Hoback Junction and headed towards Jackson Hole, the Tetons and Yellowstone. I love this area. In the Tetons I took 26 east, through Moran and decided to find a hotel in Lander and check out the area.

Lander was a smaller community, and I liked its proximity to Jackson Hole, airports and yet it was rural and open. This would be a good place to camp out and headquarter for my daily excursions. Every day I headed out in different directions, taking paved highways that led to rural roads opening a whole world of possibilities. I met with a local realtor, Patty Trimble, associated with a family-owned realty company, Trimble Realty. She had grown up here and she knew everyone and could provide local color and information. Trimble Realty was located in a small office building on the main street. Outside it had a brick face and inside it had high ceilings, large ceiling fans and wooden beams. It smelled of years of use, old wood. There was a wild-west feel to it, the feeling I would expect entering an old saloon.

"May I help you?" asked Patty.

"Yes, I'm looking for property."

"What'd you have in mind?"

"Um, well, a homestead with land and perhaps some outbuildings."

"Are you interested in farming or ranching?"

"Neither just a home-site with space," I said smiling. I knew I was not giving her clear information, but it was the best description that *I* had.

She thought for a moment and said, "Well several places come to mind fitting that general description. I have a full calendar today but how 'bout we meet tomorrow mornin' and take a look at a few?"

"Great, thank you."

Every day the weather was crisp and clear, not a cloud in the wide Wyoming sky. The surrounding mountains captivated me. There was a magnetic quality about them, these looming sentinels that stretched skyward and wrapped themselves across the landscape; like paperweights, as though they held something back or were keeping something in.

During our excursions, I learned that Patty was 29 yrs old and single. She had an early, unsuccessful, and short-lived marriage to a local named Danny Paul. He was a rancher and did some logging. He was also a fixture in the community. I wondered about living in a community where you knew everyone, and they knew you. That exposure.

When not touring with Patty, scouring the countryside for homesteads, I ventured out exploring Jackson Hole and the Tetons. The town of Jackson interested me. This wasn't a town of skyscrapers and financial districts. It was a wild-west town that had matured. The town's proximity to the Tetons and

Yellowstone helped to fuel the local economy with a steady tourist industry. Jackson Hole felt more familiar to me. It embodied lifestyles from across the country that I could relate to. I felt less isolated. After finding a hotel, I set off in search of a restaurant, intending to soak up the town. Later I took a stroll looking for a little nightlife.

The night was cool and felt open, airy. I was wearing jeans and a light pullover sweater. This was April but the country had experienced one of the coldest winters on record and this chill still lingered in the night air. I was happy that I'd thought to bring a light jacket. The Stagecoach Steak and Grille seemed like a popular spot and a good place to people watch so I went in and ordered a glass of wine. It was busy and the nightlife was just starting to pick up. There was a heavy atmosphere, noisy and charged by an energetic clientele. A local band was playing and while I pulled out my journal attempting to compose the activities of my day, note my observations and collect my thoughts, I found it hard to keep my focus. Occasionally I'd look up watching the club's activities and the local residents. They were comprised mostly of a young crowd, enjoying one another and dancing to the band.

Inside the Stagecoach, the décor was western, with hanging saddles, bridles, and tack. Photographs of an earlier era covered the walls, and the entire interior was unfinished oak. The appeal was masculine and rustic, conveying the idea that the place had survived for generations. Jeremiah Johnson, Wyatt

Earp or Billy the Kid could have frequented the establishment. I could see Gus McCrae and Woodrow Call sitting at the bar.

I had taken a seat at a table secluded in the back corner, thinking to people watch and have a little privacy. Soon I noticed that I was not the only one people watching; I noticed that I was being observed by a group of men standing on the remote side of the bar, away from the band. As I finished my glass and closed my journal thinking this might signal a good time to leave, one of the gentlemen in the group had decided to approach me. He appeared to be in his mid-to-late 30's. As he approached, I noticed his friends were watchful of his activity. He approached me with confidence. I've always admired the courage that it takes to approach another person. I didn't want to be unkind in the face of his courage, but I was uneasy. Romance was not on the agenda. He appeared to be a professional, and had a polished businessman demeanor about him, did not present as a local rancher or farmer. He was attractive and I sensed that he had some history of success in this arena. His eyes stayed on me as he walked across the room.

"Excuse me. Do you mind if I interrupt?" he said as he reached my table. "I haven't seen you here before," he continued as he tilted his head to block out the noise. "Your local to the area or visiting?"

Wanting to discourage him, I kept my responses brief. "I'm just visiting and will be leaving in the morning." I said, starting to put away my journal.

Undeterred, he looked at my empty glass and continued, "Would you object to my buying you another glass of wine?"

I was getting the impression that he was not easily rejected. I am used to men approaching me, but I was in an unfamiliar setting, out of my element across the country, yet I couldn't think of anything to say that would extricate myself and so I allowed him to take a seat. He had a blonde Nordic handsomeness to his features. There was athleticism in his relaxed approach.

"My name is John. John Lawrence," he said this as he reached over to shake my hand and take his seat. He instantly made himself comfortable and I gathered that he planned to be here awhile.

"I'm Tess, nice to meet you." My mind was trying to formulate an exit plan. He may have experience with meeting women, but I had some experience with avoiding men.

"Where are you from?" he asked as he summoned the waitress and surveyed my face.

"I'm visiting from Florida."

"Florida? Hum, I've always wanted to visit Florida, land of sun and beaches." His eyes seemed to reflect on some distant memory. He smiled. "Where in Florida?" he asked, interested.

"The West coast."

"Are you here on vacation?" Undaunted by my lack of friendliness.

"Not exactly. Actually, I'm looking for real estate near Lander."

"Oh really?" he said, pinching his brow, "I rarely get over to Lander." He had a quizzical expression in his eyes. "Why Lander may I ask and why are you moving *from* Florida?" Cautious at this inquiry, the response seemed too complicated and offered too much information about me.

Choosing my comments, I replied, "I'm not sure why Lander and I really haven't made any decisions. I'm just looking. Do you live here and what do you do?" diverting the conversation away from myself.

"Yep, I'm a native, lived here all my life. I grew up here. I left once to attend law school," he said, peering around the waitress who had arrived to deliver our drinks. He ordered a Coors light, "but when I finished, I decided to return. My parents still lived here with my sisters and their husbands, and the area offered opportunities for legal work that appealed to me," he said shrugging. "I do criminal defense and the age group of the regular population here provides for a busy practice. A friend of mine already had a small practice here and so I joined him. It was an easy fit. And to be honest, I like it here." He smiled. I smiled too. The area is popular for extreme sports enthusiasts and *a living on the edge* genre, with lifestyles potentially rife with drugs, alcohol and run ins. I had worked with attorneys and so my comfort level with him was relaxing me.

"But you didn't answer why the move from Florida." He said as he took a sip from his beer, watching me.

I looked away, not sure I could explain 'why', I managed, "Just some wanderlust, I suppose, the sky is always greener somewhere pangs, really just looking." I shook my head and smiled. "I'm interested in your practice, tell me something about it."

He settled into a comfortable conversation about his practice. His partner was part of the group, and he pointed him out as one of his companions still standing near the bar. He discussed some of his recent cases. This energized him, and I could see passion for his work in his face. He was in his element. He liked a challenge that was easy to see. "I try to look at my work from the position that the people I represent are entitled to their day in court and I try to help them by giving them the best defense given their circumstances. I realize that some of my clients are guilty but that isn't my focus. I try to set my judgment aside and find the best line of defense to acquit or get a reduced sentence." He looked into my eyes, "I hate losing." He smiled a confident smile. It was contagious.

"Are you hungry?"

"No thanks, I've eaten."

"Then how about I escort you onto the dance floor?"

"Sorry, but I have no sense of rhythm, that grace went to my sisters." Smiling apologetically.

"You don't look like a woman without rhythm," he leaned in with an engaging smile.

Not sure what a woman with rhythm looked like, I said, "Seriously," I cocked my head, "No rhythm, no kidding." Smiling, I found myself enjoying his easy manner.

"Alright, alright, I'll let this go *this* time" he laughed.

The conversation turned to the local community and outdoor activities. This was another area where we had a shared interest. He seemed impressed when he learned about some of my adventurous vacation activities ~ I had done some backpacking, hiking, camping and whitewater rafting.

"I've been skiing since I was able to walk. My family loves to ski. Do you ski?" he asked.

"No. I am interested in skiing, but I just haven't been able to put together a trip to learn." I shook my head and shrugged. "The time has never been right. I started once or twice to plan a ski vacation, but it seems that there was always a deterrent that interfered with my plans."

"Well maybe I can help with that?"

I looked into his eyes. I thought about it. We both smiled.

"Perhaps if you find yourself out this way again, I could introduce you to the sport?" Our eyes locked on one another, both considering this prospect. "And since we already have this date for a dance, I could teach you to ski and dance all on one vacation! Have you had a better offer?" He looked at me innocently, as though this was do-able.

"No, I honestly can't remember a better offer, at the moment..." I said smiling as my eyes took in his face. "Okay... maybe... I don't know…" We both smiled.

He started to further this thought when his friends approached, and he was reminded that they had other plans for the evening. I was introduced to his friends; he seemed hesitant to leave. I couldn't tell if he was trying to think of some way to prolong the evening with me. I helped him out by gathering my things. Tomorrow, I planned to head back to meet up with Patty and if nothing was found, head back towards Salt Lake and a flight home. An end to the evening seemed wise.

Surprisingly, he was intent on making a connection with me. He wanted me to keep him in the loop should I find property and settle here. "Listen, here's my business card. I'd be interested in staying in touch," he said this with an earnest hopefulness that indicated an interest that was more than friendship. His friends gave him a quick look and started to move away. He gave me his business card and went to leave with his friends. As I stood up, I could see that he made a quick assessment of me. I felt warmth spreading across my cheeks. I have never been comfortable with that type of perusal.

During our conversation I had learned that John was 33 yrs old, divorced for several years, more or less; with two children, Maggie 9yr and John Jr. 11yrs. There was a hint that he was over the moon about his kids. My impression of him was confusing. Romance potentials throughout my life entered at times least expected or wanted. As is often the case with me, the timing was usually wrong. This seemed to be the case again. I tucked his card into my wallet, where it seemed destined for the annual purse and wallet housecleaning.

As I stepped outside into the night air, I felt flattered and didn't take it lightly that I was admired. I am grateful for attention. I had been married once and there had been several men encounters. They helped I think, because they offered the potential that romance was still on the horizon, always possible. But so far that special relationship has not happened.

Walking back to the hotel, my mind rewound the evening. I was smiling.

Chapter Two

Compelling ~ A Driving Force

I returned to the soupy Florida heat and home. The year came and went, and Patty Trimble had continued her search. She would routinely send me photos and real estate publications profiling available properties.

One day she called excited about a place that had just become available, she wanted me in on the first viewing. The prior owners had walked from the homestead falling on hard economic times. The homestead consisted of a three-story main house that included a barn and an adjacent building. The property sat nestled in a glade between the Rockies. There was a water source on the property, which consisted of 20 acres of hardwood stands of ancient woodlands. It offered the possibility of a ranch or a small farm. Arrangements were made to fly out.

In Patty's phone call she advised, "The property was abandoned by the Lewis'. They couldn't keep up with the mortgage. One day they were just gone. The place hasn't been empty for long, and I haven't had the chance to fully assess the property or house, but I did do a quick walk-through. They left the house clean, and it appears structurally sound. But there's not a lot of upgrades." She paused, "Tess, it looks a lot like the kind of homestead you said you were looking for. I really think it's worth taking a look."

When Patty called me in Florida to tell me the news of this available homestead, I was in the midst of putting my own home up for sale and working through years of roots. I had lived most of my life in Florida and this had been my home. An unexpected sense of loss hovered, and fear of the unknown. What was I doing? This was a big move and a big change. I had a great life. Surrounded by people that loved me and more importantly, that knew me. Thoughts that I did not *have* to *do* this ... Often, I had dreamt of living somewhere else and now it seemed that the West called ... The reality of this dream had wings, yet I felt paralyzed. Part of me wanted to retreat, stay *here*. But I also knew that at some point in my future I would come to regret the easy path and come to see it as a betrayal to myself. I knew I had to answer this 'call', get outside my safe zone. I couldn't let safe and familiar continue to run me.

I flew to Jackson Hole.

Patty met me at the airport. The following day we rode north out of Lander headed towards the Rockies.

As Patty chatted, I sat quietly taking in my surroundings. The forest outside my window transported me back to my days backpacking in the Smoky Mountains National Park. This reminded me of those trips; entering those woods and driving along a canopied highway that took me to my gateway, the entrance to the trailhead. The anticipation of isolation, the remoteness of my proximity to any humanity was always a thrill and this reminded me of that. This felt familiar.

As the car turned into the drive, I got my first glimpse of the house. It sat surrounded by huge Bur Oaks and White Popular trees. Stepping out of the car I stood still under its shadow. The house was three stories, sheltered by the large Oaks. This was a lot of house. Standing still, I got a sense of the mood of the place, peaceful, protected.

The house was turn of the century old, with oak hardwood floors on every floor. Double front entry doors were directly ahead. Patty unlocked the front door, and it swung open to reveal a large hallway. Stairs leading to the second floor rose upward to the left. The first floor consisted of a living room with a fireplace, a library, and a kitchen that exited to a rear deck. Both rooms are fronted by large bay windows. Light in a home is important. I walked around the house taking in everything, filing it away for later review.

There were four bedrooms on the second floor with a single bathroom. That seemed inconvenient and might be a remodeling project. The third floor was a fifth bedroom with a bath. The stairs leading to it were steep and located down at the far-right end of the second-floor landing. On the third floor, the walls were lowered on two sides to meet the pitched roof. On the main floor the kitchen was a ranch style, small and straight with little imagination. It could use more space and updated appliances. My mind started working on another remodeling project. Doors from the dining room opened onto the rear deck. Looking out from the back deck a barn was visible. A barn. What am I going to do with a barn? Later.

I liked the house. I had a lot to think about as Patty and I drove back into town. We discussed the possibilities.

Being here brought to mind another subject, so on our drive back to Lander I asked, "This may be a crazy question coming from a Southerner, I'm curious about how people live in such a remote setting. Where I live, we practically live in one another's living rooms, you can reach out a window and brush your neighbors' teeth or check their mail…. I guess I'm trying to get my head around some of the isolation that separates lives here. How do people handle isolation?" I asked, a little concerned. "Not only the isolation but what do you do about medical emergencies?"

"You're talking about the homesteads outside Lander, most have grown up here, been here for generations. It's a way of life, what we know," replied Patty. "I suppose we handle life here by being prepared. Most know some first aid, and we take care of each other. Our first responders are exceptional and most everyone has some medical know-how; or has a family member that has been a first responder. We have police, medical clinics and the regional hospital nearby." I could see she was thoughtfully reviewing her community. She looked over at me, "We're a close-knit group in the sense of emergency situations, but we are also an independent group, we like our privacy and I suppose we've developed a certain amount of confidence in ourselves, our personal abilities. Suppose we have too. Honestly, don't think many 'round here give this that much thought. It's what life is out here."

"How do people from other locations transition here?"

"Most keep their homes here as second residences. The winters here can be hard, and it takes some getting used to … some take to it, some don't." Patty reasoned.

As she drove it was the first time that I had seen any Native Americans. A pickup truck was waiting at an intersection for us to pass. I was startled. I could barely make out the appearance of the driver but what I could make out appeared strong and wild. As we passed, his windows were down and for a fleeting moment our eyes met.

Patty knew him. Clint Pierre.

Something I couldn't name shifted in me when I saw him.

I quizzed her on the Native American population. "What should I expect? Are there any cultural differences that I should be aware of?"

"Many work the land and own livestock. They're good horsemen and mostly they keep to themselves. I don't usually go on the rez. I like the Arapaho. I've never had any problems. I don't know, we have always lived near them and vice versa, so can't even say that it impacts me much, or anyone else." She looked over at me matter-of-factly, "I wouldn't expect much contact with them, but I also don't think you'll have any problems." She was quiet then continued, "Most around here farm or ranch and have for generations. It's most of our way of life. We pretty much co-exist."

She stared out her window then looked over at me smiling, "Most of our excitement around here concerns locals. Every once in a while, there's a weekend run-in that usually involves alcohol and local bars, breaks up the monotony. Something to talk about on Monday." She smiled.

I was curious, "Have you ever wanted to leave?"

"Yeah, sure. I think about it but just never seem to get around to any real effort to make that happen. My folks and brothers live here, and I suppose I'm comfortable. I love the area. This is God's country," she said, her head nodding towards the landscape outside the windshield. "I'm used to it here. The winters can be hard and long but they're what I know, I suppose. And if I get bored my friends and I go to Jackson for entertainment and variety and so I guess it all works for me." She looked over at me. "I'm curious about you and this move. I understand it a little, but I am not sure I can relate to it. You're doing this alone, leaving family? Did you grow up in Florida?"

The *alone* comment struck me.

"Mostly, it's where my roots have been, but I think that in the back of my mind I never thought that I would live out my life there. With regards to the move, I'm not sure I understand it myself. It's like a *compelling*. Like a force that's driving me. Not sure what I can relate it to that would make this clearer. The only thing that comes to mind would be a missionary that feels this compelling to take off for the mission field. Many speak about a *calling* that had arrested them. They almost can't do anything else but go; something that they *must* do." I searched my brain for a better description, "Does that make it any clearer?" I asked, looking over at Patty, I could see she was mulling this over trying to place this in some familiar setting. It wasn't that clear to me either. Decided to give up on this explanation.

"I get it, I think," she started, "I've thought about moving, but can't really say it's a calling, as you describe, more of a whimsical fantasy or at times just a need for change. Things can get close here, if a romance goes bad, fall on hard times … as you mentioned earlier, hard to be anonymous, it might be harder to put some things behind you because everyone knows."

We sat silent, both taking thoughts down private roads.

"Curious about what you do for a living," Patty said, breaking the silence.

"I worked as a paralegal."

She looked over at me with a quizzical expression on her face. I could see that she was trying to put that occupation in this neighborhood; but guessing that further conversation about work opportunities wouldn't be a good tactical move.

As I left, I told her I would get back with her soon on my decision.

I flew home.

Chapter Three

Permissive Will

I needed to be sure of this move; certain that this was God's will and not some romantic sentiment that could very easily derail me. This could be a serious mistake that could take years to rectify, not to mention costly.

While making coffee one morning, standing in my kitchen, my best friend, Madeleine (Maddy), popped in on one of her frequent visits. I decided to feel her out about this move.

"What do you honestly think about my plans to move?" I said as I turned to look at her. "I'm struggling with this decision. I know it's partly cold feet but," I started rubbing my temples, "I can't seem to get a firm assurance that this is the right thing for me." I needed to be honest with the depth of my fear about this to her. "When I am *here*, I feel this 'call' out *there*, but when I am there things feel unfamiliar, I feel scared and want to be home." I said this perplexed.

We stood looking at one another, "Ya know?" she said looking over at me, sighing heavily as though she had sensed the difficulty this decision was causing me, "Rob and I talk often about moving out of state too. More remote areas to raise the kids. Traffic's a nightmare, prices keep going up. It isn't the Florida where I grew up. Even the beach situation. When was the last time you went to the beach and enjoyed them. It takes forever to get there, hotels line the beaches with little access, parking lots and meters ..." she said, shaking her head and staring at her feet.

It was true, things in Florida had changed a lot over the years. I finished making coffee and we moved to the living room, settling in for a visit. I curled up in the corner of the loveseat with my feet tucked up under me, sipping my coffee and pondering my misgivings.

She continued, "Tess, it's not as though you can't come back. And we'll come for visits. The place sounds wonderful, very similar to what you said you were looking for. I'm looking forward to seeing it." She seemed more excited about this than I felt at the moment.

"Fear of things scare me and trying new things is right up there." I said looking in her face, "It keeps me grounded in safe areas, even if it isn't where I want to be or what I want to do. It really has kept me from exploring what I want in life. I guess I need to know if my reservation is my continuing problem with fear, because I know I need to overcome that, or if its wisdom telling me not to go. I need a sign." I looked at my friend, shook my head and smiled weakly. It was a bright, sunny, Florida day and sunbeams streamed in filling the room through the large front windows. It gave the room a warm, friendly feeling. It was always a comfortable place to sit and talk.

"Well, don't you think this visit was *that*? A sign? You've been through a pretty messy time. Change and new surroundings may be just the ticket. Think of it as an adventure, 'a finding Tess' adventure. You may never have another shot at this, a time to explore life and find your calling." She looked out the window, "Most of us get tied down to life's furniture, handcuffs… careers, mates, children, mortgages; all the usual suspects that anchor you to one place." She looked back at me, "I kinda envy you this freedom to fly. It's exciting and even a bit romantic," she said smiling.

Smiling at her life's metaphors, I took a closer look at my friend, picturing shackles while serving kids breakfast and a handcuffed chauffeur. Knew she loved, loved her family and she was blessed to have found early *that* love, Rob. Still, none of that, I realized looking at her, answered all of life's plans or hopes. She wouldn't trade 'em, but …she has regrets? Here, I am pouring out my stuff and she has hers.

"Anything you want to share? Nothing going on with me could ever mean I don't have time for you."

"I'm not being dramatic ~ it isn't my meaning. I'm good. I have it all and know it. Nope, just trying to help you find your path. Mine's good."

"Okay," studying her face. "I don't want to over think this or over talk this or even over analyze this, I would just be happy with certainty."

She nodded "I get it. You're grounded here and this is a big move. Tess, you've talked about moving somewhere else for years and the doors are opening. You've always said that open doors are a sign of God's permissive will and our obligation is to step through them? Right? When God wants them closed, He'll close them." She's looking at me for affirmation to the truth of my lifelong theology.

I nodded my head in agreement.

"Honestly, it all seems as though it has His stamp, and I really think you'll regret not going." She paused, "Hey, if you blow all your money, I can always use a live-in babysitter."

We both smiled. Not sure she and I could live together. I adored her but she is me, and I am a handful.

"Look, there is always the phone and a flight home. Try it. Give it a year or two. If you know you can leave it may make staying easier. You have *options*. No one is consigning you to a prison on a remote island. You can always sell."

Hearing things said out loud helped me to get a handle on them, get perspective and insight.

"This is your time," she continued. "I've never really seen this fear in you and have never seen you shy away from anything. I honestly think you'll regret not going."

Our conversation turned to lighter matters. She and Rob had plans for a well-earned weekend date-night.

I'll go.

The move to Wyoming was a production. The house sold. The amount I received on the sale of the house allowed me to buy the property in Wyoming outright and have a small stash for some remodeling. I also had my savings. Work was another chapter in my life. I was leaving a place I had worked at for many years. I didn't want to face the tears and goodbyes. But even *this* grief had to have its time. Some of my best friends worked here and I was leaving them behind. I was looking forward to being on the other side of this plan and its pain.

The sheer busyness of the packing and moving helped. I had two dogs in tow, and I was moving a house full of a lifetime's accumulations.

Close friends, Chuck and Anna, accompanied me on my move out West. We caravanned, following a moving van, Chuck driving a U-Haul and I followed in my car. Maddy and Rob planned to fly out in a week to help me settle in. I think we all felt much more comfortable having everyone involved in my move. I needed their support and they needed to connect with my new home and life.

There were no friends there unless I counted Patty.

As I drove west, I felt comfortable with the move, certain that I was making the right decision. It felt right. I did not think that *right* meant perfect, I knew better, but I did believe that there was a plan for our lives and when we lived it, it felt this way.

We finally arrived after a week on the road. Chuck and Anna took an immediate liking to the homestead. Between the three of us we got the house semi ready. We made several visits to Lander for goods, food, and stuff. Always stuff. We found the local grocery store.

Dogs were another matter. I owned a husky, Kai. The call of the wild was always at the center of his mindset. I had finally purchased a shock collar back in Florida to introduce restraint into his deliberations and bring sanity into the home. I was given Kai as a young 2-year-old adolescent, and he was always running off and usually the neighborhood got involved in the chase. Everyone knew my dogs (by name) but I don't think that that leant to any thought that they would be missed. The collar helped and I knew without fencing on this Wyoming property that this collar would become a fixture until he could acclimate and settle into a routine and boundaries. Sprite, the female dog of the duo, was a pit-bull hound-dog mix. She was three legged but that was not an issue for her. She had enough pit-bull in her that she held her own in any setting. Her problem was her stubbornness; she could be absolutely immovable. That's my family.

Happily, the prior owners had cared for the homestead and the issues facing me were more of personal taste along with renovation projects, enlarging and updating the kitchen and installing new decks.

Here Patty was a huge help. She recommended Clint Pierre, the native American in the pickup truck I saw that day, was it a year ago? "He's well known for his work, Tess. I would trust him to work on my house." She trusted him and I trusted her.

He turned out to be a gifted carpenter.

I had flown to Jackson Hole prior to the move to meet with him. The plan was to meet at the house to discuss renovations. This gave me a chance to get acquainted with my new home, feel its energy.

Shortly after arriving at the house, I heard his pick-up truck drive onto the property. I found myself nervous remembering the internal shift I felt that day with his appearance in the truck.

Curious about him, I watched as he exited his vehicle and approached the house. He walked with a straight-backed easy stride. I greeted him at the front door. His height and broad shoulders filled the doorway; intense dark eyes met my gaze as I opened the front door. When he entered the house, from the way he carried himself, he immediately exuded a quiet strength and masculine confidence that made me take a step back. There was economy in his movement, and as I came to find out, he was a man that didn't waste words.

Introductions over, with a simple nod from him; I led him through the house. His eyes took in everything with focused attention. In the kitchen his calloused hands examined door frames, checking the bones of the house. He didn't talk, just listened to my ideas on renovations.

Finally, he spoke, "The house is solid," he said in a low deep voice. "It has good bones," his dark eyes penetrating as he studied my face … He clarified my ideas on the renovations, then asked, "When did you plan to start?"

We agreed on a plan for the renovations and finalized a start date.

When we finally arrived, I found that Clint had made significant progress. You could see the integrity in his work, his craftmanship. However, getting to know him was another matter. I found him distant, aloof. Yet, he and Chuck struck up an easy relationship. I heard them talking one day. They were discussing the land, briefly touching on its history. Listening, I saw the land differently through his eyes, the stewardship, kinship Clint felt for the land, not ownership.

I found myself studying him when he wasn't looking.

Maddy and Rob arrived the next week. Maddy, Anna and I made short work of most of the move-in projects. Every day we took walks, roaming and exploring the property. My friends walking the property with me helped me familiarize myself with the land.

"I like it here. Don't think about Florida for a while, give this place a chance to grow on you" Maddy advised. "Honestly, I get scared having you this far away because I rely on you so much for support." Maddy, Anna and I have been friends since fifth grade. "A lot of that is phone support and we still have that. Right?" She looked at me with total sincerity, then at Anna for confirmation. "It takes time for a place to become a home, doesn't it? Give this place that opportunity." I knew this was hard on her too. She was almost a twin soul to me.

One morning while making breakfast, Maddy and Anna joined me in the kitchen. Anna commented, "What do you know about Clint?"

"Very little."

"Will he still be working here after we're gone? Seems the strong silent type." I wasn't sure I was detecting concern, or just interest.

"I don't know, I think so. Yeah, I know. Not big on conversation, but Chuck seems to be able to get him talking and smiling and according to Patty, he has a good reputation, if it's a concern for *me* I'm detecting."

"Yeah, I can see the workmanship, and it is great but you're so, and I hate to say this, but well, isolated. Have you thought about purchasing a gun, just for protection? Not that I'm saying you have anything to fear or that Clint has some nefarious purpose, but just to have." Pausing, she then leaned in to add, "But I also have to say that from a strictly female perspective, he's not hard on the eyes."

I took a quick look at her and past her outside on the deck. Clint was not in my field of vision. He had put me off with his behavior and so this thought had not really occurred to me.

Stepping into the easier topic, "I've always thought that my having a weapon was tantamount to my furnishing my intruder with a gun. Never comfortable that I had the strength or fortitude to use a gun and that any hesitation might be a big mistake."

"Okay, but given your current situation, you may want to revisit that." Still pushing, "Soooo, do you think that Clint is attractive?" She turned to Maddy with a knowing look as though this had already been a topic of discussion between them and Maddy gave a nod and a wink.

I stopped cooking and thought about the man, "Yeah," visualizing Clint. "There's a certain formidable presence around him but truthfully, he has been so closed towards me that I see that quality more when I see him. Not sure he likes me much, so I tend to avoid him. Doesn't really lend itself to other thoughts about the guy."

"Okay, okay, okay, whatever…" Anna chuckled. "Still … By the way, did I tell you both who I saw a few weeks ago?"

"Hun-un…"

"Remember Adriana from high school?"

"Sure, the girl that had it all in high school, cheerleader, homecoming queen, you name it, she owned it."

Anna nodded, "Man, things have changed with her. She was at the shelter where I volunteer standing in the food line. I hardly recognized her. She looked ravaged; open sores, skin thin and gaunt, hazy, distant stare … I waited until she found a seat and stopped by her table. I introduced myself and asked if I could join her? She barely looked at me but nodded. I sat down and tried to strike up a conversation. She wouldn't speak. I told her that I was here every week, if she needed anything. It's hard to know how to help."

"I know. Funny how things change after high school." I mused out loud. "The minute it's over the world shifts and what mattered then no longer matters. Sorry to hear that about her. What happened?"

"Drugs apparently." Added Maddy with a knowing look.

"I remember her, beautiful, talented, and funny. Wow, frightening, if that could happen to her … I remember her, she was the star of the senior high school play." I looked up remembering. "It was about Helen Keller. She played Helen. She and the girl that played Anne Sullivan went from classroom to classroom acting out a scene from the play. Her confidence was intimidating. I don't recall drugs associated with her in school. How'd that happen?"

"Oh wow, that's right," commented Maddy.

"Not sure really, rumor is some guy she fell for introduced her to drugs, but I'm not sure of that," said Anna.

I wondered about that beautiful girl, how her life could upend so tragically.

Chapter Four

Good is Ahead

The home was surrounded by woodland that backed up to scenic mountain peaks and grilling out seemed a good way to enjoy the out-of-doors in this Wyoming wilderness. On one cookout it was decided to have a bonfire to celebrate my new beginning and the finished first phase of the renovation. Chuck asked Clint and his helpers if they'd care to join us, and they accepted. We were introduced to Duke, Jones, Steve, and Jimmy. Jimmy was Clint's youngest brother. I liked him instantly. They were teenagers. He was the polar opposite of his brother.

As darkness set in and we all settled around the fire, I had to pinch myself to keep a lid on my joy. We sat in the darkness under this broad sky lit up with a thousand stars, the light of the flames illuminating faces. I sat there looking from face to face, listening to their chatter, memorizing the moment, and smiling into the bonfire. I felt at peace. Arousing myself back to the conversation, I found that everyone was quietly listening to Jimmy as he told the history of his people.

"In our culture we pass down our history in stories, from generation to generation, the legends of our ancestors." The steady glowing crackle of the fire added to a reverential atmosphere as we listened while Jimmy recited the legend of their ancestors' beginnings. After Jimmy ended this recitation, I could see his pride in his heritage. I smiled. The legend started with a colossal flood that destroyed everything. As I sat there listening to Jimmy, I was reminded of the other flood story, the one in the Bible. Maybe it's the same story.

There's quiet strength in the brothers; realizing their connection to this land, they were part of the earth itself.

My gaze found Clint, his quiet silhouette outlined by the flame from the fire. Our eyes met; I couldn't read the expression in his dark watchful gaze … warmth flooded my chest and I quickly looked away.

After our guests left, and everyone went inside, Rob and I lingered by the fire. "Tess," he started, staring into the fire and then turning to look at me, "You're going to be okay here, I know it. I have no worries. But if you need anything or have any problems, we are just a phone call away. I remember your counsel once during a particularly hard time for me where you told me to review my life's prayer successes, its history, that it would be proof of God's constancy. We always overcome. So, I'm confident that this will turn out okay for you and if it doesn't, like Maddy's told you, doors remain open in Florida." He glanced at the fire ring and then looking back, he said, "Okay?"

I smiled into his face, "Thanks," I said as the somberness of the moment caught me, "I know I'll be fine," I said looking into his concerned eyes. "I know that I have you guys as support, Rob, I do trust that God would have closed this door if this wasn't His plan for me. I'm nervous about what's ahead and a new life here, I won't lie," I said. "But I agree that I have to take this step."

How well I knew that discussions that reached into deep waters were of short duration with Rob, so I wrapped up my comments, less was usually better. Still the sentiment of his emotion and care weren't lost on me. I knew they loved me and worried about me. I gave him a quick hug and went inside.

Over the days ahead, the dogs found endless reasons to run off in pursuit of some harmless animal. I kept the remote close.

Two weeks passed and everyone was readying for the flight back to Florida. I steeled myself and took a deep breath as I drove them to Jackson Hole airport. I would have to make this trip twice.

Each goodbye produced an ache in my chest. Hugs and kisses and gone.

As their last plane took off, reality set in. It ran up so swiftly that I felt a bolt travel up my legs to my brain. I was literally struck with the knowledge that I *was alone.* I was across the country from the people I loved most in the whole world. Uncertainty and the realization of what this decision cost, along with old fears, being completely alone, kicked a panic attack into high gear and while trying to stay upright, my brain was looking through a sightless veil, not understanding my surroundings, while my heart was trying loudly to thump an exit out my chest. I needed to be somewhere safe … I found myself sitting in my car. Panic attacks don't occur often anymore, and I hadn't had one in so many years that they had faded from memory, but they were always bad.

Just minutes before, the car had been full of the noisy presence of my best friends, but they are more than that, almost an extension of me. It's truly inexplicable, we've been through every imaginable situation, yet, until this moment I don't think I really got its depth, guess it was expected to always be, no relationship concerns … I know they aren't gone, I know that, but they are away from me, and I hadn't experienced *that* before. Or understood the depths of its roots and unconditional love. Now there was just an awful silence. The car was empty. There was the utter absence of them. How could I do this?

Eventually I arrived home. Darkness and quiet surrounded me as I sat in my car. Looking out the windshield, I scanned the house and yard. I think I hate it here. It had taken me away from the comfort of my prior life, this silly romantic notion of … what?

Finally, a bark aroused me. The dogs needed me.

I walked the short distance to the front porch. Walked up the steps and unlocked the front door. Everything now seemed unfamiliar. I did not realize until this moment how profoundly interwoven my connection to my life in Florida was. Especially how much I had come to rely on my inner circle of friends. Their support during and after the divorce was immeasurable.

I unlocked the door and stepped inside.

The dog's excitement at seeing me had always been so welcoming, but now it became a chore that needed my attention.

The emptiness in the house was worse than the car. More silence. There were signs of their hurried departure. As I went into the kitchen to retrieve dog food, I noticed the dishes in the sink, the full trash can. God where are you leading me? I know *good* is ahead because You promise that, but I am overwhelmed right now. In this moment nothing felt *good*.

I needed to get a grip. I fed the dogs and stood outside in the back waiting on them. Everything here seemed like a foreign country. Fear hit me. This isn't my home. This isn't my life. I've made a huge mistake. I recalled that it wasn't unusual after initially purchasing a home to have buyers' remorse. Hope that's it. Exhaustion from so much emotion and activity was weighing on me, I told myself to tackle one thing at a time. Dogs.

Kai and Sprite ran back to the house, tails wagging. At least they were happy. Inside they raced from room to room. They were still young dogs, and I found their energy level at the moment annoying. I drug my body up the stairs. I sighed. Stairs. I had chosen the room on the far-right corner of the second story. No stairs at my home in Florida. More energy is needed for this simple act. I found comfort in what was now my sanctuary. At least all my furniture was here and that brought some measure of familiar comfort. My faith had taught me that God was not interested so much in my comfort as He was interested in my character. Can He depend on me to always trust? Working on it, Lord.

I took a shower and ambled down the hallway to my room. Note to self, I need a bathroom in my sanctuary. The dogs and I climbed into bed, into my inner sanctum. I grabbed for my Bible and let the power of the words comfort me. Scripture has always been alive for me. It had never failed me, and tonight was no exception. After turning out the lights, I slipped out of bed and knelt on my floor. No prayers, no words, just looking for His face.

I stayed on the floor for some time. Finally, I climbed into bed and allowed exhaustion to take me.

I felt the morning sun on my skin. The lightness of the dawn filtering through my bedroom window illuminated my closed eyelids. I sat up acclimating myself to my surroundings. Remembering my aloneness, I told myself to focus on just doing the next thing. Coffee. Feed dogs. I had this idea that the simple act of washing my face, brushing my teeth, and sitting outside with a quiet cup of coffee was a positive and as much happiness as I was currently capable of obtaining. I changed my clothes and headed out to the front porch with coffee, Bible, journal, and remote in hand. Both dogs needed exercise.

Morning here was very quiet. *Quiet* can be heavy, I realized. I sipped my coffee and gathered my thoughts. I would put these feelings in my journal. I found some measure of peace as I sat watching the activity on my front lawn; birds flitting about, squirrels scampering for nuts and the sway and beauty of these trees. Can this be home?

The phone rang and I jumped at the interruption. Answering, it was Maddy. I was happy to hear her voice. "We got in late last night at Tampa Airport. We were dog-tired. We didn't get home till close to midnight. We had a great time, Tess. I was wondering how you were doing on your first night alone. Things, okay?" I assured her I was *fine,* and she rambled about this and that. It was comforting.

Clint and his workers arrived shortly after the call, so I had company. Friendly "Hi!" from Jimmy followed by shy hellos from the others. Nothing from Clint, not even acknowledgement. I prepared more coffee and returned to the porch. I was happy for the company but still needed to gather my thoughts and grapple with my aloneness and I needed to do that alone, away from witnesses. The other contractors followed within minutes, so I decided to wrap up, putting my thoughts into my journal. Then I busied myself with more unpacking, endless my ownership of things.

The house was filled with contractors working on installing cabinets and counters, rearranging plumbing, and rewiring. I tried to stay out of everyone's way. I provided coffee, water, and lemonade along with subs for lunch. It kept me busy and provided a distraction.

As the days moved slowly forward, Jimmy made himself available to me often and I found myself really taking a liking to him. The boys would work before and after school for money.

Jimmy loved music and the income helped him make purchases for their band. On their short breaks he would come over and talk to me, always smiling.

"What's Florida like?" Jimmy asked one day, with an expression that told me he thought it was exotic.

Jimmy asking me about Florida took my thoughts back. I looked away for a moment, feeling a sudden ache, remembering my life there. I started with the first thought that came to mind: "Hot and humid."

He frowned.

My mind filled with images of home; the years spent there quickly passed in front of me. I tried to pick out images that would interest a teenager from the Wild West. "Hum… Well… Florida is pretty much as you probably picture it. It has lots of palm trees and is surrounded on three sides by the ocean and beaches. There's a lot of diversity there in lifestyles from retirement and pre-civil war communities, migrant farm workers to South Beach residents in Miami. The beaches are surrounded by the Gulf of Mexico on the West Coast, which we call the Gulf, and the Atlantic Ocean on the East Coast." I looked over at the boys, they were listening. "The state has lots of springs, not something it's too famous for, but they're beautiful. Much of the state sits on limestone aquifers and the springs are the result of rainwater that has filtered through the limestone exiting again at openings in the surface." Searching my brain for more info, I added, "Most of the state has nine-month summers, tropical and humid. In fact, some days the humidity is so bad, until you adjust to it, it can feel as though you're trying to breathe through water. And then of course there are the Theme Parks, Universal, Sea World, Busch Gardens and Disney. There's Key West, a tropical hot spot that attracts serious partiers and sunbathers. And, of course, the state attracts the college crowd during spring breaks that converge on our beaches. Florida has a history rich in Pirates and inland portions of the state and the everglades still have remote communities. Pretty diverse state now that I think about it." I didn't bother mentioning mosquitoes.

Jimmy's eyes lit up and I could see he was visiting those places in his head, and I could tell the others were still listening as they worked.

"I like Florida," I continued, my mind reviewing my life there. "I grew up there. Florida has manatees, the Everglades, coral snakes and alligators." Their looks belied the impression that I had just spoken of some faraway exotic animal. "Alligators to Floridians are like cows in most places. The sightings of them are so common that sometimes they get ignored, although they are not quite as docile as a cow," I said laughing. "What do you think Florida is like?" I asked Jimmy, interested.

Jimmy grinned "Oh, Miami Vice and Spring breaks!" He blushed and the others snickered at him. He turned to them "Hey, you guys think the same thing!"

"Oh, so Florida is adventure and girls, girls, girls!" No response but lots of blushes. "So, what's life like here?" I asked. "In Wyoming and on the reservation?"

Jimmy was trying to reach for some interesting tidbit to make it seem as exciting as he thought Florida sounded. I had not thought of life in Florida as exciting. Why do we romanticize everywhere but home?

"Well..." He looked over at Clint for help. "Hey Clint, what goes on *on* the rez?" Clint looked up, his eyes rested on me for a moment, then shook his head. A half smile crossing his face. Jimmy turned back to me. "Well, we live... um, we farm and run a ranch. I go to school on the rez and I play in a band. We ride horses and I have a favorite swimming hole. I'll have to take you 'round to see my favorite spots." He smiled broadly.

I got the quick idea that his male mind would not pick out the details and the color of their lives that would interest a female mind. Still, I welcomed a male view of life here. Would probably have to save this discussion for hopefully future female friendships.

"What do you do in the winter?"

This animated him. "We have snow mobiles that we fix up and ride!" He told me about their adventures riding around the reservation in the snow. "We play a lot of games on the computer in winter, and we hang out. There's school and my band meet a couple of times during the week, and we have gigs on weekends!" Everything with Jimmy seems to be an exclamation point.

The others were listening to our exchange but did not join in the conversation.

Thanks to Jimmy I started to get some feel for their community.

"Hey, how about I take you around and show you the rez? And you could come and listen to the band when we have a gig at our community center!"

"Great, I love the idea. Any time, just let me know." I jumped at the idea. I needed to stay busy, and this would help me become acquainted with my new community, maybe even meet people.

The kitchen was coming along. Clint had made a lot of headway, unsupervised, I realized. He had followed my plans. I wanted space in the kitchen. I wanted a kitchen that facilitated storage of food for long winters. I had the pantry enlarged and was now in the process of filling its shelves with a variety of starches, spices and just about every imaginable culinary need. My eye was to the long term where we might experience protracted isolated spells due to winter storms. (The 'we' being myself and the dogs) My thoughts and ideas tried to cover every imaginable problem that we might face. I stocked the pantry with batteries, flashlights, candles, matches and the linen closets with blankets, sheets, towels, and pillows. I had the well and pump system revamped to accommodate a vegetable garden but also sunk the well deeper to ascertain availability during isolated spells. I purchased a whole house generator and bought large propane tanks. My prayer was to be prepared in the event of any circumstance given the isolation of this homestead. I wanted the homestead to be self-contained. Sometimes I would bravely approach Clint for his thoughts regarding winter concerns. Florida did not prepare me for Wyoming winters. Politely he always offered his insight, and this became instrumental and the reason for the well, pump and generator.

When all was completed most of my funds from the sale of my house would be depleted. I was so grateful to be able to get all this done and not have debt because I had no idea what the future held. Now … I had to make a life.

Chapter Five

High Mysterious Intellect

Waking early most mornings. I would lay in bed listening ... always a hushed quiet. Stretching, I let peace flow into my body, breathing air deeply into my lungs. It was a form of meditation, getting my body into a meditative state for morning devotions.

Musing over my appearance of late, realizing it had taken a backseat to everything else. I had an athletic body, thin and healthy, but I didn't have an active interest in fashion. Some items in my wardrobe spanned 10 years. I could be trendy, but shopping wasn't a priority. My shopping was more confined to *spells* or needs. I was comfortable in jeans and tee shirts, my uniform.

As I lay in bed, I heard the movement of the contractors as they started the day. Ugh. Did I oversleep? I had hoped to get up before them and have a quiet cup of coffee before the thud of hammers and skill saws. The work was almost complete, and I was starting to see the realization of my vision. With this new life, I was aware of my freedom. Nothing owned me here. I was my own master. But there is joy and pain in that. Joy, real joy still evaded me, however. The initial pain of aloneness was subsiding and there was some nesting. I was finding my footing. My days proceeded as *I* planned, not as ordered by someone else, which was a new experience for me, and it took a little getting used to. I *was* working on happy.

I had taken to walking around the interior of my house visualizing décor but maybe I was imprinting it, making it mine. Because I was alone, perhaps somehow walking around room-to-room made the house more familiar. I couldn't fill it with other human presences, but I could fill it with mine. With every picture hanging and every flower arrangement, every piece of furniture move, it was becoming my home.

Today I planned to do more exploration of the property. I had been told there was a stream on the property and today I wanted to locate it. I was interested in the water sources on the property. I love water. Had always lived near water and realized that it was important to me, not in the obvious sense of sustenance but the tranquil clean beauty of water.

I jumped out of bed and washed my face. My blonde hair was usually tucked up in a knot at the back of my head. It was an easy look requiring a large tortoise colored plastic pin to hold my hair in place. Donning my usual wardrobe, I put on my boots and headed downstairs to start coffee and the day. Grabbing my Bible, journal, and coffee, I headed outside to sit on the front porch, read my devotions and convert my thoughts chronicling my life to my journal. A comfortable routine was helping me to adjust.

Clint was already at work. He still rarely spoke. I had almost gotten the impression that he didn't like me, but I couldn't place any reason or fix on any event that I felt might give basis for this. I gave him a wide berth only because I felt he preferred it that way. The other contractors were finished, and he was just days from wrapping up what was left of my remodeling projects.

Soon I had packed a small backpack and headed out. I wanted to explore the property behind the barn and find the creek, or stream or whatever water source I was assured existed on my property. Quickly, down the back deck stairs, across the lawn I reached the barn. I cannot quite get that I own a barn. Nor can I find an immediate purpose. Stables, maybe? Cow? Probably not. Entering the barn, I was reminded of my early childhood visits to relatives. Several owned farms and this smell was that smell, the smell of animals and earth, musty from decay and musty from animal excrement and life. I stood there taking in the moment. Transported. I loved this barn. It was old. It was real. I found myself wandering around it, looking at the remnants of prior occupants. Stalls, old hay, loft and old wood. The earthen floor made solid from years of use, was now as hard as concrete.

As I stood there, movement in the corner of the barn startled me. I let out a surprised yell. A snake! He did not seem to notice me, and I stood completely still trying to determine whether it was venomous or not. I wasn't afraid of snakes, more fascinated than frightened, but I didn't want a venomous snake in my vicinity. The thought occurred to perhaps do a Steve Irwin capture and release to a more remote area where we would both be happier. I had not startled the snake, but I had startled Clint. He ran into the barn and several others followed. Now I felt silly. There was real concern on Clint's face. This was unexpected.

I stuttered 'Ssnnaake..''and found his eyes running to my gaze.

He sent the others back to work and moved in the direction of the snake. I followed peeking behind him. It was in fact a rattler.

Concerned for both Clint and the snake I mumbled, "Can we try to catch the snake and release him?" Clint did not appear to be listening. He grabbed a stick and an old gunny sack. I was utterly transfixed by his grace and confidence. Within moments he had apprehended the snake and placed it easily within the sack.

Clint looked at me for a moment, "Are you alright?" he asked, genuine concern on his face.

"Yes," I said, catching my breath, startled at this sudden concern.

Clint made a slight nod and without saying another word, he took the snake to his truck and gave instructions to Duke. Truck, Duke, and snake left.

I walked to the barn door opening and stood there watching him move with ease around the renovation site; the patient calm manner in which he gave instructions. His obvious grounding in his own masculinity, not showy, not proud … is it his heritage or the man?

And where are the dogs? I realized that I had not seen them most of the morning. I went inside to retrieve the remote. I think Clint thinks my need for the remote and not having my dogs under voice command is funny in some way because when he sees the remote, he smiles. I called for the dogs … nothing. As I started to step off the deck, Clint whistled. They came running. When had he gained mastery over my dogs? Lamely I thanked him, feeling lame often around him. He dismissed them and they followed me. Nice.

I decided not to think about Clint or my dogs.

Off on my adventure, now realizing that boots were a good call. I headed out behind the barn. The land was not maintained, and I had tall grass, fallen trees and thick shrubs to navigate. Could I get lost on my own property? Would Clint have to rescue me a second time today? Not a chance. I got my bearings and tried to keep sight of landmarks behind me. If I do this a little each day, the area will become familiar.

I stepped carefully, vigilant to snakes and any movement. Soon I was caught up in the woods. The beauty. The quiet. Here and there sunlight filtered through the trees, and I would look up to find openings allowing gold to penetrate across the forest floor. The high grass was drying from morning mist and sending wafts of pollen airborne. Feeling light, airy, and weightless in this timeless environment. I could hear water but could not locate its source. I searched for what seemed an hour or so and then gave up.

I headed back.

My next plan was to head into town. I had forgotten to bring any art supplies. I wanted to purchase some and start trying to regain some mastery over a dusty talent. It seemed to take less time to recover the ground back to the barn. Clint was alone working on the deck. In town I managed to find a craft store, made my purchases and dropped in to say hello to Patty.

Patty seemed pleased that I appeared to be settling in. Our relationship had not grown yet to include her in my inner sanctum of relationships, and vice versa. But we had an easy relationship. I was curious about her single life but didn't ask. Patty had short brown hair. She kept it coiffed, and I could tell her appearance took some time and expense. Wondered how she saw mine of late?

"How is the remodeling going?" Patty asked.

"It's almost finished," I said, settling in a chair near her desk. "I am glad you recommended Clint, he's done a great job and works independently, never asks me for a thing. Already I can see how the house will look and it's beautiful."

"Yeah, everyone says that about his work and he is not bad to look at, if you know what I mean," she said with a knowing smile. (She must know Anna) "He has the interest of more than one local lady, but he's never been approachable that way."

Intrigued, I asked, "What do you mean?"

"Around here he gets more than a few heart rates up. He's gorgeous and adding to that is the fact that everyone thinks well of him. But if he dates it isn't obvious. No one turns his eye and there are few details on his personal life. Maybe on the rez there's a girlfriend. Does he talk to you?"

"No, I pretty much experience what all the ladies experience, aloof and distant. He barely ever says a word to me. But I'm glad to hear this because I felt his distance was somehow related to something I had done. Good to know."

"How is your social calendar? Meeting anyone?"

"No, not really. With the remodeling and people on the property throughout the day, I've stayed pretty much close to home. And I'm still unpacking and settling in. I'll get around to that." I smiled.

She seemed convinced of that. "Why don't we get together again for dinner, or something? Hey, speaking of good-looking guys, what about that guy we ran into at dinner that night in Jackson? He was very attractive and seemed interested in you. A story there?"

She was referring to John Lawrence; he was having dinner in the same restaurant.

"Oh, he is just a guy I met him when I was searching for property last year. It was just an evening thing. Nothing *really*." She was looking intently at me as though she was not buying my explanation. "Really, it's nothing," I reiterated.

We made plans and I made a mental note to dig out more of my wardrobe to add some variety to my appearance. At least I could make more of an effort when I ventured into town. When I returned home, the workers had left and I was alone, again. This was the time of day that went either very well or not so well. It was quiet. There was good quiet and not so good quiet. Some quiet is actually *disquieting*. Called Maddy while preparing chicken quesadillas. Favorite foods and good conversation usually cheered me. We chatted about this and that, she always managed to find ways of comforting me. I was missing some interpersonal interaction. Decided to make a point of following up with Jimmy on his offers.

After a shower I got on the computer to check emails. There was an email from John Lawrence. I recalled that second run-in with him shortly after I had arrived. Patty and I had gone to Jackson for dinner one night and he had recognized me. If he felt slighted that I had not followed up on his suggestion to stay in touch, he didn't let on. I did not tell Patty, but he had been in touch ever since. He seemed to be moving forward in a direction familiar to me but one that I was not sure I was ready for. He was suggesting dinner Friday night in Jackson.

Right now, in this empty house, the company was sounding pretty good and so I accepted.

Thursday morning arrived, and the morning ritual was repeated. I decided to ask Clint if he knew where the water source was located. I walked outside and found him putting the finishing touches on my deck railing. I realized that they were days from completion and days from not returning. A rush of panic went through me.

As I stepped outside, Clint seemed to sense my mood as I stood hesitating, reflecting on this future aloneness. He waited for me to speak. His eyes were black and penetrating. His hair was long, and he sometimes wore it braided and tucked behind his ears or let it hang loose. Occasionally he wore a ball cap. On the rare occasion that he smiled, his teeth were perfect and white. I didn't know why he didn't smile more because it totally transformed his face. He makes me feel like he knows things. I see a higher intelligence than mine when I look into his eyes and it disarms me; it doesn't encourage conversation from me, quite the opposite, I find it stifling. Added to this is the beauty of the man. His face is beautiful; his body is beautiful and the graceful economy in his movements and his obvious confidence add to his overall power. A virile masculinity exudes from him. He is intimidating. I remembered Patty's comments about female interest in him; I got it, his magnetic power was palpable.

Shaking loose his stare, I found my words. "I was told that there's a creek on the property and I'm trying to find it. Are you familiar with any water source on the property?"

He nodded, "Yes, I knew the Lewis' and they mentioned a stream on the property," eyes studying my face. "If I remember right, it's to the right of the barn. Think you are headed in the right area," he said nodding in that direction.

I stared into his eyes for a brief moment before breaking the connection. "Thank you," I managed. Finding my feet, and turning toward the woods, I wondered at the intensity I often found around him, was this normal?

Heading out more to the right of the barn bushwhacking through shrubbery. This resulted in casualties to my skin. My arms were cut and scratched, and one area had started bleeding. I used my shirt to stop the bleeding. While standing nursing my cut I could hear water. This was close. Pushing through more shrubs and high grasses, over trunks and around thick vines and dense foliage I came upon the stream. It would take work, but this area could be cleared with a path back to the house.

I was happy that the water was this close. It could be my sanctuary, my quiet place. I realized with the work almost completed; my entire property would be a 'quiet place'. I sat down next to the stream. It ran clean and fast. Fish I couldn't identify populated the stream indicating it's health. The streambed was a sandy dirt mixture, not covered in bottom grasses, I could wade here.

The water was a light blue from the mountain runoff. Brisk and frothy as it moved over rocks and around root systems, swirling and falling, pushing constantly forward away from its beginning to some unknown destination.

The stream banks were populated here and there by a thick root base interwoven along the banks. Dense tree cover and wild shrubs lined the stream. The width of the stream swelled, accommodating deep and shallow pools. I took my boots off and plunged my feet deep into the inviting water up past my shins. It was freezing and instantly I pulled my feet back stunned by its temperature. An intense stab of pain traveled from my feet to my brain, like eating ice cream too fast. Rubbing my temples, I quickly put my socks on trying to generate heat.

As the numbing left and my feet warmed, I looked around. The place had a spiritual element. I sat listening to the gurgling of the water and feeling cool, breezy air on my skin. The woods surrounding the stream brought quiet, offering protection and solitude. Laying back, I closed my eyes with my arms folded across my forehead. Breezes flowing through the leaves whispered, hushed, tinkling sounds that moved from tree to tree carrying their sound through the woods. Were they talking? The gentle movement allowed flickers of sunlight to dance across my closed eyelids. The peace of this place gave me a sense of lightness. Clouds moved overhead casting shadows as they passed. Somewhere overhead I heard a woodpecker with its short bursts of tapping. Wyoming had three toed or black backed woodpeckers. I couldn't identify either if they fell on me.

Not wanting to move, the stress of many mixed emotions seemed to melt into the earth; like a magnet pulling them downward. Eventually I sat up sitting cross-legged, examining myself. My mood. Checking my progression. My spiritual life elevated my love and enjoyment of everything in nature. Nature was an expression, a part of Him. Love created this planet for our needs and our enjoyment. Watching every moving thing, large and small, knowing that He had given each its own instinctive behavior and life span and that they all worked in harmony, in balance with one another. The profound flowing organization of nature and the high mysterious intellect that held everything together, His intelligent design. Gentle unseen breezes brushed my face and cooled my skin, a simple pleasure.

Things get lost out here. Time and civilization don't touch it. I laid back, resting my head on the ground. Relaxed. Waves of peace floated over me, feeling oneness with my surroundings, my blood twittering in response to Him. Cocooned in what felt like an embrace.

Chapter Six

Complicated Resurrections

Heading back, I smiled with the realization that I had found the stream. I owned a stream. Peace lingered as I came around the barn.

The workers were gone except for Clint who was just loading up. He saw me and I picked up something in his demeanor. Had he been waiting?

As I walked, I volunteered hesitantly, "I found the stream. Thanks for your help."

He nodded, and his eyes went to my scratches.

As I approached him, I said, "It's pretty close," smiling. He nodded, and I sensed an openness in his posture. Something almost friendly in his eyes. The usual tense seriousness on his brow and around his mouth was gone. We both stood for a moment looking at one another.

Clint started, "I didn't think you'd have trouble finding the stream," he said, friendly, "I see you met with some obstacles," looking down at my scratches, the blood stains on my shirt and back into my face.

I blushed. I was having difficulty finding conversation, shoot, I was having trouble thinking. To gain composure, I looked towards the deck. "How is the deck coming?" I asked weakly.

A new feeling was stirring, a feminine side that had been dormant; I was aware of the male female thing standing there so close to him. I had felt peaceful, and now intensely feminine. Confusing warmth flooded my abdomen ...

At this question, he seemed to pause, his eyes retreating a little. "Fine, I should be done with everything in a few days," he said, studying my face.

Wondering about him I asked, "Do you have more family here other than Jimmy?" stepping back to gain control.

"Yes," he nodded, noticing the movement, his posture still friendly. "My mother, another brother, and two sisters."

"Do they live around here?"

"Um hum," he said, "My youngest sister, Dinah, and Jimmy live with my mother and I, and Joseph and Tamara have their own homes on the rez, Tamara is married. Dinah and Jimmy are still in school." His continued focus fueled the intensity I was feeling.

Staring up into his eyes, I managed to nod. "Where's your dad?" I quizzed.

"He died a few years ago," he responded.

"I'm sorry," I said, searching for some latent pain in his face.

"Thanks. It's fine," he said, eyes shifting. "It was years ago."

I asked, "Does your entire family live on the reservation?"

"Yes. We have the ranch that my dad left us." At this he broke his gaze and started towards his vehicle. Looking back, he said, "I'll see you tomorrow." As quickly as the conversation started it was over.

I stood confused about what had just happened. I made several milestones today; I'd found the stream and there was an ever so slight improvement in my relationship with Clint. As he drove off, I turned and walked into the house, my mind occupied with Clint and wondering at these new stirrings.

It was Thursday and tomorrow was my 'date' with John.

I located the animals I had left indoors. Sprite was three-legged and had trouble navigating the underbrush. She would get caught and I had to keep a close eye on her. Today I wanted to find the stream and did not want Sprite causing difficulty. The dogs had been trapped indoors all day and I felt bad. I let them outside to run. I went inside to retrieve my journal and formulate something for dinner.

Back outside I sat on the top step. I could see the work that had been completed today. I had to admire Clint's work. I turned and looked back at the house, at his additions, the workmanship. The additions added so much inside and out to the character of the home. I realized, it reflected the character of the man who built it. Turning back, my eyes went to the last place we spoke, my eyes squinting trying to remember the encounter, the new Clint. I was aware of something new between us, or was it just me, was I misreading this?

Inside for the evening it occurred to me that I really needed to take stock of my appearance for tomorrow night. How did I feel about this? I didn't honestly know. Relationships were elusive for me; I was not sure why. Nothing stuck. Was it me, or was it God keeping men at arm's length for a purpose all His own? I had no answer. I had toyed with the concept that I was called to a life of singleness. Since my divorce, I felt fit for that and most of the things in the female heart that are receptive to romance had either died or fallen asleep. Since I had not been the cause of that, I assumed this was God's will. If He wanted romance for me, a mate, I trusted that He would resurrect it, and either way I wasn't worried. But I was cautious and wary about tomorrow. These thoughts led me into preparation for my date. To stay calm and not overthink the 'date' I decided not to think about it at all. I would just focus on cleaning up. It seemed a productive way to spend the evening, doting on myself. Hadn't done that in a while. I prepared a bath for a long soak.

I woke Friday morning with a lot on my mind. Stream, change in Clint and date.

As I sat outside engaging in my morning ritual, devotions, journaling, and coffee, I wondered about life ahead. I had been here several months, and it was time to start testing my wings and exploring my surroundings … off my property. Lord, what are your plans for me? Jimmy may provide an open door.

Sitting there a noise startled me. I looked up and saw something or someone running back towards the woods. I could not make out what it was, but too small to be an adult, and since this was the *woods* after-all…. I decided on a small animal.

While thinking of Clint, I could hear his truck as it entered my property. He parked and stepped out smiling at me. Good sign.

"Mornin'," he said, while stepping out of his vehicle. He unloaded his truck and started walking towards me, still smiling.

Totally disarmed by this friendliness; I returned his smile. "Good morning," I said as I watched him approach, again this warmth. "How are things?"

"Fine and you?" he said standing near the deck looking at me with a replaced openness that I found put me under his spell.

I'm good, thank you, your work is beautiful, Clint. You have a gift." My tone had conviction in it. I gushed, "Everything is as I had imagined it. I really love the way it has all turned out." I tried to look away to hide my embarrassment at my chatter, but I found I couldn't. Finally, all I could manage was a faint smile.

He was standing comfortably with one arm resting on the railing, looking at me. A flicker of a smile crossed his face as he said a quick, "Thanks." Then breaking his gaze, he prepared to start work.

Why this nervousness around him? Maybe intimidation. He disarms me, that's for sure. Funny this feeling at not seeing him every day? My mind briefly toyed with finding another construction project.

I went inside the kitchen wondering about this feeling.

Leaning against the kitchen cabinet, I reviewed what I was doing. There's a purpose for this move, ministry. I could, at least, do something about that and a good place to start might be to find a church body to belong to. Clint was becoming a distraction. I thought about a church, seemed like a good idea. Hum, how to go about finding one? Maybe Clint knows?

As I walked to the back door and looked out, Clint was preparing to put sealant on the wood deck. Am I looking for reasons to talk to him? I stood at the door for a moment. Feeling nervous, I stepped outside deciding to approach him about local churches. He looked up. "Hey, I'm looking for a local church. Do you have any information about churches nearby or on the reservation?"

His eyes squinted for a moment as though processing churches and me. "Yes, there's a Community Baptist church close, it's on the rez," and he gave me the directions. He wasn't sure of the times services ran and he gave the impression he didn't attend.

He went back to applying the sealant.

I filed the information away and filled the day catching up on emails, paying bills and general household chores, aware of his presence outside. Laundry and unpacking filled the rest of the morning. Some boxes held no interest, and I had pushed them into one of the bedrooms now relegated for my stuff. I phoned Patty to get the local news and updates. She knew about my 'date'. We discussed it.

"He's hot, if you're not interested, point him in my direction!" She laughed. "Where are you two going to dinner?"

"Skinny Crow in Jackson. Have you heard of it?"

"Oh yeah. It's a popular restaurant and I hear the food's good. I haven't eaten there. Do you have any plans for after dinner?"

"Not that I'm aware. John might but dinner is as much as he's communicated. I'll let you know more later. I'll call you early in the week. Okay?"

"Okay, very interested in how the evening goes. Want all the details! Call me on Monday and maybe we can fit in a lunch or dinner?"

"Great."

My life seemed surreal. I couldn't even call it my life. I still didn't own it. Roots were slow moving. Hopefully a year from now will find me on the other side of this feeling.

The day was quickly passing, and the time was nearing for my date. I wasn't sure I could give John good directions here, so we agreed to meet at 6:30 in Jackson.

I found myself happy. This was a high point. I was enjoying the idea of putting on something feminine. My heart raced a bit. Nervous? Yes. I hated first dates. It always felt like an interview. I told myself to relax. Getting ready gave me something to do. I decided on a simple dress with cropped sleeves and found my favorite sandals, a constant from my Florida wardrobe. I checked myself one last time and headed downstairs.

Fed the dogs and as I was sending them out back for one last romp before sequestering them for the night, I checked myself. Clint. For some reason, I didn't want to face Clint right now, heading out on a date. He had my head turned around and he seemed unaware of his effect on me. I opened the door and let the dogs out ahead of me and stood in the doorway watching him. He was still working when I stepped outside. He raised his gaze as I walked out onto the back deck. Something flickered behind his eyes as he scanned my body. It occurred to me that my appearance was new to him. I blushed, feeling the same warmth. He continued to look at me. It was making me uncomfortable, searching for something to say that would relieve the moment, I asked, "Are you almost finished for the day?" He nodded slightly. Lamely I added, "I have dinner plans in Jackson, and I'll be leaving soon." I offered, not clear why.

From his scrutiny and change in expression, I felt he understood my evening activity. Putting the dogs inside, I left Clint to finish up.

As I drove towards Jackson my mind was on Clint. What had happened? Could *he* have some interest in me? I shuddered and tingled oddly at the thought. I admit, I found him attractive. There was an increase in my pulse at the direction these thoughts were taking me. How does this work, date with John, thinking about Clint? Sighing deeply, I tried to clear my head and focus on the evening ahead.

Chapter Seven

Obscured Boundaries

The Skinny Crow was a popular local establishment that exuded an atmosphere that promised good food and privacy. John met me inside the front door. Our email banter had been friendly, he was interested, asking a lot of questions. Email helped me keep boundaries. Tonight. Not sure about tonight. My control of my boundaries was becoming blurred about both men.

We were seated in a corner booth. Intimacy. Why does that scare me? I buried my face in the menu, ordered water, wine, and a grilled chicken Caesar salad. John ordered a beer and a steak platter. We both sat back surveying one another.

He looked handsome yet I sensed a similar unease. Hates first dates too? A moment passed before either of us spoke. He quickly examined his hands resting on the table and I looked away at the activity outside the booth. There were a lot of couples.

"You look beautiful. I love that smell," he said, as he turned, studying me.

"Thank you," I said, shy at the compliment. My heart didn't race with John. I found my thoughts complicated by the man I left working at my house. Which only added to my angst over first dates … never clear on protocol and less certain on expectations.

"How's the remodeling coming along?"

This relaxed me, I was happy to start the conversation with a topic that felt safe and that I could be animated about. I went through a list of everything that had been done.

"Unfortunately," I told him, "I could spend hours talking about the move, the construction work and settling in, making this my home. The last few months have taken me from my home in Florida to Wyoming. It's been more of a 'Whew', just getting things accomplished," I said smiling.

He chuckled with an appreciative glint in his eyes. Told him of my concerns and preparations for the pending winter and the fact that I had zero experience with northern winters.

This made him smile. "Florida, oh right!" Laughing, "I'll have to make a point of visiting you in the dead of winter. I am curious as to how Wyoming winters will look on a Floridian. Don't get to see that that often," he looked relaxed. His smile reaching his eyes as he gazed into mine.

"I'm happy you find amusement in my situation," I replied with a smile. "But really, tell me about winters here," a little concern showing.

"I suppose they can be harsh, but I think, rather hope, that you'll get used to them." I felt the hidden meaning. "Just be prepared and I really don't anticipate that you'll have any problems. Tess, if you need anything, I am available." He smiled warmly. "Besides, no one has died from exposure around these parts for years." He laughed accentuating 'years'. "Most people stock up on supplies," he said speaking as an authority on this subject, "and many have an extra freezer and food in the event of prolonged confinements. You'll learn as you go along and besides, I'll be more than happy to come by and check your winter readiness," he said beaming warmly.

He saw the concern. "Tess, really, you'll be fine." He reached over and gently touched my hand to reassure me. "You'll probably be more bored with the imposed indoor activities than anything else, so I suggest that you hon up your game interests and skills. I have lots of board games and can't think of a better way to spend a long evening than beating you at Scrabble or Monopoly. I'm the king of board games!" He had an infectious laugh.

"Oh really, what makes you think you'll beat me? I have a pretty fair command of English *and* real-estate. I'll warn you; I may not be easy to defeat," a teasing smile on my face.

This romantic thing called 'connecting' was developing, a good start at a friendly emotional level. Not bad I thought. I felt tension drain off my body.

"And then, of course, there are outdoor activities," he added, "that I think you might like, skiing, snow mobiles and we have several outdoor concerts and festivals. I think I can find ways of keeping you from boredom." He smiled.

By the time the waitress brought our meal, I found myself warming to John.

"I'm curious as to how you are managing being alone. Are you feeling isolated?"

Tensing up whenever I hear any comment regarding my future aloneness, I replied, "So far, I haven't been alone, *yet*. The last of my contractors will be finished shortly so ask me again in a few days." A sudden ache at thoughts of Clint caused my gaze to stray, turning toward a passing waitress. "So far, I'm managing," I said, turning back to face John, "I found a stream on my property, plus I'm still organizing and putting stuff away. It's *okay*." I said managing a slight smile, "I'm staying busy… just letting every day happen John, I suppose. The word *alone* spooks me a bit I admit. Sorry if I seem melodramatic. It's a transition but I'm a big girl," I said, straightening my posture.

"I can see that," he said speaking more softly, "Now I'm the one that's sorry, feel maybe I was being a little nonchalant about your challenges Tess. Sorry, really. If there is anything I can do to smooth this transition, let me know. I can swing a hammer, believe it or not and I'm pretty handy around the house, yard work, you name it. All you need to do is ask, and I mean that." He was oozing sincerity ... and warmth.

Feeling grateful for his offer, "Thanks John, I appreciate that. I'll keep that in mind," I said teasingly. I paused, revisiting other concerns, "I have an old relationship with fear, being alone is maybe more of that." I looked over at John and took a deep breath. Fear has run me in the past and is now monopolizing the conversation. "Don't think I realized how much this was building in me with no interpersonal outlet. I'm taking it out on you, and I *am* sorry! You'll just have to take my word that my conversations are not usually this dramatic. Really," I said with a promising nod and slight smile.

"No, I'm glad that you're sharing. We can all relate to fears. I have my own - difficult ski runs, challenging cases, formidable opponents and of course relationships," he said, smiling warmly. "I understand completely and sympathize." He reached over and stroked my hand. "I don't know if I can make your fears go away but I am only a phone call away, and I hope that you take my offer seriously," he said, moving closer.

I nodded, acknowledging the offer, mindful of his closeness.

"Ah, relationships. Maybe the scariest," I said, staring at our hands, "because I think we have to let our guard down, be vulnerable for any meaningful emotional connection to occur, for me, at least I find that dangerous territory." I looked in his eyes, moving my hands to my wine glass. "People should come with resumes, background checks and sworn testimonials from friends and family," I said smiling. John laughed.

He sat studying my face before speaking. "Agree, there's a lot of variables to dating … age, experience, agendas … a lot in play. Hard to find out about people if they want to stay hidden." He was quiet for a moment, looking down then back at me. "Age and inexperience were the culprits in my marriage. It's a typical story, met in college and got married between semesters when I was in law school. Unfortunately, several years into our marriage and two kids later we realized that we didn't agree on our future. She wanted a bigger city practice for me, and I wanted to come back here. We drifted and she found someone else which ended things. I don't know, maybe there wasn't enough of a relationship to hold it all together to begin with…" I could see he was still carrying some residual pain from this.

An interesting topic given this was our first date. I was surprised at his candor.

"When were you divorced?"

"Well, I guess it's been about 4 years now."

"I hope this isn't a painful subject, John, I was just curious," I said, concerned.

Taking a deep breath and smiling warmly, he replied, "No, Tess, I'm over the relationship. It was a hard time for all of us; I don't know, maybe I feel as though I failed them. I don't want to be back in that relationship, but I think Maggie and JJ would like that. Not sure I buy staying together for the kids." He looked into my eyes searching for that answer.

My gaze traveled from John to couples at other tables. I looked back at John and smiled gently. "I don't have an answer to that. That can never be an easy call, kids, and divorce. I'm divorced too and I know all the mixed-up emotions that come with it. Do kids benefit from unhappy parents staying together or suffer at the loss that not having both parents bring to their foundation? I don't know. Maybe the answer is to marry the right person the first time? But then we're back to background checks and sworn testimonials." I said, smiling. "We're pretty starry eyed when it comes to love. And formulas and playbooks aren't exactly romantic. Love is mercurial. You know, I think selfless love is about as good a guidepost as we are going to get and that goes to raising children and loving each other." As I said that, my thoughts wandered back to my marriage, the tumult and anger. How does love get that bad? I hadn't thought of that in a long while.

John looked hard at me, his concerned eyes wandering over my face.

I cheered, "Dating is almost a deception," I continued lightly. "We put our *best* foot forward. We're hardwired for love, and it creates this *want*. But so many things can distort it. So often we accept levels of relationships with people who may not be right for us, and we think, rather hope, that things will change or work out and therefore be okay." I paused for a moment, then looked over at John. "My marriage had some of those elements. I don't blame people; we're created to be relational, engineered for closeness with a need for love. Because it's an emotion, wisdom is not often in play. Sorry, John, dialogue is the product of an over-analytical mind. And you are probably thinking about now 'Man, what did I get myself into'?!"

We both laughed looking warmly at each other. He was easy to talk to and open. I got the feeling there would be no boundaries on subjects we could talk about if this conversation didn't cause him to run. This thought enhanced my feelings for him.

"Again, I agree with you, it's hard to separate emotion and wisdom and make the right call. Well, it's obvious you've given this some thought. I confess I don't give much thought to relationships, and by *that,* I mean understanding relationships; a lot of the emotional stuff tends to be a mystery to me, I'm sorry to say. So, I tend to let relationships flow and see where they go. Maybe it's a male thing."

"Venus and Mars!" We both laughed, tension gone.

"True." John was silent for a few moments while he looked over at me, staring, taking me in.

To break the moment, I asked John about his children, and he lit up like a candle. I learned his pet names for them, their pets, their favorite games, and sports. I loved seeing his love for his children transform his face. I loved that he loved his children. His selfless care for his kids made him very appealing.

After dinner things became more relaxed. There was a subtle movement by John that put us physically closer. Close enough that I could smell his cologne and sense his masculine power. I found myself responding to him, it made me quiet.

John seemed to sense this change in me, and his tone softened. His eyes didn't leave my face, he seemed to be trying to penetrate my thoughts, a thoughtful analysis of the woman he was sitting next to. I was starting to enjoy his attention. His arm found the top of the booth and he casually tilted his face towards me. "I thought we could take a walk, and I could introduce you to my town. I could fetch a jacket from my car?" He was waiting for my response, hopeful.

I nodded.

As we walked, his hand found mine and I realized there was a power in Jackson Hole walking under the night sky and the shadow of the great Tetons that fueled romance. It was powerful.

John was warm physically and gentle emotionally. This surprised me. He had come across as confident with work and with women. He almost seemed shy with his uncertainty about me. I hadn't been gushing or rushing into a romantic relationship with him.

He must have wondered about this. He was the persistent one in keeping the contact going. I was receptive but not responsive, until now. I found I liked John. More than once he noticed my watching him as we walked. This made him smile and he squeezed my hand. I was responding.

He stopped at the neighborhood park on the south side of the Stagecoach where we had first met. He turned towards me, hesitating, staring into my eyes, then gently his hand reached to cup my face tilting it towards him, his thumb tracing the outline of my jaw. I liked the face looking back at me. There was a different kind of beauty in John's face, his Nordic-chiseled face, just starting to be etched by life and age, lines deepening when he smiled or frowned. His lips were not full but there was a cute dimpling at the edges leaving one with the impression that he was rarely upset, often happy… But at this moment his green eyes were steady, focused on my face, with a soft intensity, glittering – everything stood quiet and still.

"Tess," his eyes searching mine for something that told him to proceed. I was open but not sure about this. He sensed this. I felt his warm lips kiss my forehead then my lips. He was gentle, his kiss soft almost reverent. Moving back, he looked down reaching for both my hands and stared at them, looking back up he said, "I was hoping that I would get an invite out to see your new home, to see where you've been keeping yourself hidden these past months."

He was stepping closer into my world.

"Okay ....," my heart racing, hesitating I managed, "When … when can you come by?"

"What are your plans for tomorrow? I have most of the day open," he said looking gently at my face.

"Okay," I said with a nervous laugh, "tomorrow will be great."

We agreed to meet in Lander tomorrow morning. Tomorrow? As he walked me back to my car, I couldn't help but feel confused. He had just stepped into a more assertive role in the relationship. There was so much to think about as I drove home. My mind reviewed the evening. I kept replaying John's face, his words, his power, and gentleness.

I arrived home dizzy with emotion. I was having a hard time collecting my thoughts and he will be here…tomorrow. Was I ready for this? Not even remotely. But what was there to prepare for? It's a visit. I felt hesitant happiness.

Chapter Eight

Life is Your Ministry

Saturday morning quiet time brought more than a few concerns. Things felt a little out of control. Suddenly my heart was reacting to romance, and to make matters more complex, it involved two men. The fact that I wasn't sure about Clint's interest didn't alter the fact that he has stirred something in me. Romance has not been part of my story for several years now. Why is romance such a problem for me? Maybe because there's is no controlling the heart. Control is counter to romance, a deterrent to romance. Sometimes close relationships have felt like a trap, like I'm in a closed closet, suffocating, or that more will be asked of me than I'm capable of returning. Since few things in life are this intimate, for me I fear that a relationship will touch some buried problem or shortcoming.

Exposure.

Movement again in the brush! Running! This time it set me in motion. I ran towards the noise. Is some animal living nearby? To the left of the barn, I investigated the brush. Pushing through I found an area that was clearly depressed, as though something had been sleeping there. Some of my garbage had been pilfered, the debris of leftovers strewn about. Searching the area, I found a little path that took me to a fork, one leading up the mountain and one leading out to the road. I went up the mountain trail but didn't see any signs of anything; nothing to indicate the identity of what I heard. No clues. I'll have to make more of an effort to contain my garbage. The last thing I needed was an animal problem.

I walked back and took the trail to the road. As I stood there lost in thought looking back up the trail, Jimmy and Clint stopped by. They were not usually here on Saturdays, so I was unprepared for them.

Clint. I felt myself blush, my pulse reacting. Don't think my heart is sleeping anymore. They had stopped by for some tools Clint had left here that he needed for a job today in Lander. I was headed in the same direction. I wondered if we would run into one another while I was meeting up with John. Suddenly, totally uncomfortable with the direction my life had gone. Complicated emotions running rampant in my heart. What's wrong with single and simple?

Jimmy was talking and I realized he was talking to me. He was staring at me asking me a question, and when I didn't respond, Clint looked over at me. Both were now looking at me. I roused my senses and stuttered, "I'm sorry, what were you saying?"

"My band is playing tonight, can you come?" His enthusiasm was beguiling and infectious.

"Sure. I think. What time and how do I get there?"

"Oh, no problem, I'll come by and pick you up."

"What time?"

"How about around 7:00? Band goes on at 8ish and we need time to set up."

It's another date. This one a lot less invading on my heart and I thought it might allow me to control the day with John. My calendar was starting to fill up. Dinner with Patty was also planned for next week. I was looking forward to getting a woman's perspective.

Watching them leave, I remembered I had to meet John in an hour. We had agreed to meet at the parking lot of Trimble's. Now hoping Patty was not working. Why hadn't I picked another parking lot?

John was waiting for me. I rolled my window down and said a quick hello. He smiled and I motioned for him to follow. "This was the plan, right?" He nodded.

At home I parked my car and motioned for John to park anywhere as I stepped out. I met him at his car. As he exited his vehicle, he stood and surveyed the property. "Wow Tess, this was not what I was expecting. Do you live here alone? It is beautiful. I had no idea a place like this existed outside Landers. How much property is there?"

"Thanks, twenty acres. Let me show you around."

Standing in front of the house he commented, "This is a beautiful home, Tess. I like it, although it seems like a lot of house for you." He looked over at me quizzically with a curious wonder filling his face. I could see that he could not put me together with the house.

"I know," and now looking at it, it does seem a bit much. "There was something about the house John that just felt right. It is a lot of house, but it offers a lot of possibilities and the price was right. To be honest, I am not entirely clear on the reason for purchasing it myself." I trailed off, didn't share my ideas for potential missions work on the property.

We walked slowly into the house. He was taking in the scope of the property, and I was trying to see it through his eyes. I took him on a tour of the house, and we walked through parts of the property. Tripping on a narrow trail John caught me. As we walked around the property, I could see he was deep in thought. When we returned to the house John commented, "I am probably overstepping boundaries here, but what happens if you get hurt?"

I studied his face trying to understand where this concern was coming from, "I know the property comes with risks, what doesn't? I can't explain something I don't fully understand myself. Buying this house just felt like the right call and it was the only property that I felt that way about. Sometimes you just have to go with your instincts, right?"

"I'm not questioning your ability to take care of yourself Tess and I meant what I said last night about being available for you." We were standing on the back deck facing one another. I could see that he was genuinely concerned.

I looked down at my feet and then moved towards the back door. Standing on the deck I asked, "Are you hungry? I can make some lunch."

"Sounds good."

I made lunch while John got better acquainted with Kai and Sprite. They have no loyalties. I watched John interacting with my dogs, sitting comfortably on my back porch. I found that mentally I was putting him in my world. Women do *that*! Men hunt and we nest.

I brought lunch outside and joined John on the deck. I laid the sandwiches on the table and walked to the railing Clint had been working on. Leaning forward I absently stared towards the barn. It was a beautiful September day. Rumors of rain this week. My first. But today was perfect. Neither of us spoke for a few moments. I turned and looked over at John who was munching on a sandwich and watching me closely. It sent a chill through me.

"Tess, you've really made a good investment here. The house has good bones, and I can see why this place attracted you." I was happy he thought so. "I can, however, understand it if you feel a little isolated and alone. Having some difficulty understanding you're going from a busy congested city to this. This seems extreme," he said looking at me. He seemed to see me differently. He continued, "I'm fascinated, I can't figure you out. Leaving everything and setting up a new life out here all by yourself. I don't know many women that would do this or possess the strength and courage it must have taken to do this alone. A true pioneer lady." He smiled warmly, as he stared, assessing me. "I'm glad we've met, and I have a feeling that getting to know you will be nothing short of an adventure." He put his sandwich down and looked intently into my eyes. "I'd like to get to know you. I'm not usually this direct and I am hoping this doesn't send you running for the hills. I don't want to scare you off. I've been attracted to you since that first night at the Stagecoach. I know this is early in our relationship, but you're on my radar Tess."

I found myself staring at my boots, cross-legged with my hands resting on the railing. Looking up I caught his gaze. "Well, that scares me," I said with a half-smile. "Sets the bar a bit high for me, funny to see myself that way. I'm pretty certain that I'll have trouble with this high assessment, and it seems to leave nowhere to go but down. I'm thinking you're headed for disappointment and I'll have to keep you at arm's length to prolong your fascination," saying this my smile widened.

"I'm fairly certain that once you get to know me that I will not measure up to being even mildly interesting." I said sincerely.

He chuckled as he stood "Ah, and humble too. I like that. You are probably too close to see what others observe about you. In my occupation, I have to be a pretty fair evaluator of people given the nature of my clients and opponents… check the waters for deception and sharks, having said that I may be better at assessing people in a work setting rather than social situations, so, I'm not setting myself up as an expert by any means. Whether you acknowledge it or not it took courage and confidence for you to come out here, live out here alone, it makes you maybe more than a bit interesting. I like what I see and what I see is a very beautiful, loving lady, especially after hearing you last night talk about relationships – I loved the 'selfless love' comment. It's how I feel about my kids, and you nailed my feelings. Intriguing. I'm not looking for danger, but I like confidence and strength in a woman, with an edge of adventure. I like that you're about more than appearance. Deep waters in you lady," he said, smiling as he stood and started moving around the table towards me.

I was transfixed. How could he believe those things about me? Clearly, he sees something in me I don't see. Within seconds my thoughts were interrupted by his touch. He was now standing confidently in front of me, both hands on the railing on either side, pinning me, a smile playing on the edges of his mouth, his eyes fixed on my face. I was holding my breath. I could feel his power, and he had without question taken a leadership role in the direction of this relationship.

His eyes looked deeply into mine. Surveying my face, he leaned in slowly, his lips brushing mine gently as his eyes held mine, his kiss deepening, we both pulled closer, the kiss becoming more ardent. Finally, he pulled slightly away and stared into my face, studying it. It had been a long time since anyone had touched me like this and I found I had a yearning for more ... this touching so close ... he was getting to me and it felt like an answer to a long lost need ... sweet and intimate ... the two of us standing there, close enough to inhale one another's breath. His hands had moved to my waist, and he looked down at my body. His eyes took me in ... what I felt from him wasn't lust, it went to another feeling, a deeper connection flowing between us and he leant in, his kiss becoming intense, ardent. I responded. Breathing heavily, his face inches from mine, "I plan to hang around to find out more about Alessandra St. Michael. In the meantime," he whispered, his green eyes staring deeply into mine, "walk me to my car and tell me when I can see you again." He said this, leaning in for one last kiss, staring into my eyes, then releasing me and stepping away. As he released me, he took my hand and led me through the house.

When he reached his car he turned, a focused gentleness in his eyes, "Look, Tess, I really don't want to rush things with you." His hand still holding mine. "I have ideas about this relationship, and I want to take things slower than I'm used to. See what develops before other things interfere." He searched my eyes as I nodded, not sure what I was hearing. "You know, I don't have your phone number!" he said as he sat and reached into his glove box for a pen and something to write on. He retrieved a loose pen and the back of an envelope. He took down my number and told me he would call tonight. I remembered that I had plans. "Tomorrow then."

I nodded.

John drove off leaving me standing in the front yard with my dogs and something more than warmth in my heart.

When had I given him my full name? Had he run a background check?

Okay Lord. What was this? I had talked to my pastor when I was going through my epiphany, telling him I thought God had called me to be single. He told me he doubted that. He told me God would probably bring someone into my life when I had found my ministry, someone to join me. I knew that your life *was* your ministry. How you lived it day-to-day, walking out you're calling and finding a way to live your faith in the trenches of life. I honestly don't know what to think or how to process this in light of what I thought I had been called here for. Could this be another distraction to sideline me?

I turned and walked back into the house not seeing my surroundings, head, and heart full of stuff. I couldn't find any clarity. I grabbed the remote and headed out the back door towards my stream. I needed to talk. This time I took the dogs. Shortly, we were by the stream, and I found the quiet soothing as I sank to the ground. I listened hoping for a repeat of the Thursday quiet. No movement but I was pulling strength from above. I was part of something permanent and higher than I knew I could fully comprehend.

In the quiet, my thoughts turned upward. Romance makes me think of You, Lord. You *are* love, the love that fuels romance. You caused everything. Love is air, earth, fire, and water; it's Your currency. As proof, we seek it constantly, we possess almost a primal need for love. You love me passionately, as I *am* and not because of the possibilities you see in me, but today, at this moment in my completely flawed state … You love *me*. You *are* our mysterious romance. Our *capacity* for love comes from You. Relationships open our hearts so that we can understand the loving relationship possible with You. There are soul relationships here that You intend for us, to show us this love, unfortunately, most of us don't wait to find them. We hunt, seek, and settle, never knowing the exhilaration, passion, and depth of being in a relationship engineered by You, to be totally, completely loved by someone. If romance is in my future, I only want that man who has my name engraved on his heart. Keep me protected from anything less.

Jimmy! That startled realization brought an abrupt halt to my thoughts. Later.

Chapter Nine

Romantic Maelstrom

As I arrived back at the house, I checked the time. 5:30. What did he say, 7:00 pm. As I ran upstairs the phone rang. It was Patty. Yes, she did see me today in the parking lot. Who was that following me in the beamer? Remember John at that restaurant? Same guy. I have to run. Can we catch up later this week at dinner? "Sure. Looking forward to it," she said, a hint of excited anticipation in her tone.

Quickly showered and washed my hair. Once done, I stepped out to hunt for something to wear. Definitely jeans. No boots. Sandals and jeans were an old familiar wardrobe, but I decided against a tee shirt and found something dressier, a pink button-up shirt. It was a date of sorts, and I was in the mood for a different appearance. It was just 6:15. I decided to eat something, as I was not sure that the date included food. Rummaging through the refrigerator I found some leftover manicotti. Last on the agenda were the dogs.

I headed down the stairs to locate my things as Jimmy was driving up. Perfect. I couldn't wait to see more community.

Jimmy looked good. His hair was pulled back into a ponytail. Duke was with him, and I had to sit in between them. Duke seemed uncomfortable around me, and why shouldn't he? I am a generation away from relating to him. But Jimmy and I connected, and an excited conversation flowed about tonight's plans.

We drove out of my 'street', turned right, and headed north towards the reservation. The road was surrounded by hills and deep ravines. The mountains loomed in stark contrast to a landscape that was punctuated by green forests and sporadic rushing rivers. The forests stood defiant and proud next to these ageless mountains. It was a diverse landscape. As we entered the reservation. I saw homesteads, and I could see signs of ranching and farming. We turned off the main road and traveled a few miles to the community center. I found that it sat near the Community Baptist Church. Across the street was a convenience store that offered the hope of coffee later.

While they unloaded, I wandered inside the center. Only one portion of it was open. They had put up dividing walls. Reminded me of the bands I used to watch at the old Armory. There was a stage set up along with seating. An open area was situated in front of the stage for dancing I presumed. There was a concession set up and I headed that way. Happily, they had coffee, which I purchased and took a seat interested in everything I saw.

The band set-up and they did a preemptive rehearsal warm-up. I located the bathroom and as I stood I could see that people were starting to arrive. Young people. There was electric anticipation reverberating in the air as they arrived, an expectation of fun and maybe more. Some were arriving as couples while others were looking to be a couple. Each gender was eyeing the other for future potential. Looking for love. I remember those days. Others arrived and were mostly spectators, watching to see what happened, or just here to enjoy the music and hang out with friends.

I headed back from the bathroom, secured more coffee, and found my seat. The band was surprisingly good. Jimmy was the bass guitarist. It was obvious they took this seriously, and obvious enjoyment between them in what they were doing. Maybe it was a system they had developed but each seemed to understand the other without words being spoken. I didn't know why I was surprised that Duke was the lead singer and guitarist. Jones was on drums and Steve was another lead guitarist. They also made up the group of Clint's helpers. I wondered if Clint had any involvement with his brother's interests.

And there were girl admirers, hanging near the stage. I smiled watching them. No one asked me to dance, no real surprise and I was grateful because I had no grace. I saw evidence of adult supervision, but it was quiet and unobtrusive. The youth gave them little cause for adult intervention.

While sitting there I was approached by a young woman. She introduced herself as Jimmy's sister, Dinah. She looked like Clint; a beauty and I could see a family resemblance. "Hi! It's Tess, right? I'm Dinah, Jimmy's sister! Jimmy talks about you alllll the time! He told *everyone* that you were coming and that he was bringing you!" She laughed at her brother. She was stunning.

I stood up smiling, "Hello, Dinah! It's wonderful to meet you. I think Clint told me he had two sisters, Dinah and…."

"Tamara." She helped.

"Right, thanks." I smiled warmly at her. "Jimmy is a favorite of mine. I love his energy and enthusiasm. Always smiling. I can see a family resemblance between the three of you. I am very happy Jimmy thought to invite me."

"Yeah, he has more energy than the entire tribe put together!" We both laughed in agreement.

"Well, I am having a great time, and it is nice to meet new people. I hope I see more of you. Please feel free to drop in and say hello anytime," I said warmly.

"Thanks!"

We could not continue the conversation due to the noise level and a boy pulling her onto the dance floor. As she left, she yelled back over her shoulder, "This is Tommy!" And she turned and joined her excited partner, laughing and dancing on the floor. It felt good to watch them. I find myself smiling more often.

Sitting back down, I got caught up in watching all the activities. People watching. I was so engrossed that I didn't notice someone approaching. He was an older gentleman, with a badly pocked and scared face, stocky and solidly built. Everything about the man spoke of a hard life and his eyes reflected some hidden bitterness or deep hatred. I shuddered. I was an easy standout in this crowd, and I guessed he saw me as a curiosity. His blatant interest, however, didn't strike me as friendly. He found a suitable place near a column where he stood observing me. I became nervously uncomfortable, and I tried to ignore him, but occasionally our eyes would meet. The encounter felt malevolent.

Just past him, my eyes caught the movement of a couple entering the center. It was Clint. For a moment my heart reacted. He was not alone. He caught sight of his brother on stage and smiled. I noticed his female friend. She was attractive and they stood close enough together that it was obvious they were a couple.

My eyes moved towards where the older man stood, and I found that he had disappeared. I made a quick check of the room. He was gone but Clint had spotted me. He smiled. I returned the smile. I relaxed a little, his presence made me feel safer.

The music had picked up to a heated electric beat, and the animated dancers threw themselves into its rhythm. Clint and his friend walked past me on the other side of the center to join the other adults hovering in the background to the left and ahead of me. I could barely see Clint, but I was struck by his friendliness with the others and his popularity amongst them. The female seemed to have the same opinion. He was relaxed and laughed easily with them. I felt a twinge of something. I wondered what it felt like to be the recipient of his focused attention.

As the evening progressed, I was struck by the realization that I had ridden with Jimmy. I would have to stay until the band loads up. Why didn't I think of that? They were having a great time, and I could see potential for this continuing on into the early hours of the morning. At his age that is exactly where I would be and what I'd be doing. To my surprise Jimmy ran up during a break and, apparently, he had already thought of this. He told me that he had asked Clint if he would take me home. Clint agreed. Would I mind? I think I did but what choice did I have? I put on a smile and told Jimmy that that was fine. Right behind Jimmy, Clint was walking across the hall towards us, alone. His manner seemed to suggest he and his friend had plans and dropping me off was not in them.

He reached me shortly after Jimmy left. "Do you mind if we take you home?" he asked looking in my face. I couldn't detect agitation, just ….

Looking up at him, I responded, "No, that's fine. I'm really sorry about this Clint, and that it has interrupted your date.

Whatever works best for you both," I said as I tried to avoid his face.

Instead of hurrying me towards the door, he stood still, and I could see intensity clouding his dark eyes. Thinking this look meant he would like to leave now and return to his plans, I turned to grab my things. He stepped closer, almost hesitant, "Has anyone asked you to dance tonight?" I was happy it was dark in the hall because I didn't know if I had turned white with the thought of dancing or blushed with the thought of dancing with Clint!

He was standing waiting for a response, watching me and I couldn't figure out what to do next, but I could hear that it was a slow tune. I thought I could manage that. So, I nodded and stepped forward. I followed Clint onto the floor.

Jimmy was grinning from ear to ear.

As he moved close and put his arm around my waist, I reached up to rest my hand on his shoulder. My free hand in his. I felt a swirling rush of warmth like a rush of air that moved fast down my spine. I was finding the sensation confusing and hot. Instantly I realized how romantic and physical slow dancing was, mixed with the lighting, the music, all of that adds to the atmosphere and fuels the mood. It was like a tonic, and I was finding it hard to stay clear-headed. I grappled with composure and so tried to find something to say that would give me control.

"I wasn't expecting to see you tonight. Do you usually attend Jimmy's performances?" trying to keep my voice steady and my breathing normal.

Looking into my face, he responded warmly, "I usually stop in to check on things. It makes him happy, and I like his music." He continued, "He's mentioned to anyone that would listen that you were coming. He really likes you," he said, the warmth deepening. "You look great, Tess," his eyes gentle and deep, penetrating, not leaving my face as they took in my facial contours, resting on my lips. I shivered; I think this was the first time I heard him say my name.

I managed to breathe, "Thank you."

His warmth pulled me in, inviting but not safe. I stepped in and he moved close to take the lead. I could usually follow if it was slow. The realization that he had his arm around my waist and was holding my hand against his chest, near his heart caused an increase in my pulse and I wondered if he could tell. Twice in one day a man had gotten my blood moving through my heart at a pace that took my breath. He led me gently through the steps. I felt him pull me closer as he leaned in. His cheek next to mine. I had his full attention, his dark eyes not leaving mine. I tried looking away but there wasn't anything else I wanted to look at but his face. It captivated me. His dark eyes, his straight nose and strong jaw, his high cheekbones and full lips …. Everything perfectly placed and perfectly proportioned. There was a gentle grace in his movements, a protective quality about the way he hovered over me. The room, the dancers all disappeared. All I could see were his dark eyes and the beauty of his face. I was lost there. I didn't want the moment to end. I tried for control so that he could not see how strongly he was affecting me. But soon my arm moved around his shoulders, pulling him closer, my hand resting on his neck. We both stepped in, bodies touching. I could feel the length of his body against mine, his heat, his power ... breathing each other's breath, eyes locked on one another.

There was movement behind him, it was his female friend, and I realized the music had stopped. I must be blushing. I could see confusion on her face; it matched the state of my mind. Clint seemed aware of the situation, but we were still staring at one another. I wanted to be alone with him. Just to touch his face but the moment was gone; it had to be unless I wanted to continue dancing. The fast pace of the next song made it clear that that was not going to happen. I corralled my emotions and stepped away from Clint.

"Thank you for the dance," I managed to mumble as I turned and moved towards my seat leaving them both standing together. I needed distance and a clear head. The panicked realization that I was supposed to ride home with them struck me. The evening moved forward slowly. I did not chance a look towards Clint. I was lost in my thoughts. Needing fresh air, I stepped outside to clear my head. As I stood there, I could feel some measure of control. Lord? Returning to the dance I still felt confused but calmer.

As the evening wore on Clint approached me alone, asking if I was ready to leave. He was not smiling but I felt a softening in him towards me. Was that confusion on his face because it mirrored mine?

Again, outside in the parking lot, in the night air, I found some composure. He opened the passenger side door of his truck, and I stepped in trying to avoid him. We headed off the reservation for my home.

I was afraid to ask about the absent girlfriend. With the elevated stirrings that had been occurring between us, energy between us was not entirely unexpected, but the dance was. I would not have exposed myself to his power and not sure what his thoughts were at the moment he asked me to dance. Hard to know her perception or his, but certainly things had changed. I sat staring out the window watching nothing as images of the Teton Range ran past the window and flickered shadows on my unseeing eyes. His presence in the cab remained powerful.

I remained quiet.

He pulled up to my darkened house. The silence in the vehicle was thick.

"Thank you, Clint," I managed to say. "I'm sincerely sorry I've interfered with your plans this evening." I wanted to say anything that would bring clarity to the situation for both of us, but I didn't know what to say that would straighten this out and not knowing what else to say, I took a breath and pulled on the handle. I got out of his truck, closed the door and headed toward the house. I found my key, unlocked the front door, and went inside. He started his truck and left.

Kai and Sprite greeted me inquisitively. After letting them out, I went upstairs, took a quick shower, and went to my bedroom.

As tired as I was back at the hall, I was now completely awake. My whole body was alive. What had been sleeping in me was thoroughly awake. I opened my Bible; I needed wisdom and direction desperately before anyone got hurt or I made a colossal mistake and harmed the reason I was here. It's not like I haven't been in romances before, doesn't history count for anything? I felt like a teenager. I wanted what I wanted. What I want now, as an adult, should carry with it the weight of responsibility. Accountability. The mistakes of my past learned. But how do you proceed with your head in a matter of the heart?

I had no idea where my heart was at this moment, caught up in a romantic maelstrom.

I got down on my knees.

Chapter Ten

Feral Shadows

I had no idea when I finally slept but I woke up in a state of confusion. Wherever my thoughts had taken me before I fell asleep, they had not helped the confusion. As I laid there my thoughts went to the events of yesterday, in particular last nights. Who *is* this man, Clint?

The thought drove me out of bed. What would help clear my head? Will he be here this morning? Oh, it's Sunday. No. Sunday. Church. That might help. I felt like a purpose had been given to me. What time was it? 7:30. I found the number for Community Baptist and called for its service times, I knew its location, next to the Community Center on the Wind River Indian Reservation. Did last night with Clint really happen? Will I see him?

I had time.

Quickly I went downstairs to get coffee and take care of the dogs. I ran back upstairs and took a shower hoping that the water would penetrate my brain and clear it. It didn't but I felt better.

I took my journal downstairs and onto the front porch. Sitting in a chair, I stared out over the lawn. This is such a peaceful place. I mused that things had taken a turn I had not foreseen. Romance. No longer clear why I was here. I stared out over the lawn and further out towards the hovering mountains. In such a short time, things seemed to have gone off road. But romance is God's plan also, right? However, this situation did not feel clean. I knew the enemy threw distraction in our path, to keep us from our purpose. For some reason, I thought if God intended someone for me that God would escort His 'someone' up to my front door and introduce us and I would just know. This involved the hearts of two men. Since there was no behavior bordering on forethought, was I guilty? How had I brought this upon myself? I think I was feeling a little ashamed about last night. And yesterday. The hearts of two men have been touched by me and vice versa. It would serve me right to be the one hurt. Are you teaching me about the inner workings of my heart? But realistically Lord, how had I brought *this* on myself? I *know* I didn't encourage either man, nothing close. I had been in relationships before that proved to be wrong for me and I knew that they were time-consuming, and you could live with the consequences for years. I didn't want that. I didn't think I had the luxury of that now.

I thought about both men. I liked them but not entirely the same. Examining my heart, I realized that my heart quickened when I thought about Clint. There is danger there. There is a solid quality about John. Solid felt sure and familiar. Settling? What I expect? Clint definitely offered the unexpected. There seems to be a wild quality about him like the day when I first saw him in his truck. But he hasn't done anything wild. The opposite, he is responsible and has a good reputation in the community. Maybe he just seems less tame; the masculine, animal quality in the male that women find compelling; the warrior, the fighter, the protector. I felt an intense warmth at this thought. So, what would make him dangerous? His appearance was wild and foreign; his culture had a wild romantic history and the likelihood of our culture's blending seemed less certain. Danger.

My thoughts turned to John, that feeling at the railing and standing under the Jackson night sky… My heart reacted with warmth to his face and his presence. But neither image gave a hint at clarity in where relationships with either of them might be headed or if either one was that person.

My thoughts stalled. If I stopped musing and listened, You'd give me guidance, I was certain of that. I relaxed. Someone loves me more than I can fathom, and He runs the universe. Protect our hearts, Lord. I'm giving this situation to You. I promise to obey. Or try really hard. I know I am willful. But I think that romance is the most complex, *the* most complicated because wisdom flees in the face of it. It's not a product of reason. Who we love is not dependent upon calculated decision making; we love whom we love, inexplicably.

The church's proximity to the community center brought back memories and the ache of last night.

A woman at the door greeted me warmly and handed me their service brochure. I thanked her and found a seat in the back row. I read the brochure. It provided information on events involving the church for the week, Bible studies, youth groups, community events. Pastor Peter Allen. Is that a Native American name? The service started and I found the pastor was a young man in his thirties. We sang a song and sat as he read the brochure of the upcoming church events. More singing and a short meet and greet. I was the immediate focus of several, but most could not seem to find the courage to say hello. The woman that I had seen at the door introduced herself as Rosa. I liked her immediately and she came and sat next to me.

Here was a place that felt familiar to me. Since my salvation, church has always been a holy reverential experience and it does not matter the denomination, because in all of them I feel His presence. My salvation experience was cataclysmic. It was a breaking event that started with an ecstatic high that lasted on and off for years. It also started me on a new path, and a new me. Church excites me because it's where He lives. I fell in love with Him, and I've never known anything close to this relationship. These highs still punctuate my life.

After the service Rosa and I spent a little time getting to know one another. She invited me to the church Fall Festival this Saturday, and I invited her to my home for coffee. Now that the contractors were finishing, I could use some company. She already knew where I lived ...? Rosa was 46yrs old and had three children between the ages of 14 and 20. She worked at the church part time and at the Reservation office, housing the Bureau of Indian Affairs. She seemed like she might be a potential new friend. I was delighted to make her acquaintance. Rosa introduced me to Pastor Allen. He was a small man, but I could sense there was a big heart housed there. He was very welcoming and interested. He mentioned the Fall Festival next Saturday at a local park. Just bring me. Rosa and I exchanged numbers, and we set a time for coffee, next Saturday morning. As I left the church building, my eyes checked my surroundings for any sign of Clint. Rosa walked me to my car, and I drove slowly out of the parking lot.

On the road home I remembered John. He was supposed to call today. John. Was it just yesterday that he was here? It seemed like a distant memory. Too much had passed through both my heart and my mind since the last time I saw him. Unfortunately, I didn't want to think about John, I wanted to think about Clint.

I pulled up to my house. It is *my* house, I realized.

After changing and a light lunch I looked for solace on the back porch, the whole day ahead of me. I walked out into the back yard towards the barn. I loved this barn. As I walked over to the barn, noting again the smell that made me think of family farms and pioneers, I turned and stood in the opening of the barn door, leaning against the open-door frame. Looking back at my house I was startled to realize that the house was finished. Finished and he had no reason to come back. Didn't I still owe him money?

It's hard for me to explain to myself how he had become so important to me. We hardly spoke. I knew almost nothing about him, yet he had entered my heart and captured a part that was not making room for John. I hadn't consented to this, the stealth of Clint, under the quiet cover of daily life.

I grabbed my boots, the remote and headed towards the road and the places I had walked with my friends. I thought about the stream, but I needed to move and clear my head.

The day was spectacular. There was an autumn chill in the air. The trees were starting to change colors. No palm trees. This is one of my favorite seasons. I love the changes, the world falling asleep. The dogs were beside themselves with the joy that running and exploring brought to their noses and limbs. Back in Florida I didn't take Kai for walks, it fell more into a category of 'sniffs'. Nothing standing vertical was ignored.

I took a side trail just off to the right. The trail offered a varied selection of the forest and there was a glade about half a mile up that had the last growth of red Indian paint and Heartleaf arnica.

The pace was sporadic due to the dogs. Not sure what would happen if the wolf in Kai were allowed unsupervised reign. He was all white and people often mistook him for a hybrid wolf. He was smart, and I was pretty sure that he knew his way home. Sprite was a whole separate matter. They had both escaped in Florida and she had gotten arrested. She jumped into a police cruiser. Maybe that makes her smart. While she doesn't project smarts, she is tenacious. They paw printed her at the pound and released her to my custody. Kai, however, was at our doorstep at 6 am. It's what Kai can encounter out here that concerns me … bear, mountain lion, and real wolves.

The glade was just starting to exhibit signs of fall. The last of the wildflowers mixed in with the tall meadow grasses looked like a painting and I wished I'd thought to bring my camera. I found a cool shaded area under a Bur oak, and I sat inhaling the scenery. Leaning back, I closed my eyes, listening to the breeze and woodland sounds, but all I could see behind my closed eyelids was his face, his intense obsidian eyes outlined with black eyelashes. There was a hint of gold inside the black in his eyes; flecks of light that seemed to dance when he showed interest. They reflected fierce confidence. I wanted to get to know him. He had grown on me - his quiet strength and confidence had grounded my first months for me, without realizing it I saw that I had come to rely on his daily presence, my feelings had gone from unrecognized comfort at having him around to genuine interest in wanting him around.

I decided I needed to keep moving. I found a new trail that I had not explored before that took me up past the meadow. The trail was pocked with large boulders and roots presenting a more difficult terrain, requiring more exertion, but it felt good; it kept my mind busy and the feel of the sun on my face and the cool air running through my hair was invigorating. The trail wound around large rock outcroppings. As I climbed the steep trail, I noticed that there were caves. Maybe these are home to the animal stalking my home in the early morning hours? The tree density was becoming more sporadic and more of the rocky skeletal substructure of the mountain was evident. Trees fanned to the right and the left, creating an opening for a glade of high meadow grasses. The tall grass was plugged in sporadically, surrounding rocks and boulders like tufts of hair on a bald head. This glade moved up the mountain, which was topped with stony outcroppings that were roofed by slow moving cotton clouds floating over a brilliant blue sky. I loved everything about this land; the ruggedness, the wildness, the idea that it belonged to no one. It offered escape from human problems.

Standing in the sun, I surveyed the mountain. I felt light, weightless here. This felt good, like a 'soul' massage. My heart lifted and open to nature and all its surrounding beauty. So blessed.

Just off the trail to the left I noticed an odd solid brown shape embedded in the tree cover that captured my attention. It was nestled just above the trail between Bur oaks and Ash trees. There was a side trail nearby and I decided to follow it. I found that it ran up to what I now recognized was a cabin. Is this still my property? Cautiously, I moved in closer investigating the cabin. By the looks of it, it was an old hunting cabin. But there were signs of life, recent newspapers strewn around and a recently used fire ring outside. Broken bottles and charred cans had been left in the ring. I found a stick and flicked around in the coals causing a small swirl of smoke to escape. I could still smell the burning wood. Who used this and *was* it on my property?

I knocked on the cabin door. No answer. The cabin was not locked, and I opened the door wide. It appeared to be vacant, so I stepped inside; it was empty. The cabin consisted of one room. Hesitating, I moved slowly around the room. Cans of beans and soup were stacked on a shelf along with a box of matches, salt and pepper. There was an old mattress and tattered blanket to the far back right. Someone is using this. It was drafty inside and newspapers covered the windows on either side of the cabin and were stuffed into cracks. Walking back outside, I sat down on the front rock steps. Maybe someone will come back? Looking southeast, is that the roof of my house? ... Do I have a neighbor? I could hear water and a short distance behind the cabin I found a small stream. It was a convenient water source. Walking up to it, I stooped down to inspect a small dam that had been made with rocks that corralled the cold and fast-moving water creating a spout, which I suspected was used for collecting water. I noted that there was a clear trail that led back to the cabin. I pivoted around, looking back at the cabin. Someone definitely appeared to be using it. Could they be hunters?

Straightening up, I walked back to the cabin and waited, hoping someone would show, finally I left. I wondered if Patty knew who owned this cabin? And was it on my property?

The dogs were inspecting everything. I called them, and we headed back down towards the main trail. Upon turning towards home, I found another side trail that appeared to head to the back of my house. I took it. This turned out to be the trail I had taken the other day in the chase. This was that other trail that forked up the mountain. I stood for a moment and looked back towards the cabin. An unsettled feeling came over me. I needed to find out more about the cabin.

Walking back to the house I found that Jimmy was there. He had brought his sister Dinah. They both smiled when they saw me. Can I get free of Clint? Still, I love his brother's company and would miss him, I realized.

"How long were you waiting? It's good to see you, Jimmy and nice to see you again, Dinah" I told them as I walked towards them.

"Dinah has been wanting to meet you officially" He grinned. Dinah blushed. "What did you think of the band?" anticipation all over his face.

"I thought the band was great and the evening was wonderful! You guys are *really* good, and I mean that. You have talent and an unusual sound. It was amazing to listen and watch you guys. Stay with it."

Jimmy was elated.

"Would you both like to come in for something to drink?"

They both nodded and smiled.

Inside we sat at the table in the small dining area. I had soda left from the contractors and offered them each one. I grabbed some water. I asked Dinah about herself. She must be the quiet one because Jimmy instead offered the family bio. I learned Jimmy was 18 and Dinah was 17, the youngest and the other siblings, Joseph 22, and Tamara 24.

"How old is Clint?" I asked, leaning forward, curious.

"Oh, Clint is the old one!" Jimmy laughs, accentuating *old*. "Mom was married the first time at 15 and she had Clint at 16. He's 34! Can you believe it? My mom's first husband left them, and she remarried. Our dad died of tuberculosis a few years ago." I blinked hearing the diagnosis. They still get that in America? I recalled now that Clint said *his* father had died. He must have considered his stepdad his father.

"Where's Clint's dad?"

"No one knows," Jimmy says, acting like he doesn't want to talk about it.

So, I asked about their mother. "Does she work?"

"No, my dad left her the ranch, and she takes care of things. Clint helps and pretty much supports the family. The rest of us help out. Dinah and I go to school on the rez." He added, "I'm a senior and she's a junior," he says nodding in Dinah's direction. "I want to play music, but my mom wants me to go to community college." I could see he was unhappy about this. He continued, "Then there's Joseph and Tamara, they're older and Tamara is married. She has two kids. She and Jackson, that's her husband, live on their own ranch not far from us. He's a rancher."

I learned from Jimmy that Clint is a tribal elder and Jimmie bragged that Clint was an ex-Marine and could track and find anyone or anything. He was a decorated Vet, Purple Heart. It was obvious that he not only loved his brother but that he admired him. He provided a brief Clint bio. Bragged Clint had been the high school standout, lettered in sports, was the quarterback and that he joined the Marines out of college. He said that Clint had been married before, but his wife, Nina, had died in childbirth leaving him with Oliver. They call him 'O'. The family helps raise O. When Clint got out of the military, he moved to the family ranch.

Suddenly, I saw this man in a new light, he has suffered deep pain and crushing sorrow, shouldering heavy responsibilities. His father's disappearance, his wife's death, a single parent; carrying the weight of his family and the tribe.

My mind went to the dance, his face, his touch.

"The lady last night, his wife?"

"Oh, no, that's his fiancé, Joannie? Did he introduce you?"

"I guess he didn't get around to it …"

"Yeah, *maybe*!" Jimmy laughed "Too busy dancing with you! Boy, she was mad about that. They got into a fight after he took you home. Rather she did. Clint didn't say much."

He asked Dinah, "Did they break up?"

"Jimmy," Dinah looked over at him as if to check the conversation and I heard her speak for the first time today. Shooting him a sharp look, she said, "Clint wouldn't like us discussing that. He'd be upset and besides, I don't think it's over. Joannie called today and they're seeing each other tonight." There was gentleness in Dinah and a protective quality for her brother Clint that I admired.

"Dinah, Clint and Tess are friends. He danced with her." Jimmy offered.

Quietly Dinah replied, "Still, don't think we should say anything." She looked down at her lap. I sat there with my eyes shifting between the two, following their dialogue and decided it was time to change the subject, so I asked Dinah about Tommy, hoping this was not also forbidden territory.

Her eyes brightened, "He's just a friend," she commented but her action belied something more.

"Right!" Jimmy scoffs. "He's at our house every day! My mom has to chase him off!"

She's blushing. "I am surprised just *one* boy is hanging around. You're such a beauty," I told her.

My phone rang. It was John. "Can I call you right back? I have company."

"No problem, Tess, talk to you soon."

Jimmy and Dinah left promising to visit again.

Evening was approaching, I fed the dogs and let them outside one final time.

I wanted to clean up before talking to John. Needed a shower to help me relax.

Before calling I went downstairs and wandered the house, looking at each room, my house, wrapped in stillness. I went to the kitchen and rummaged through the pantry trying to satisfy some desire or comfort me with … I didn't really know, I was restless. Nothing looked appetizing. I moved to the back door and looked outside, night was settling in. I decided on a cup of coffee.

Coffee in hand I went out onto the back deck to chill before calling John. Am I stalling? It was dark outside, but I didn't turn on the deck light, I wanted to look up into the night sky and see the heavens, see stars. They're supposed to be more visible away from city lights. And they were, they were out in the thousands. Like sparkling diamonds. Listening, I could hear crickets chirping and the shrill of cicada's; bats careened and flitted from tree to the barn and back so fast that I couldn't follow their antics. The crescent moon was partially hidden behind tree covered mountains. For the first time I heard off in the distance the lonely, haunting call of a wolf. Why do they cry at the moon? Still closer was an owl, hooting for its mate. I've always loved owls. In Florida an owl had nested for months in a front porch column and at night I could hear the sweet trilling through my open window producing sweet peacefulness.

Night held its own mysteries. Remembering my days backpacking. Images flooded my mind of my hiking treks in the Great Smoky Mountains National Park. The park had been created when pioneer communities had been bought out by the Federal Government, specifically to create the park. Some communities lay buried under the Fontana Dam. There were still signs of the early settlers in the park and often, in the stillness of the grassy meadows I passed when I hiked, I could still hear voices of children running and playing in the filtered sunlit mornings or horse drawn wagons moving slowly along hushed, shaded, one-lane dirt roads. Occasionally, I would find the hint of a lane that led to a forgotten homestead, or wild cascading roses, or pass by a partial boundary wall or chimney that stood defiant against the encroaching wilderness, as stubborn proof of the lives lived there. When I walked in the hushed silence of that great Park I always felt the echo of the early settlers; their Sunday gatherings, the emotion of their lives captured and destined to haunt the mountain wilderness. There was a side trail near an old homestead on the Old Settlers Trail, that led me over a rise to a forgotten family cemetery. Their graves marked by rough rocks; some with etched names and dates from the late 1800's still visible, I felt humbled to share in their family's legacy. They *had* left a legacy. The feeling I got then, hiking, I felt again here, the quiet voices of pioneers.

We're all sojourners here, we're just passing through.

Suddenly, a shiver ran up my spine, I felt I was not alone. No scuttling movement, just a creepy sense of something, as though peace disappeared. Opening my eyes I surveyed the property. Scanning I soon found a spot, a deepened shadow on the left side of the barn. The shadow was not a familiar shape for the backdrop. It was a thick shadow, almost the shape of a man. The shadow didn't move. My senses were heightened. I tried to make out what I was looking at and reasoned what *could* be out there? It couldn't be a person, could it? I felt I would have heard something in this stillness, footsteps, rustling of shrubs. But if it was a person, they were watching me. An elevated anxiety seized me, and I became acutely aware of my isolation. I felt my pulse rising. Squinting hard into the darkness, I tried to prove to myself that it was just a shadow. I called out. "Hello?" listening. "Is anyone out there?" My heart was thumping hard. I decided that I needed to get inside but remembered the trash. Securing the lids, I turned back towards my house and looked towards the barn, the shadow was gone. My imagination! I felt relieved. But as I walked back to the house, I turned again from my place near the chair to take another look, the shadow was gone from this vantage point also …

Backing towards the back door, I found the knob and turned to go inside. I chanced another look and could now see underbrush where the shadow had been … I felt hysteria rising in my throat. That won't help, I knew, and I pushed it down. Forcing myself to be calm, I closed and locked the backdoor and leaned my head against the doorframe. My hands were shaking. This had to make sense. Why would anyone be out there? It didn't make sense. My frightened thoughts reminded me of the cabin I found earlier today. Was I spotted and followed here? Trying to think … Slowly I secured every window and door. My years backpacking had found me in some frightening moments, and given the shear isolation and remote settings, I'd had to work through fear. I knew from those experiences that fear could paralyze me and make me a victim.

The dogs were *not* 'watch' dogs. Unfortunately, Huskies are known to aid and abet a thief and show them the easiest route to safety. Sprite was worse. She was a bad-ass dog if you were a cat or squirrel. Otherwise, she just wanted to be loved, by pretty much *anyone.* Anyone entering with criminal intent stood the chance of being licked to death. Still, their presence in the house calmed me. Whatever I faced, they would be there with me.

Before going upstairs, I tried another peek outside but now it was entirely too dark to see anything. The deck light would illuminate the deck, not the barn. Upstairs, I locked myself and the dogs in my bedroom. I was having a hard time shaking this feeling that I was not alone outside. *Now I felt isolated.* There were no contractors coming tomorrow. Unless I reached out, I would be alone here. I can't be frightened of shadows. My home was surrounded by shadows all night. I wondered how to think about this. Is someone watching me?

Shower, devotions & I climbed into bed and called John. "Geezzzz Tess! Calling right back must mean something different in Floridian!" he said laughing. It was good to hear his voice.

"I'm sorry. I just got tied up. How are you? What did you do with your day?" sounding more nonchalant than I felt. Should I say anything? But then he would learn of my delay in calling him.

He gave me the rundown of his day. I liked listening to John and rarely interrupted. Finally, he said, "Hey, I've been doing all the talking. What did *you* do today?" His tone was meaningful, warm, and working on intimate. I felt the direction he was taking the conversation. He doesn't want chit-chat, he wants more. I started to relax, propped up my pillow and pulled my comforter close around me. Talking to him helped chase away the shadows and I could feel his optimistic energy fill the room.

"Do you have plans next Friday night? I was thinking pizza and beer in Lander. Are you up for it?"

That sounded great. "Will this include a big screen TV and a game?" We both laughed.

"You sound like a girl."

"Because I AM a girl..."

"I'm quite an admirer of that fact." I could feel his warm smile. "Is it a date?"

"It's a date. What time?"

"How about sixish?"

"See you then."

"Looking forward to it." He paused, "Good night, Tess," he said, his tone close and warm.

It made tonight's event seem trivial.

After the call I slipped out of bed onto my knees.

Chapter Eleven

The Confession

Flickering sunshine woke me. It was morning and nothing happened. I must have been imagining things. I felt relieved. Stretching my limbs to work out the tenseness from last night, I rolled over punching the pillow under my head. There seemed to be no reason to hurry in getting out of bed, but my mind started working on the week ahead.

Dressed, teeth, Bible, journal, dogs, and coffee.

Kai and Sprite seemed to sense my reserved mood.

I moved slowly through the house.

Remembering last night, darkness and shadows were always things that made me uncomfortable in the woods, even when backpacking. Maybe last night was just an old childhood fear; like things that go bump in the night, the bogeyman that I was sure lurked under the bed or the ghouls haunting the closet. I reminded myself again for the millionth time since childhood, *nothing* ever happened, ever.

While I made coffee, lost in thought, considering possibilities, images of Clint and John filtered through my head. Life seemed to have its own agenda and was speeding forward with me hanging on. I didn't feel in control at all. I realized I didn't need to have answers, at least not at this moment. I decided to wait and see how God orchestrated things. This was His call not mine. It relaxed me.

I was startled out of my reverie by a presence on the back porch. I turned to see Clint standing on the deck, resting against the railing, watching me. Seeing him arrested my movement, my heart and my breath all at the same time. Was he here last night? Somehow, I thought I would have *known* it was Clint. I felt sure he wouldn't have stalked. I looked at him and I could feel blood rushing to my face & the intense thumping of my heart. I started towards the back door happy to see him but afraid to show it. I couldn't fathom why he was here and why he didn't knock? It didn't matter.

A quiet "Hey" was all I could manage as I stepped out the door, letting the door close behind me as the dogs rushed out. Kai ran to Clint sitting at his feet. Clint reached down, petting him. Releasing Kai, he leaned back against the railing, looking at me.

As I moved outside, I watched as he exhaled deeply. He was studying my face; his gaze then lowered to the deck. As he looked back up, his eyes found mine, "Tess," his words came slowly. This isn't the first time I'd heard him pronounce my name, but the sound of his voice saying my name, sent shivers down my spine. Hearing him say it touched something that I couldn't identify, like a voice my soul *recognized*. I stood breathless, quietly waiting for him to continue.

Studying my face, it took him a few minutes to continue, his eyes focused on mine, "I wanted to come by," he said quietly, "to try and explain about Saturday night, about what happened," intensity clouding his eyes. "I didn't want to leave things the way we left them in the truck. This is probably not the right time to tell you this, and maybe coming here is a bad move," he said, emotion shifting behind his dark eyes, exhaling deeply, "but I've been in a struggle since I met you." He paused for a long moment. Looking deep into my eyes he said, "I'm attracted to you, Tess. Have been almost from the first day I saw you." His eyes black with intensity.

I found myself holding my breath, a shiver running through me.

"When you answered the door the first time we met and I saw you … I recognized something, felt something connect …" he was looking at the backdoor, towards the front entrance, remembering, he said, "I don't know" … his brow furled, conflicted. "Tess," his gaze now fixed on me, searching for words, "I'm not sure how to describe that moment or since, but you've been constantly in my thoughts." He was searching both my eyes, "I haven't been able to clear my head or keep from thinking about you and working here every day didn't help. That night watching you at the bonfire when your friends were here…" he looked at his feet as his thoughts strayed.

He continued, looking up, still this intensity in his dark eyes, "There's something about you that touches me," he said, shaking his head, studying my face, "your spirit, your energy. Against my better judgment, I prolonged this job because of how I felt," he said quietly. "Every day I'd follow your routine; my attention was constantly aware of your location on the property. On those days when you headed into the woods, I worried and couldn't leave until I saw you return. One day I almost went in search of you. The relief I felt when you came around the barn," he said, his face a mix of emotion; trying to be understood on something he clearly was conflicted about himself. He searched my face to see if I was processing what he was telling me, looking for my reaction.

We both stood there looking at one another. I *was* trying to process what he was saying… because somehow, in spite of his declaration I sensed this was not going to turn out well. Standing completely still, my attention focused on him, not sure I was breathing.

He continued, "Tess, I didn't really understand the depth of this attraction, but I did think that I could handle it." Belief of this was evident in his eyes. Sighing heavily, "I knew the job would end; I really believed that that would take care of things ... I hadn't expected what happened Saturday night. When I went over to speak to you about taking you home," he paused, searching both my eyes, "Tess, being close to you at that moment I felt an overpowering need to touch you, and

I used the dance as my excuse. Saturday is all I've been able to think about. Your smell, the feel of you next to me, the joy of having you move close. When you put your arm around my neck and leaned in, the thought that you might feel the same was … overpowering …" Looking deep into my eyes, looking for recognition. "I couldn't take my eyes off you; I felt it was what was holding us together. Tess, what I felt *in* that moment is something I've never had with a woman, nothing I've ever felt before." Shaking his head, his breathing deeper, more strained. This conversation was hard on him; I could see that. "Because of how I was feeling, I knew it was a bad idea and I hurt Joannie." I saw his eyes shift. "I can't pursue you" he said with determination, clear-eyed, "and this may not make sense, but this is the closest I've ever come to feeling this way. I want to keep this, the memories I have of you, of touching you, the dance. But I can't live with the memories unless I make this right in some way. I didn't honestly know how to do that except to come by and face you." Firmness in his eyes, he was no longer looking for understanding, the set of his face spoke of his conviction.

I was struggling with, "I can't pursue you…"

With a pained look he said, "Joannie and I ended things Sunday. I knew I was being unfair to her even before I met you. We don't share the same feelings, but I had thought that both being Arapaho, having our culture in common would be enough. I like Joannie, but I've never loved her that way."

He looked spent, emotionally drained as his eyes took in my face. His struggle over this and his broken engagement had all taken a toll on him. He looked older. I was happy that he hadn't taken any of this lightly, it elevated him.

Resignation in his eyes, "More than anything, I want to pursue this feeling I have for you," again he was searching my face for understanding, "but I don't know how I can and not hurt the tribe," a different man now looking out through his eyes. "I have obligations to the tribe. I'm an elder and I've been a strong advocate with the tribe about keeping the race pure. I believe in staying within the tribe for relationships, otherwise we stand to lose our culture and our identity." He scanned my face for understanding as he ended his confession.

There it was. No matter what follows, I knew he felt what I was feeling. I think it was hitting us both simultaneously, Love? I'm not too sure I know what that feels like between a man and a woman, but this …this was new for me also, as though I had stepped into another dimension, one where the molecules in the air that I breathed were more alive, I was more alive; and the cause of that was this feeling I had for Clint.

I knew it was my turn to say something.

He had leaned back, both hands on the railing, his face tense, focused on mine.

His confession created mixed confusion for me … cares for me but can't pursue me. My forehead crinkled trying to force my brain into some intelligent response; I was still working through understanding my own feelings. As I looked at him, I tried for words that would bring clarity; help me name to myself what I was feeling. Softly, watching him intently, I began, "Saturday night took us both by surprise." I took a breath, looking at his face. "Before I came here, romance was not a part of my life. I wasn't looking for it. It's been a while since I've had any feelings for a man … You've also touched me, Clint," I said softly, searching his eyes, watching his reaction to my admission, wondering if my admission would somehow …

Could this really be our first and maybe only chance to connect with each other with what we were both feeling? So maybe we both needed to hear this. He is saying this can't happen, yet his eyes betrayed him.

"You've awakened something in me that I haven't felt in a while. And now listening to you, knowing we both feel the same way," as I said this, the focus in his eyes shifted with this acknowledgement, I saw them soften. "I would like to see you, get to know you. I wasn't looking for this Clint, but now, I'd like to see where this goes. I think I understand what you're telling me, and I don't have an argument about the purity of the concept, keeping your culture preserved, but life isn't always clean or neat. I don't have any idea how I could compete with your tribe. I don't think I would want to. I don't want to harm anyone but how is caring about someone wrong in any culture? It doesn't cross boundaries or cultures?" I looked away, feeling emotional, hoping to shake his belief. "I understand the concern, I do," I said looking back, "but feeling the same way about each other, I honestly can't understand why *this* can't happen. We are not the whole tribe; we're just two people."

My eyes were questioning as I looked hard at him, "I suppose it's my turn for confession ..." I sighed as I met his eyes. "You put me off when I first met you. I almost felt a dislike for me from you." searching both his eyes, he was listening. "But recently ... things started to change for me towards you, and I've been in a struggle trying to get my arms around what this feeling was and the dance, whether intended or not, brought some form of clarity for me. I've been reliving the dance also, but it's not just the memories of the dance and being close, touching, but everything about you. And then the dance ... I felt the same way. You were all I wanted to look at, touch. I confess that before Saturday night I was starting to... *notice* you," I searched his eyes for his reaction. He looked down when I said this, a smile playing on his lips. "But it confused me." Looking back towards me, his eyes a deep black ... I had to struggle to continue because the intensity in his gaze was diverting my senses. "Saturday night changed things, maybe illuminating what was happening. But at the same time threw me into a tailspin," I smiled weakly. I looked around at the work he had done, "You've been here every day since I arrived. Your image is stamped everywhere I look." I looked at his face, searching his eyes. "Not sure how this started, but now that this has been awakened, I *want* to get to *know* you, and so I don't clearly get how a belief can make *affection* wrong, caring about someone wrong," I said, shaking my head.

In three strides he had me wrapped in his arms. I buried my face and my arms against his chest; felt his face in my hair, my neck as he pulled me tight, hands at my waist, and around my back. Completely encased by him, pressed tightly against his chest, I found my emotions were reaching my eyes. He pulled back slightly, taking my chin in his hands and moved my face toward him. Searching my face, his look was gentle, tender. He saw the moisture in my eyes and I saw his concern. His eyes moved around my face as though memorizing it. Wrapping me again in his arms, he gently kissed my forehead, my eyes, my cheeks, my neck; the corners of my mouth and then his lips were on mine. As his kiss deepened, I reached up, putting my arms around his neck, pressing him to me, my whole body responding. He responded, pulling me tighter. Bodies locked together. His kisses became more ardent, more insistent, hunger growing and I found that I matched his desire. I could feel his heat, feel our hearts thumping together. Not sure how long we kissed, uncontrollable passion building … finally, I felt him pull apart. I was trembling. Both breathless, moving back, I could feel the tremble in his hands as he took my face in his hands, surveying it, his eyes settling on mine. He moved a strand of my hair behind my ear. There was a sad half smile on his face, as he stared into my eyes. As my pounding heart steadied, I felt peace standing with him next to me. We both stood for long moments staring at one another.

He was leaving. I could feel it. Pulling away, he whispered "This is hard, Tess. I have to go." I heard the pain in his voice, and I nodded. He released me, looking down memorizing my face. Leaning in for a final gentle kiss, his hands found mine as he turned to leave. He left the deck and turned to walk toward his truck, started his engine, he drove away.

As he left, standing where we last touched, I started to cry … What was I feeling? Is this love? Is he my soulmate? And he's gone. His character, his strength and even the strength of this conviction moved me. I wasn't sure I'd ever met *anyone* like him. He brought so much to everything he touched, his family, his work and his name. Even my dogs sensed something in him. There was another man in the same royal occupation also with dark hair and eyes. Is that what pulls my heart to *him?*

The day passed in a tearful blur.

Chapter Twelve

The Dark Secret

Tuesday morning.

I got up slowly ... earlier than normal... it was still dark outside; but I wasn't sleeping anyway... once again, not sure the point in getting up and not sure the point in staying in bed. My thoughts refused to think about anything but Clint. Still tearful, I reviewed everything. The intensity of my emotions had drained me. I sat up in bed, still under the covers, hugging my knees, looking out my bedroom window ... remembering.

Face, teeth, journal, Bible, coffee, and dogs...it's my *best* today.

I went downstairs. I had this intense need to see him, wanted to get in my car and drive to his house, sit in the dark, just for a chance to look at him. Maybe keeping alive hope that he was still possible in my world. I might have if I had known where he lived. Thankfully, I didn't. At this moment facing this loss, I think I could accept love on those terms, if I could see him, it would be enough. I found myself crying as I walked through my dark, quiet home. Unbelieving that this man and this emotion could not be mine. Why did it come? Totally uninvited, I was getting angry. I walked back to the deck where I last saw him, reliving every word, every touch, the sweetness, the passion and feelings that fueled our moments. I wanted him and I think I wanted a life with him. No idea what that would involve but I was pretty sure it involved more of what we both felt yesterday. And just gone?

I sat outside in the darkness, signs of morning appearing over the mountains.

Feeling deep hurt and sobbing, I prayed, Lord, I'm desperately hurting and confused. I think Clint is that man and I've been allowed to experience sublime emotions. I'm not understanding this, why this came and why this left. It's one of the most important experiences one can hope for and it's being dangled in front of me; to become a tantalizing cruelty. Is it some punishment for something I've done or not done? Offered then taken? I know that's not how You operate, You love me, more than any love we feel here on earth. You've given me so much and I know that *all* good things come from You. Help me understand this trainwreck. I know that earth isn't my eternal home, but it's all I know right now. And all I know at this moment is that it feels like the air has been sucked from me ... passionate emotion filled my heart and now nothing. From an exquisite height to a bottomless emptiness. Why?

I sat rehearsing my history, my relationship with my Father in my head, all the victories, guidance and that in everything I have always seen His hand that went ahead of me. I also know that the most important experience I have is knowing Him. There's a reason for everything that I go through. Character. *What* I go through is not as important as *how* I handle what I go through, my response. In the middle of pain, heartache, failure, what I *believe* and how I respond determines the outcome. I know this. I believe this. I trust You. Here I am Lord. Look at me!

Dawn was just cresting. It was the earliest that I had been outside sitting on the deck.

My prayer calmed me, and I was sitting quietly, sensing my Lord when I heard movement again. The yard was still cloaked in morning darkness ~ but now a shade of gray was beginning to illuminate the yard. I was up at that moment, operating on all cylinders, determined to know what this was. Running into the shrubs I caught by surprise the object of the noise. A child! I might have been more surprised than the child, although the child was hysterical and fighting for dear life. I wouldn't let go. I had no idea what I was going to do but I knew I needed to solve this mystery. Clapping my arms around him I struggled to get his fighting form back to the deck for a better look. I was shocked when I could fully see him. He was terrified and filthy, more like an animal than a human. I was reminded of children raised by wolves. I had to get him inside and contain him. I figured that he would not make this mistake again and this might be my one opportunity *to* solve the mystery.

My heart was racing. But my woman's heart was also engaged. I had no intention of letting him go until I could figure out what was going on and how to help him. Struggling, I reached the deck and sat there with an iron grip on this child. He had quieted and as we sat on the deck, he became very still. I looked in his face and saw so much fear – tears filled his frightened eyes and streaked his face.

"Shsssh" I repeated soothingly trying to calm him. "It's okay," I whispered.

It took some moments, but he finally calmed a little.

"Do you understand me?"

He nodded.

"Are you hungry?"

He stared at me, no response.

"I am going to take you inside the house and make you something to eat. Is that okay? Don't be frightened. I won't hurt you. I want to help you. Can you understand what I am saying?"

Again, no response.

I started to my feet still with a firm grip on my little ward, helping him stand so I could pick him up. In the kitchen I sat him at the table and immediately went to get something for him to drink. Rummaging through the refrigerator, I found eggs and bacon. As the smell of cooking filled the kitchen he remained very still, sipping juice and watching my every move, but sipping the juice and the smell of the food seemed to ease his stress. Breakfast in front of him, overcoming his fear he ate hungrily.

Sitting next to him, I was able to observe him better. He was filthy and had on a tee shirt and jeans that were in the same state. His clothing didn't appear to be worn or tattered, making me think his situation might be recent. I noticed his dirty sneakers, but at least he had them. No jacket in this cold, no hat. His hair was cropped short, not professionally, at odd angles and lengths. He had big frightened brown eyes and they and his nose were running. I judged his age to be around four years. How was a child his age alone and rummaging through my trash? He watched me cautiously, timidly and I was afraid he would bolt if I took my eyes off him.

As he ate, my mind searched for anyone that I knew could help. Not Clint… I thought of the woman I had met at church, Rosa. We had exchanged numbers and so I called her apologizing.

"Good morning. Is this Rosa?"

"Yes."

"I'm sorry to bother you, Rosa, I don't know if you remember me from church on Sunday. This is Tess." She remembered me. "I didn't really know who to call. I found this young child on my property this morning, he appears to be Native American, and I am at a loss as to who should be contacted about this. Can you point me in the right direction?".

This was her cell; she was at work, but she assured me she would be right over.

Waiting on Rosa, I continued to sit near the child. Kai and Sprite ran into the kitchen. Initially, they frightened him, and he squirmed away from their inquisitive noses. But soon their persistence and my reassurance eased his fear and timidly he reached out to touch them. Sprite started licking his hand and the slightest hint of a smile glinted in his eyes. Kids and dogs. I could see him starting to relax, I smiled and stroked the top of his head.

Rosa was over within the hour with Chief Blackthorn. Rosa worked at the Bureau of Indian Affairs and had explained to Chief Blackthorn what I had told her about this child. Both were as shocked as I had been when they saw him.

She introduced me to the Chief who politely shook my hand.

"What happened Tess?" she said, concerned, as she went to sit beside the boy. "Timmy, are you okay?" She looked up at me perplexed by what she saw. "What's going on?" The Chief continued to stand next to me, but a look of concern was evident on his face.

His name is Timmy.

I recounted the story of the morning events. Both listened while I explained, "Several mornings there have been rustling noises in the woods near my barn and when I've gone to check the source of the noises, I didn't find anything except remnants of pilfering from my garbage cans. This morning, I happened to be up earlier than usual and just happened to catch him." I said this nodding towards Timmy. "He looks starved, and I wondered if he's been living in the woods." I said, shaking my head, incredulous at that possibility.

Everyone stared at the child. Quietly, Rosa spoke, turning her face from Timmy towards us. "I know him and his family, not well though. Both his parents are dead." She turned back towards Timmy, "Where is your brother and sister?" She waited for an answer, but I was stunned by her question.

"Wait, what? More children! There are more children out there?" My mind frantically searched for some way to understand what was going on.

She had the same worried look, "I know," she looked back at Timmy, "the whole thing is mysterious. How could this have happened?" she continued, turning to look at the Chief. "I remember the funeral of their mother a month or so ago. It was at our church and Pastor Allen held the service. It was quiet and brief. I didn't really pay attention to the children after the service. I just thought someone had them," she said, as she looked at him and back at me with a wide expression of surprise that this was possible.

"What are the ages of the other children?"

"There are three children in the family," Rosa offered. "Their mother died recently. Their father has been dead for a few years. The family has had a hard time of it. I'll check with Pastor Allen about more details and see if he knows who was supposed to have custody of the children. The oldest is James, I think he's fourteen, there's a middle girl, Jenny, but I'm not sure of her age. She may be ten. And Timmy, I think, is around five. The family's last name is Whitehorse." Rosa finished.

Timmy just sat near her with his head down. "It's okay," she said to him." You're safe here and we'll take care of you. Okay?" she said soothingly, wrapping her arm around him. She looked up at the Chief for guidance.

Chief Blackthorn spoke for the first time as he turned towards me, "It's Mrs. Michael's. Right?"

"St. Michaels."

"Mrs. St. Michaels, would you mind if I asked you some questions?"

"No, not at all."

"What time did you find him?"

"Um, I think around 6:00 this morning."

"And you think that this has happened before?"

"Yes, maybe twice before within the last week or so."

"Do you know what he was taking out of your trash?"

"I suspect he was foraging for food because the debris consisted mostly of food wrappings."

"Could you show me where you found him?"

"Sure."

"I'll call Pastor Allen and see if he can help with this," said Rosa, staying alone with Timmy and the dogs.

I led Chief Blackthorn outside.

Chief Blackthorn was friendly but carried an air of authority. He was a large, stout man with a wide friendly face and dark, intelligent eyes. He towered over me, easily six feet or more. I showed him the area where I had found Timmy and left him to investigate the area further. He walked covering the ground around the shrubs and took off into the woods. I stood waiting on the deck. He found indications of trampled shrubs, food wrappings and shoe prints but some he said he thought were considerably larger than children, more like boot prints, over near the barn. I left the deck and moved to check out the area where he was pointing. I thought again about the shadow and looked back onto the deck where I was seated that night. A chill ran down my spine that wasn't related to the weather. I looked around at the woods that surrounded my house and wondered what was going on around me. What don't I know?

"Chief Blackthorn?" I said as he was headed out of the shrubs.

"Yes." He said, still looking at the ground as he walked over to me.

"I'm not sure if this is related, but Sunday, I found a cabin up the mountain that looked to be occupied. I'm not certain if it has anything to do with this situation or not, but I wonder if it's possible that Timmy and his siblings could be staying there?"

"Hard to say. Do you remember where?" Then he added, "Could you show me?"

"Certainly. Right now?"

He nodded and while apparently reviewing the situation he said, "Give me a moment. We may need backup to help comb the area and organize a search." He nodded at me and turned grabbing his walky-talky, talking into it as he walked away from me connecting with his office.

I went inside to get my boots and a jacket.

While I was inside, I heard Chief Blackthorn call for backup and make a call to Wind River Child Protective Services. He was organizing a manhunt and starting the process of placing Timmy in the care of the tribe.

Inside, Rosa got up and came over to me. "What's going on?" She whispered.

"Sunday, I found a cabin up the mountain aways, and we're going to check it out. I'm so sorry to keep imposing on you, but would you mind staying with Timmy until we get back?"

"I don't mind staying with Timmy. Any way I can help," she said this with concern in her eyes. "I hope that James and Jenny are there," she said looking over at Timmy. "They have to know we have Timmy," she said looking back at me. "I can't imagine them allowing their five-year-old brother to scavenge for food alone. I'm suspecting that his size made him less likely to be spotted by homeowners." She continued, "They were probably nearby when you grabbed him." She looked perplexed.

The noise of my scuffle would have hidden other noises, possible, no, probable that they saw what happened to their brother. "But you know, thinking about the other mornings when I saw something, it was not large and seemed to be alone. This is the third time I think that Timmy has been here. Think I would have noticed the older children."

"Makes sense, dunno."

I nodded, remembering the allusive shadow.

"Right, odd to think that my property may have been a part of their lives and for how long? This cabin may be where we have the most success finding them. Any idea who may own it?"

Rosa shook her head.

I told her, "Chief Blackthorn called Child Protective Services, and I think they may be on their way over here."

"Good, I called Pastor Allen to see if he knows anything and waiting for a call back."

We both looked over at Timmy who was sitting quietly, watching us. We stood staring at one another, afraid to name our fears. I wasn't sure what to think at this point. Nothing in my life prepared me for this. I heard Chief Blackthorn moving on the back deck, so I nodded at Rosa and turned to join him outside.

It took us less than half an hour to locate the cabin. I led as we climbed the mountain headed for the location of the cabin. Once the side trail was in view, I could see that Chief Blackthorn was fully assessing the situation. He stood still on the main trail before setting foot onto the side trail. He was listening and observing the area. His radio squawked alive, he answered. His men were at my house mobilizing for a hunt. "Mrs. St. Michaels, can you stay on the trail and wait for them? I need to approach quietly. If they are here," he whispered, "I don't want to startle them or have them take off running." He muted his radio.

I agreed.

Stealthily and steadily, he left the main trail, heading up the side trail, slowly approaching the cabin listening and watching for any activity. On the side trail he waited several minutes. I thought about my reckless approach on Sunday, oblivious to any danger. I shook my head at my lack of caution and wisdom. He waited several minutes before stepping into what I knew to be the opening to the cleared area surrounding the cabin. Here I lost sight of him and stood there patiently waiting. It was several minutes before he returned. I searched his face for his findings. He shook his head.

"There are signs of human habitation at the cabin; trash strewn around. I went to the fire ring, and it was still warm. Something has been cooked there recently; I could still smell food in the air around the ring. But there was no one inside or outside the cabin, but it's obviously in use." Chief Blackthorn told me, with deep concern set in his face. "It doesn't look like they were staying here. Would expect more footprints. Cabin doesn't indicate multiple occupants and footprints are larger, boot size. Let's head back to your place so I can set up a search of the area." With this he sidestepped me, stepped onto the main trail and headed briskly towards my house and his men. I wondered about the shadow.

The day was a blur with a flurry of activity from the Wind River Police and Child Protective Services. I was introduced to Stephanie Hunter with Child Services. It seemed that I was interviewed by everyone trying to ferret out the details of the capture and piecing together the last few days of this poor child's life. Poor Rosa was now caught up in the situation.

Pastor Allen had arrived soon after I returned home. He went immediately to Timmy and stooped in front of him, "Timmy, are you okay son?" he said looking deeply into the child's eyes. "Where's James and Jenny?" he said gently as he reached to touch Timmy. He picked the child up and held him securely. Rosa and Pastor Allen proved a calming influence for Timmy. He listened to Rosa and Chief Blackthorn, gathering their information. He said turning to me, "We had assumed after the death of their mother and when the children disappeared, that a family member had taken them." He asked again, "Son, they aren't in any trouble, we want to find them to help them, can you tell us where they are?" Still no response from Timmy.

The horror that no family member had taken them and that they have been alone this long, was written on everyone's face. Was it possible that a fourteen-year-old was taking care of them? Where? How had they been living? I wondered about the dark secrets Timmy may know about how they have been existing, their whereabouts. If he knew who was staying at the cabin, given its proximity to my house and garbage.

Stephanie Hunter with Wind River Child Protective Services collected Timmy and left to place him in a foster home. I watched her load the lost child in the back of her car and waited as they drove away, my eyes riveted on Timmy and my mind horror struck by the hardness of his life. With Timmy gone, I felt numb. I stood around, staying out of everyone's way.

Rosa prepared to leave. She came to stand near me. I reached out my hands and grabbed hers, "Rosa, I cannot thank you enough for all your help. It's really appreciated." I said, exhausted by the emotion of the day.

She smiled warmly and we hugged. I walked her to her car.

As she got in her car, she sat and turned looking up at me, "Tess, I'll be in touch and let you know if I hear anything more. Oh, are we still on for Saturday? Coffee and the Festival?" she reminded me. "If it's too much, I'll understand."

"No, no, that's fine. I think I'll need the company and distraction." I said feeling drained and empty, had a feeling at the end of the week I was going to need this.

The day moved towards dusk as the hunt wound down without results. It was going into the low 30's tonight and everyone was concerned. They discontinued the search at nightfall.

"We'll be back in the morning. The problem is we aren't sure where the others are or if that cabin is related to them; but it's hard to believe they'd be far from Timmy. It's going to be very chilly tonight." He sighed heavily with concern on his face. "Hard to put the hunt to bed knowing this but harder still to find them in the dark and risk injury to the rescuers in these mountains."

I nodded and we said our goodbyes. After they left, I stood out back on the deck in the dark listening and watching. The biting cold finally sent me inside.

Chapter Thirteen

The Black~Hearted Knight

Wednesday morning came with renewed activity as searchers continued their hunt for the two Whitehorse children. I assisted with hot coffee and pastry at the base camp that was located in my backyard and ran into Lander for groceries for the all-day search. No one was able to get any information out of Timmy. Rosa and Pastor Allen showed up with church members to assist searchers and provide any necessary support.

I had Stephanie Hunter's business card and planned to check on Timmy's care later in the week. The day passed without locating the children. Chief Blackthorn had started an investigation on the Reservation locating and interviewing any family and friends. No family was located. The family had lived pretty much isolated from community notice and involvement. Even school attendees and personnel had little information. Teachers reported quiet children and no close friends in their classrooms. Since they were compliant and good students, there was little to draw attention to them. A search of their last known residence revealed a small two-room house, vacated for some time. Debris and animal use was evident everywhere. A search of welfare benefits or social services, EBT payments, banks, employment resulted in negative findings. How had they lived?

The day progressed with no success and as evening moved in, reluctantly searchers and volunteers packed up to leave. As night fell, I was alone again. Tomorrow the search would continue but the search would move into areas that were past the boundaries of my land. They were not expected back here tomorrow. Rosa and Pastor Allen promised to keep me apprised of all developments.

Thursday morning came with no fixed plans. I had dinner plans tonight with Patty, but the day was wide open and so it seemed a good time to go exploring. Maybe I was running away. Clint's image is stamped everywhere, and I can't avoid him or my thoughts. Each time I headed off the back side of my property I took trails to the right and so this morning I decided to head off out my front and take the road left off my property and explore the road that headed over a rise, some place where Clint's presence had not touched. I realized that my travels had not taken me in that direction, and I was happy to have something new to occupy my day.

Inside I grabbed my boots, remote and the three of us (two bounding and one walking) proceeded out the front door. The day was overcast and so a light jacket and hat protected me from the cooler temperatures. My mood was elevated once I hit the road and started off to the left; I was excited with the thought of gaining more familiarity with this new world I had adopted. As soon as I gained the top of the rise, I saw down the road and to the left an old homestead. A similar homestead sat almost directly across the street. I did not realize that I had neighbors this close to me. I could tell that both had been here a long time. The homestead on the left appeared neglected and disheveled while the one on the right was well kept. Both could use a coat or two of paint. Each had chicken-wire fencing marking their property boundaries but the one on the right also had a neat white picket fence across the front yard.

A withered and ancient man sat on the front stoop on the homestead to my left, eyeing me with mild curiosity. As I passed, I said "Good morning" smiling and waving. He continued eyeing me and gave me a barely perceptible nod. Okay. I did not see any activity at the homestead on the right. I spent the day walking and exploring and towards the end of the day I took a loop that led me home. I passed back by the homesteads. The old gentleman was still seated on his front stoop but across the street children were now playing in the front yard. I smiled at both. It felt comfortable knowing that there were people nearby.

Back at home I tried to direct my thoughts inward, to my life here, my purpose. I couldn't focus for any space of time. Everything was a reminder of Clint. Once again, I sat on the back porch remembering everything. And these thoughts were my constant companions. I knew tomorrow was my date with John. He had called yesterday but I didn't answer. I'll call tonight and explain about Timmy, hopefully, it will be an excuse. I didn't want to ghost John, he didn't deserve that and frankly, I liked John, I liked him a lot. It was late in the week; I didn't feel right cancelling at the last minute. Maybe I was looking for a diversion. I knew I wasn't being fair to John. It seemed that it would take strength to think this through and more strength to handle it and going with the flow of this date was easy. Thinking and handling this relationship wasn't something I felt capable of today.

Night was drifting in as I drove into Lander and dinner with Patty. It was a saving event, taking me away from my isolation and thoughts. Patty looked pert and pretty and put together, like she had everything in her world under her control. I envied her.

As I sat down in the booth, I could tell something was amiss as soon as I sat down. We ordered dinner and wine and got the usual civilities out of the way. She waited until the orders were completed and we were alone. There was a new development in her life.

She started with, "I met someone recently." She was not smiling.

"Okay...?"

"Yeah, ..." She said, staring out the window. I waited for her to start the conversation.

Finally, I said, "Patty, what's going on?"

Her eyes teared up and she looked at me. "I don't know how to start," she said.

I could see that she was grappling with composure. Funny to have just been thinking how good her life seemed. There's always one more thing we don't know.

As she fought for control, she started, "You and I have never really talked about our romantic relationships, and I am embarrassed to tell you about what happened. But I need to tell someone, and I feel I can trust you." Her demeanor calmed a little. "I don't date around and since my divorce no one has really interested me. But recently a developer came to town for a few days surveying potential property. Nice looking guy, polished city looks and behavior. Dad had me show him around. Gotta tell ya," she said, shaking her head, "he got my attention right away. He asked me out to dinner a few nights after we first met, and things moved quickly ending in his hotel room." At this she looked out the restaurant window, I could tell this pained her. "We saw each other every day for the next couple of weeks and I thought this really had potential. He was attentive and gentle. Man, I thought I saw love there, in fact he said he loved me, if that isn't corny. Completely knocked me off my feet." She looked at me, "Tess, I was breathless and happy and barely had time to collect my emotions, I was already looking down the road to maybe a hopeful future with him, could see it, and next thing I knew, he was just gone. That was it. Dad told me the day after he had left that Dale had left him a voice message saying that his partner had found a more suitable location."

This reminded me of another disappearing relationship; I could relate to everything she was saying.

At this she stopped. I waited for her to collect herself. It was some minutes before she began again, staring out the window. "Besides," she said as her gaze met mine, "he acted like I was the one for him also and we discussed a future together; I could go there, he would come here…" Again, she had trouble continuing … her eyes brimmed with tears as she struggled to get at what she needed to unload. "Attentive, generous, and nurturing… I haven't found that in many men. Nothing, nothing, caused me any alarm or sense he was being deceptive." She looked at me looking for some intelligible explanation for the emotional trainwreck she was feeling. "Gone, just gone." She took a deep breath, "I'm not sure what I feel the worst about, the loss, the shame, the questions, the confusion. I've never been someone's fling. Always prided myself on being smarter than that, not me. I'm the one in control. Man, I totally fell for this guy." Emotion was running all over her pretty face and finally settling into her throat. Two competing emotions hovered; my heart broke for her (and me) while wanting to kick his polished city looks into the local dumpster where I felt he belonged. It was hard to look into her pretty face and see this destructive pain in her turquoise flecked blue eyes, and harder to know what to say to her that would help.

I was in the midst of my own train wreck. I was the wrong person to come to for help.

"Tess, I'm sorry. Didn't mean to turn dinner into a confessional."

"Don't apologize. I just wish there *was* something I could say that would help. Ya know the hardest area to keep our head is in matters of the heart. No one does it well. It's the fortunate few of us that find Mr. Right and fall in love with each other early in life. That isn't common for the rest of us." Feeling my personal pain resurrecting. "But he sounds like a creep, and you may have dodged a bullet. He may do this sort of thing in every town. A long-term relationship with him cannot be a happy one, all indications are they probably all end badly and / or there may be some poor wife waiting at home, lonely and totally in the dark thinking she is the love of his life."

"That's a sick thought. I know you're right. A lesson learned. I just feel emotionally lost, confused and ashamed of myself that he could have me so easily and there is no way to redeem that."

I wasn't expecting dinner to involve a subject so close to my own pain and tried to remove myself from Clint and focus on Patty. Our situation wasn't identical, so I tried to put my head into previous life experiences that were similar. I offered, "Most of us can recount some event or behavior that shamed or crippled us, where we used poor judgment or were hijacked emotionally and physically by some handsome, black-hearted knight, the antithesis of a kingly Prince. It's a hard lesson.

We'd give anything to turn back time and enter the event again knowing more, get back the time before the loss, grief, pain, and harm to our self-esteem. No one escapes this planet without some serious scaring. If you haven't suffered at some time in your life, I can't understand that, and I would seriously question anyone making that claim. And while you don't want to hear this now, I think pain humanizes us, deepens us and eventually the pain moves on. I don't know if this makes you feel any better, but you are in a very large club of brokenhearted individuals with similar stories."

"It doesn't, not sure what will help right now."

We sat quietly for several moments while Patty struggled with her emotions. Watching her was difficult and I fought to keep my own emotions in check.

"Nothing feels familiar to me, like my world flipped. There's an unfamiliar tang to everything, colorless, empty and nothing matters. In fact, everything reminds me of him. It's a small town." She sat quietly for a moment. "I thought I met *my* prince and I got hooked. Look, I know I'm still an emotional wreck AND I know this passes, but I would prefer that sooner than later. I feel like I'm lost. Not sure what I'd do if I saw him again. I still care for him," she said looking hopelessly into my face, "and I keep thinking he's gonna call, he'll explain himself and the happily ever after scenario could still happen." Her voice quieted, "To add to this, I was brought up to respect myself and I'm so shaken by my behavior." Emotion swelling, "I'm not who I thought I was, and I don't know what to do about that." She said, looking past my face into the night beyond the glass. "I know this sounds dramatic and coming from a big city, maybe this is more common there, but it's a first for me." She stared into my face, "Tess, thanks for listening. I need to change the subject." She straightened her posture as she asked, "How is *your* love life progressing? I am really interested in hearing about this guy, John. It would encourage me to hear a successful love story."

My turn to stare out the window.

"Doubtful you'll hear that tonight." I said, shaking my head and looking back at her. I was not even remotely ready to discuss Clint so I pulled my thoughts together to recall John and piece together information that would help Patty or at least salvage dinner for her and try to bring some levity to her hurting heart. Conversations about romance did not seem a good topic item at the time but she seemed genuinely interested. So, I told her about our dinner in Jackson and then his visit to my house.

"John came out to your house?" She looked hard at me. "Oh, that's right. I saw you two in the parking lot."

Shaking my head, I said, "He liked the house but thought it was a lot of house for me, which it is. I think he was having a hard time understanding me in relation to the house. The fact that it seems isolated concerns him."

"So how do you feel about him?"

"Umm, I like him, he is a great guy, fun and interesting."

"That really sounds boring, any chemistry?"

"Yeah, there is …" my mind drifted to his smile and his touch on the deck. He definitely has a presence. "Who knows where it's headed. I sure don't but I like being around him and I think that there is chemistry, compatible interests and at the very least, friendship. That does sound boring."

"I don't know, slow start-ups seem recommended and I'm the wrong person to comment on that tonight." She smiled weakly.

I decided to open up about Clint. It was a long evening.

"You have snagged quite the duo. In my humble opinion, maybe the two most eligible bachelors for miles. Clint has been the mysterious heartthrob and seeing, meeting and getting to know about John… Man!" She took a deep sigh. "How did you manage that?" A painful smile crossed her face.

"Yeah, but Clint is not in my life. We are both suffering from very painful disappearing acts."

"I'm sorry honey. You're right. But to be honest, given my current situation, it all sounds healthier, complicated but healthier, two men. Both men have had time around you to get a sense of their own feelings. At least you know Clint's feelings towards you. And John, who knows, moving slow, never know what's down the road. Good lesson for me. Most around here would kill to have your experience with Clint, any experience and I like what I hear of John, sounds like a good guy. Not enuff of them around," she said, finally smiling.

Conversation drifted to local events, Patty's work, and social happenings. I asked her if she had heard about the Whitehorse children, she hadn't. I asked about the cabin. She was not familiar with the cabin. Said she'd check county plot plans and let me know if anything shows. Warm female conversations, shopping and local gossip ended the evening conversation.

"Patty, why don't you come out to see the changes and I'll cook us dinner? Think you could use a change of venue from the Lander scenery."

"That sounds great, Tess. I appreciate the invite. I would love to come out."

"How about next Friday evening? I'll make lasagna and a salad."

"Wonderful, and I'll bring the wine."

It was late when I returned home. I called John and reached his voicemail. I left a message confirming tomorrow night.

Friday came. I had planned to meet John in Lander for pizza. I had to do something about my wardrobe; sad at best and woefully out of style and date, digging through stored boxes provided a mindless diversion and kept thoughts of Clint in the background. It didn't help that he was who I wanted to be with.

Dinner with John was fun. He had an endless banter of funny stories, local history, and his work. His eyes shone and shimmered as he spoke. His smile animates an already gorgeous face. He sat close and was behaving like a boyfriend, but not sure that that was ever established. No matter to him; he was totally confident and undaunted. He sees us as an us. With dinner finished, we walked around Lander; he confessed he rarely came to the town. We found the historic district and walked around hand in hand as the night darkened and stars came out. The cool night breeze brought us closer. John stopped and turned to me, leaning in for a kiss. I liked John and there is chemistry. I found the kiss tender and myself returning its sweetness. His arms pulled us tight. I let the warmth of the moment linger, it took my heart and thoughts elsewhere, a shield from Clint. At the end of the evening, we were both smiling. We made plans for the following weekend. He will call mid-week to firm up details. John may be the normal in my life right now.

Chapter Fourteen

A Festival of Beginnings

Rosa stopped by Saturday for coffee and conversation. It was pleasant. I liked her instantly at church and I liked her more on this visit. She seemed a little uncomfortable and I couldn't ease her out of it, but this was hopefully the first of many visits. She agreed to save me a seat at the church festival later that day.

The festival was quite an event as it turns out. There were numerous canopies, bands (Jimmy's!) and more people and food than I had expected. It was a good composite of the Wind River community. I was surprised. Pastor Allen seemed genuinely happy to see me as did Rosa. I had an opportunity to speak with the pastor about my vision for ministry and offered my home and assistance if he found a need for it. I could see his mind working behind his eyes. He told me he would keep me in mind and took my phone number. Rosa took me around to meet people. Jimmy bounded up happy to see me. "Tess!" he yelled. "Hey, come meet my family!" I wondered if he was ever less jubilant. He is one of the happiest people I'd ever met. Nothing seems to bother him.

The realization of what he was saying hit me, "Sure... I'd love to meet your family," I said, concealing my panic. Don't know why the thought had not occurred to me that he might be here.

"This is the first time my mom has heard us play when we had a gig! Isn't that cool? She's heard us play in my bedroom before, but this is almost professional. I hope she likes it." But he smiles when he says that, and it's infectious.

"I'm sure she'll love it; you guys are good." I smiled. Rosa and I followed him. Rosa knew the Pierre family well. She and Jimmy walked over to an older woman seated by a picnic table. She was surrounded by a group of people; I did a quick search for Clint.

As I approached her, I could feel her eyes before I saw them. Same intense eyes as Clint. She seemed intent on my face, and I nervously smiled as Jimmy introduced me. "Mom, this is Tess. The lady I told you about."

Her eyes did not leave my face during the introduction as she warmly said, "Nice to meet you, Tess." I almost got the impression that she knew something about me that would interest a mother's heart. Does she know about Clint and I? That I am partly behind the broken engagement of her son? Then I wondered if I would see Joannie here. Could things get more complicated?

I replied, "Very nice to meet you too, Mrs. Pierre," while Jimmy moved on hurriedly making the other introductions and so I met Joseph, Tamara and her husband, Jackson. I told them it was very nice to meet Jimmy and Dinah's family. "I am very fond of both of them," I explained as I turned my gaze back to Mrs. Pierre and complimented her on how wonderful I thought both her children were. I could feel Jimmy beaming beside me just before he said his goodbyes and headed back to the band. Mrs. Pierre asked us to sit with them and asked Joseph to locate more chairs.

I wondered if Clint would be hearing about this tonight. The exuberance of Jimmy made it seem likely and I wondered about his reaction. I couldn't ask if he would be here today.

Joseph must look like his father, Mrs. Pierre's second husband, because he doesn't resemble Clint, Dinah, or Jimmy. Clint looks more like a full brother to them than Joseph. There is a refined, genteel quality to his features and Tamara resembles him. They are not as beautiful, but you would not call them unattractive. Joseph returns with the chairs and smiles broadly at us. I love the friendliness of this family. They made me feel warm and accepted. It was a nice day, sunny and cool. The day worked its way into evening. Jimmy's band rotated with several other local bands. We visited and ate and listened to the bands. I met Tamara's two children, Sue 4yrs and Jackson Jr. 7yrs, and Clint's son, Oliver, this rounded out the immediate family. Rosa hung out with us the entire evening. I met her three children, Mary 14, Joshua 17 and Adam 20. None of them had much interest in us and moved in and around us only to check in with their families. This felt a lot like 4th of July gatherings back in Florida.

During a lull in the conversation, I sat, and people watched. Suddenly I noticed the man from the community center standing by one of the food canopies. Was he staring at me? I asked Rosa if she knew him. Her gaze followed mine. At that instant he turned and walked into the canopied area, appearing to head for food. She *sort* of knew him, thought his name was Sam but didn't know much about him except that he didn't have a good reputation, and she thought I should stay away from him. No problem there. Since I stood out so much in this community, I found it hard to tell Rosa that I thought that someone was staring at me because most do initially; but this was the second time with this guy.

Sunday

After my usual morning ritual, I headed to church and sat with Rosa.

After church Pastor Allen approached me. "Tess, Stephanie Hunter from Child Services called. She is unable to find a foster home at this time for Timmy. I know this is soon, but I remember your comments and offer to help, is it possible that you can take Timmy temporarily until a home opens up?"

I didn't see this coming today. It took me a moment to respond, and I could see anxiousness brimming from Pastor Allen's eyes.

Deep breath, "Yes, I'll take Timmy and I'm happy to help." I replied firmly.

Relief evident on Pastor Allen's face. We each smiled weakly.

"Thank you, Tess. Can you take him today? Sorry, but they plan to take him to a juvenile holding facility. I really feel bad about this and wouldn't ask if I wasn't desperate."

"No … no problem. About what time today?"

"What time works good for you?"

"Well, let me get a room ready, so how about an hour or so?"

"Tess, I can't thank you enough."

As I headed home my thoughts were all over the place. This certainly helped put other thoughts out of my mind. Am I ready for this? Guess I'll find out.

Jimmy and Dinah were waiting for me when I got home.

"Hi guys!"

Smiling Jimmy leaning against his truck gave me an exaggerated wave, "Hey, we just wanted to stop in and say hi for a minute! It's, okay? You busy?" Still smiling.

"Good to see you guys. Come on in."

As we walked inside, Jimmy said, "You sure were a big hit with the family!"

"That's nice to hear. I enjoyed all of them too and the festival. Happy I was invited. Listen, I have agreed to help a young child who seems to have lost his family. Pastor Allen is bringing him over shortly and I have to get a room set up for him." I explained the whole situation with Timmy. They both offered to stay and help get a room set up. The discussion turned to the two missing siblings. I mentioned the cabin. This animated Jimmy. He wanted to run out and see the cabin. "Whoa…Need to get the house situated and wait for Pastor Allen."

"Can we hike up later?"

"Let's see where things are when they get here, but probably worth a second look."

Pastor Allen arrived with Timmy and Rosa. Always happy to see her. All of us busied ourselves getting Timmy situated and hopefully comfortable. He seemed more relaxed, friendlier. Pastor Allen and Rosa left thanking me again for taking this on and promised to stay in touch. While Jimmy & Dinah helped with room preparation, we discussed the current situation of Timmy's siblings. Still not located.

Dinah offered to stay with Timmy while Jimmy and I headed for the cabin.

"Not sure what we'll find at the cabin. If James and Jenny are there, I hope we'll be able to convince them to come with us. It would be helpful to have Timmy point out the cabin as the place where they are staying but weighing that against what he has been through, I thought it best to leave him here."

I asked Dinah, "Is this alright with you? We shouldn't be gone long. The cabin is not far from here."

"No, it's fine, be safe."

Just as we headed out the back door, Jimmy turned to Dinah, "Call Clint and let him know what's going on, ok?" She nodded.

My heart thumped violently against my chest wall; I couldn't help responding to his name. If I can't have Clint in my life, his siblings offered second-hand comfort. Still, how can I get over Clint with his family so close to me? Jimmy and I headed for the location of the cabin. The trail was shrouded in dusky shades of early night. The half-moon was rising and would provide some illumination. We approached quietly.

"Don't want to startle them if they are there. Don't want them to take off running," I said, parroting Chief Blackthorn.

He agreed. Stealthily we approached, listening. We stood just off the main trail that led to the side trail taking us to the cabin. We looked for any activity and waited several minutes. Nothing. Jimmy motioned that he was going to head down the trail leading to the cabin. I followed. Again, the fire ring was warm, and I could smell food lightly in the air. We turned and started for the cabin, cautiously surveying the entire property as we walked. No sign of movement or life. The door was closed.

We knocked and received no answer, so Jimmy pushed open the door. Inside the cabin, I saw that nothing had changed. If they were living here, they were living hard on little to nothing. It shook me to think of the lives they may be leading. My heart ached to find them. We had to find them soon. Fall was coming. I remembered Chief Blackthorn mentioned finding only boot prints and I went out to look. I saw what he was talking about, boot prints but not smaller ones. Lord, help them. It seemed doubtful they were using this cabin. My thoughts turned to the shadow.

It was dark when we left so we used our headlamps to head home.

Back at the house, Dinah had fed and coaxed Timmy into a bath. I grabbed his clothes and threw them in the washer. I would need a trip to town to do some shopping for him. A completely different child sat before us. He was shy but more relaxed and already bonding with Kai and Sprite. He is particularly bonded with Sprite. I wondered if her three-legged situation made him feel like there was someone that may need him? He did not initiate talk but would respond when spoken too. However, any discussion regarding his siblings met with silence. We needed to gain his trust.

I was grateful for Jimmy and Dinah's help. I had no confidence in this situation and their support was immeasurable.

Jimmy asked if Clint had called? "No."

"Let me call him about the kids. He may have some ideas on finding them." He reminded us that Clint was in the marines, "and he's pretty good at tracking." Jimmy said. All I could do was nod. Jimmy got on the phone while Dinah and I prepared Timmy for bed.

"Tess!" Jimmy called from downstairs. "Clint wants to talk to you! Can you come down?"

I caught my breath and stood for a moment. Leaving Timmy with Dinah I went downstairs. Jimmy handed me the phone. My heart was racing. "Hello".

"Tess?"

"Hello Clint," I managed.

There was a pause, "How are you?" He said quietly. I asked Jimmy if he wanted anything from the kitchen.

"Do you have any soda?"

"Yes, in the refrigerator." He turned and left the room.

"I'm fine," I said softly, "How are you?"

Silence...

"Can you tell me what's going on?" he said quietly.

I could feel my heart beating hard and my throat closed. I took a second to gain composure, I started, "A few days ago," rewinding my memory, "I would startle something getting into my trash in the mornings. In fact, last Saturday …" I hesitated … "when, when you and Timmy came by for your tools, I was just returning from following whatever it was." I said quietly, taking a breath, "The other day I was up earlier than usual when I captured the culprit. It was a small child named Timmy, Timmy Whitehorse. What I learned was that both parents are deceased and there are two more older children that can't be located." I was quiet, feeling myself tear up. I wanted to touch him. I couldn't continue, I needed a moment.

He was also quiet before speaking, "James and Jenny. I know the family. Okay. Any info on where they *might* be?" he asked softly.

"No," trying for composure, "Police were here for two days and conducted a search. They didn't find any sign of them. I discovered a cabin up a trail from here…"

"Cabin? Where?" Clint interrupted.

"That was where I was coming from Saturday. It was up that trail some distance, off to the left. I had just discovered it when I ran into you guys," pausing, "Do you know anything about that cabin, who owns it?"

"No … Alright," he sighed, "Thank you for the information. It helps." Very quietly he said. "Good night, Tess."

"Good night, Clint." I hung up the phone, wiping my eyes and staring at the phone

"What did Clint say?" Jimmy said, returning from the kitchen.

"Not much, just gathering information," I said as I rushed upstairs to help with Timmy.

"Don't worry, if anyone can find them, it's my brother," he yelled.

"Thanks," I yelled back." Are you guys staying the night? There's room."

"We have school tomorrow, but we can stop by after school and help."

Jimmy and Dinah left. I checked on Timmy and found him sleeping. Children, dogs, and teenagers. The mix worked like medicine, or therapy. Timmy was responsive to Dinah almost immediately. I wondered if he connected with her as an older sister. Like Clint with wood, she had a gift with children.

I fell asleep thinking of Clint.

Chapter Fifteen

Impossible Evil

The next day was busy with feeding Timmy, playing with him, and running into town to get him a wardrobe and toys, things that would help him acclimate to this new home and help him feel safe. I let him find toys that interested him. I found he likes trucks, all kinds of trucks and GI Joe's. I found some books that I hoped he would enjoy, especially when putting him to bed at night. We shopped at the grocery store, and I introduced him to various food items that I thought he might enjoy. After a busy day putting his room together, decorating, dinner, bath and spending time reading to him, he fell asleep. Sprite slept in his room. We stayed away from the backyard as I wasn't sure what memories it might provoke. He needs to feel safe and happy.

With Timmy securely tucked in, I left his door ajar with a night light and I went outside to sit on the deck. Night had settled in, and those amazing stars were out in profusion. Odd to see so much sustaining and enduring beauty with what felt like so much chaos. I tried to clear my head and review recent happenings. Clint, John, now Timmy. Clint, what do I feel? The pain wasn't ebbing; I cared deeply for him. I admitted that I had hoped that with time, things would change. John. I honestly wasn't sure. Clint stirred my heart and set it on fire, but my heart was warm towards John. I cared about them both, in widely different ways, but my feeling for John was growing. There are different kinds of romantic love I was beginning to see. Wonder how John will see my being Timmy's caregiver? I felt certain Clint already knew. Lord, I need Your peace and some guidance here.

Another disturbing sense that I wasn't alone came over me. I perused the property. Checked the left side of the barn. I couldn't see anything in the dark, but the feeling didn't leave me. My alarm was heightened, maybe it is James and Jenny? There weren't the usual night noises, as though nature was holding its breath.

"Is anyone out there? James, Jenny?" … Quiet … Squinting into the dark, I couldn't see a thing, but this disturbing sense that something was out there had grown. I got up and let Kai out. Immediately he ran to the barn and disappeared. I heard movement in the bushes. Kai does not bark. I ran after him. Pushing through the bushes I called to him, "Kai! Come!" Following, I reached the trail. After several minutes Kai leaped back onto the trail. I stood still, looking for sign that someone was out there, but, remembering Timmy alone at the house, we returned home.

I decided to call the Lander PD. I explained that I felt someone may be watching my house and asked to have an officer come out and check around my property. They promised to send a patrolman out shortly. Officer Thompson arrived, and I went over this concern that someone might be watching my house. Using his flashlight, he headed towards the barn looking for footprints and I showed him the trail Kai followed and assisted in getting him to the main trail. He took off up the trail searching for a possible intruder. After waiting some time and he did not return, I called the Lander PD again and explained that Officer Thompson had not returned from his search. Additional officers were dispatched. By the time they arrived I was in full alarm at the disappearance of Officer Thompson. Again, explaining what had occurred, I showed them the trail. For a few minutes I stood on the trail watching the lights illuminating the officer's movements. Wondering WHAT was going on and if *they* would disappear or locate Officer Thompson.

Returning to my house, I stood in my front yard waiting. Looking around, still this uneasy feeling, a creepy frightening sense that someone was nearby watching. The night was very quiet and chilly. I had a strong urge to run inside and call Clint.

Shortly after, my property was converged on by vehicles hurrying into my yard with lights flashing. Officers piled out of vehicles and met with the two officers that had been up the trail. I noticed the arrival of the coroner and a paralyzing realization of what that meant. Trying to keep hysteria down but desperate to know what was happening, I moved to where I could see the trailhead and watch the activity.

Inside, I could hear my phone ringing, it was Chief Blackthorn. He called to let me know there were no leads on the missing children. I updated him on current events. He said he'd come over. This may be related to the children.

While on the phone, I heard someone knocking on my front door. I ended the call and met Detective Anderson; he was the lead detective assigned to this case and needed to ask me some questions. Once again, I went through all the events. He informed me that they found Officer Thompson off the trail with his throat slit, no struggle was evident. They were searching the woods for suspects. I told him about the cabin. He was aware of it, and it was already being searched. Chief Blackthorn arrived shortly after this visit and joined in the search.

It was now after midnight. A helicopter and police dogs assisted in the search which went on until morning. I was living in a nightmare.

I called Pastor Allen and Rosa and told them what had happened. "Is it possible for Timmy to stay with Rosa for a few days? Don't think he needs any more stress and I'm not sure this doesn't in some way involve this property. Not sure we're safe."

Rosa was working with him today and he will ask her. "I'm sure that won't be a problem. He can come here to the church school during the day, and we can take care of him. I'll be right over."

I called Patty, "Good morning, Patty. How are you doing?"

"Better I suppose. Day at a time as they say. How are you girl?"

I got right to my reason for the call, "Were you able to locate the owner of that cabin and is it located on my property?"

"No. Someone built it without pulling a permit and since there's no record of it, not sure if it's on your land or the land next to your property, which is owned by a corporation, Wellers Inc, who purchased it several years ago. A hundred acres. Why is everything okay?"

I updated Patty.

"Are you kidding! Are you okay? What the h-ll! Do they have a suspect? I'll be right over," she said, quickly ending the call.

All at the same time, Detective Anderson, Chief Blackthorn and Rosa appeared at my front door. I looked at both police officers, hoping they could provide me with some information. Detective Anderson spoke first; he had been updating Chief Blackthorn.

He provided details of their search. "The dogs picked up on a scent that led to a cave, not to the cabin. There was a makeshift camp set up inside the cave. We didn't find anything that identified the occupant. The scent continued up the ridge and over, where we located an old logging road that had recent tire tracks.

"What did you find in the cave and how far is it from the cabin?" I asked.

"Empty food containers and water bottles, sleeping bag and blanket, cigarette butts and a few articles of clothing. All is being bagged for DNA analysis. Some porn magazines along with empty liquor bottles and we'll follow up with the stores where they may have been purchased. You can see the cabin from the cave." Detective Anderson noted.

"Were there any signs of the children? Could this person have them?" I asked.

"We are continuing to search but so far, no sign of the children has been found. Only adult boot prints. You saw him outside your house?" He inquired intently.

"I didn't see anyone. The first time that I was aware there might be someone here, it was just an unsettled feeling of being watched and I thought there was a shadow and then last night again a sense of something watching me, so I had my dog investigate and I think he might have chased something up to the trail." I paused, "I don't know any reason why anyone would be watching the house or me for that matter. Chief Blackthorn later mentioned finding a boot print at the same location by the barn. Could the boot prints be the same person?"

"You never mentioned anything about the boot print being related to someone you suspected watching your place." Chief Blackthorn interjected.

"That's because I wasn't sure what was going on to be honest, what they meant. I still don't."

Turning to Detective Anderson, Chief Blackthorn said, "We're willing to assist any way we can. This may be connected to two missing children we have been searching for, and this person may be involved.

"Thanks. We're not a big department; any assistance would be appreciated. Do you own a gun?" Detective Anderson asked, turning towards me.

I was stunned by the question. It brought home how seriously real this was, "No, do you think I need one?"

"It may not be a bad idea, just for protection." Offered Detective Anderson.

Chief Blackthorn and Detective Anderson exchanged a look, said they'd be back in touch shortly and both left together saying they wanted to check the area around the barn for footprints. Outside Detective Anderson and Chief Blackthorn continued their discussion as they searched the property near the barn.

At the barn, Detective Anderson turned and said, "Tell me about these missing Whitehorse children."

Chief Blackthorn gave Detective Anderson a rundown of all the information they have on the two missing youths.

"Recently we've had several missing person reports. All young, late teens to early twenties, mostly female. Mostly troubled teens out on their own. Parents report regular contact but now they're not hearing anything. We've just started investigating these," advised Detective Anderson.

Chief Blackthorn mentioned, "Well these two youths are part of a family of three, Native kids but they're apparently off the reservation based on the fact that they were pilfering food from Mrs. St. Michael's trash cans. They could be part of whatever is happening to the kids whose disappearances you're investigating."

"Could be but it doesn't make sense that Mrs. St. Michael would be a person of interest in our investigation due to the age and living circumstances of these youths. Not sure why our perp, if there is one, would be here watching her, again, if that's what's happening here. The Whitehorse kids could just be runaways. Still, it's too early to know facts but it's a disturbing coincidence since these disappearances involve seven kids plus now, possibly your two."

Chief Blackthorn nodded. He appeared lost in thought. "Nothing like this, kids disappearing, is being reported on the rez and these kids leave and now disappear. Not ruling this out. Any developments with your case?"

"None, but it's early. This killing of the officer doesn't make sense and seems isolated to Mrs. St. Michael or something or someone nearby. Her intruder may be living off the land given the cabin and the cave. Maybe a hunter or squatter living there? Could be someone's getaway or … not sure. This is probably an entirely different investigation and not connected to the missing kids."

"Maybe."

"I don't want to prioritize one over the other. Could be a serial situation with the missing kids and a focused situation with Mrs. St. Michael, if she is part of the equation. Her place may just be situated nearby and not really involved," said Detective Anderson. "Something else, I didn't share this with Mrs. St. Michael about what we found in the cave. There was a collection of blood-stained clothing items, and the porn covered a nasty variety of deeply disturbing obsessions."

"I'm afraid to ask."

"Violent torture and sexualized ritual killings, snuff stuff, caged slaves like animals, visually explicit stuff, this included children. You can't imagine how dark this stuff is, but it offers some idea of the person we may be looking for and the obvious need to catch this guy now. I've sent everything to the FBI to have a profiler analyze the kind of person we may be dealing with. We may need help."

"When you say ritual, are we looking at a satanic cult?"

"No, more along the lines of torture that has a systematic pattern. An appetite."

"Good idea on getting a profile. Unfortunately knowing this new information, I'm imagining the worst for these kids, all of them." Chief Blackthorn stared off into the woods and looked back searching his brain for some clue as to who this person could be. Most of these kids are not Native. May not involve James and Jenny. He felt this was probably not a tribal matter.

"Keep what I've told you confidential. Don't want people around here scared till we know more."

Chief Blackthorn nodded.

"I'll keep in touch." Detective Anderson turned and headed towards his car.

At this, both officers left Tess's place.

Back in the house Rosa had been standing in the background wide-eyed with fear at what she was hearing and seeing. I was lost in thought staring out the back door, watching the officers, wondering what they were discussing and wondering about their delay. I watched them drive off. I turned and realized I had forgotten about Rosa and Timmy. "Rosa, let me check on Timmy. Sorry I don't have him up and ready."

We both headed upstairs. It was still early, and we found him sleeping. As we headed downstairs, Patty rushed in. The three of us made coffee and rustled breakfast for Timmy.

My mind was reeling, am I in danger, should Timmy stay here at all, where are his siblings and who is this person and is that person after me? I was reminded of Sam. Could it be him? The three of us sat and tried to make sense of everything. An officer murdered. Near here. Last night.

Patty looked truly frightened. "This never happens around here, I mean never. Do they have any idea who did this?"

"No."

Pastor Allen arrived. We busied ourselves getting Timmy up, fed, and ready.

As they started to leave, Rosa turned and said, "Tess, I do not live far; in fact, I live just up the street. I can be here in a second if you need anything."

"Where do you live?"

"Out your drive to the left, first house on the right. The first house with a white picket fence."

"I've seen that house. Children playing outside?"

"Yes, I occasionally run a daycare there."

Funny she never mentioned this. After gathering all the news, Rosa and Pastor Allen finally left with Timmy.

"Maybe you should come and stay with me," said Patty.

"Thanks, I appreciate the offer, but I have the dogs. Kai did chase something last night and whoever it is knows about my dogs now. That may be a deterrent."

"Honey, I don't know. From the sound of things he may be watching the house, it seems he would know about the dogs. Listen, I have a .38 revolver you can borrow. I'll run home and get it. Have you ever shot a gun before?"

"No"

"Okay, I'll be right back, and we can practice shooting at targets. Okay?"

All I could do was nod. I couldn't get my head around everything. I couldn't understand any of it. It made no sense. I needed a diversion from Clint, but this wasn't what I had in mind. I liked the idea of her returning today.

As she headed out the door, Patty said, "Listen, the offer to stay with me is a standing offer. And by the way, I know some guys that would be more than happy to help in a meaningful way, if you understand me."

I smiled, "Thank you honey, I do appreciate that." Not sure how I felt about the suggestion.

Lord let me sense You here now. I know You have me and nothing is happening outside Your will. Give me discernment and wisdom. I'm at a total loss and clueless on what I should do. Amen.

Chapter Sixteen

Beyond Redemption

Patty left and I was alone with my thoughts. A few minutes later there was another knock at my door, it was Rosa.

As she stepped inside, I could see she seemed worried, "Tess, I'm sorry to bother you but something occurred to me about your situation that I think I should tell you about." She came in and sat down. She studied her hands for a moment then looked up, "Remember the festival and that guy you pointed out by the food canopy?"

I nodded.

"I don't know why but I started thinking about him just now. I know a little more about him than I said the other day. I'm not sure if he's involved, but he has a bad reputation. Really bad," she said looking concerned. "I thought maybe I should mention him. His name is Sam, Sam Raven." She sat quietly for a moment, then looking at me continued, "He and his family were well known around here years ago." She went into his backstory. With a deep sigh she started, "Sam grew up very hard. He was born on the Crow Reservation in southern Montana. Both his parents were Crow. I heard his dad was an evil guy. Always in trouble and heavy into drugs and alcohol and usually some kind of brawl when he was around. He couldn't keep a job, worked as a day laborer, and he moved his family often. Sam's mom wasn't much better, but then neither of them grew up better either. They had five kids. I heard the dad moved the family often due to the many problems he caused. Heard he finally moved them to California, where he worked as a migrant worker. Quick money, and no roots. They always lived on the fringe of society. Not sure if the kids were in any schools. The family lived in lean-tos, plywood propped up for shelter; dirt floors, food cooked over fires. Very barebones lives."

I interrupted her asking if she wanted coffee.

While I was preparing the coffee she continued, "The dad drank and gambled in the evenings," she said as she joined me in the kitchen, adding "leaving the mom to manage on her own at their camp, scrounging for food and clothing. I heard that sometimes, when he ran out of money, he would gamble his kids for drugs and alcohol, feeding the filthy appetites of the men in camp. All five kids were later found abandoned alongside Interstate 5 near Anderson in California. Don't think they ever saw their parents again. The kids were placed in an orphanage near the Crow reservation."

We both stood there … her remembering and me pondering. I was imagining this family whose days and nights consisted of endless months and years of horrific terror, abuse, and an unfathomably desolate existence.

"As soon as Sam turned 18," she continued, "he joined the Army and eventually got accepted into the Rangers."

I had this feeling listening to her that there was more to this story that concerned her than she said. Seemed like a lot of intel from random rumors.

Rosa continued looking at me as though this news carried with it something almost private and hard to share, there was a struggle flitting behind her eyes. "I've met him. He's a quiet man, and I could tell he doesn't trust people and doesn't talk about himself. Even during the twenty plus years he spent in the Army Tess, heard he didn't make a single friend. Good place maybe if you want to be isolated. I've heard he's a dangerous man, very skilled at killing." She stopped her conversation here … stood lost in thought. I stood watching her, waiting.

I guessed the Rangers was the first time he found any power over his circumstances. And I suspect it provided an outlet for his anger and rage. I was picturing this man whose life began in a loveless, inhumanly deprived, and depraved home, certainly a formula for insidious hatred, festered in a life of abuse and hopelessness. A chill went down me when I realized who I might be dealing with. Still, I felt a sadness for him, growing up in a loveless, inhumane foundation, his life so far removed from mine. I thought about feral animals. I knew he wasn't an animal, but does feral apply to people? I didn't think so …

Breaking the silence I asked, "Why did he retire?"

Rosa looked up at me, "He didn't really. He was discharged due to a severe knee injury. So, he returned to Montana and the Crow reservation, but he couldn't fit in."

I suspected the military did not necessarily give him the tools to reenter society, especially if he never felt he belonged in the first place.

"Why would he be interested in me if he is the person doing this and why watching me?"

"Well," she sighed, "that's why I mention this, he came home with an addiction to drugs because of his injury, and if he's watching you there may be several reasons. When he returned home, he gravitated to prostitutes, they were willing companions for a time, but I was told he was violent with them. Soon the word was out about his violent abuse, and he found it difficult to find any companionship. This has probably isolated him even more. You're an attractive woman. It may be more what you represent. But I'm not sure." She added, "He became well known to the police on the Crow Reservation and it's possible everything has pushed him further into isolation. Think the military life had given him some structure." She stopped, looking frankly at me. "We see him from time to time on Wind River, like at the festival. Don't know where he's living, but it made me wonder about that cabin, if anyone can live off the grid and, in the backcountry, it's probably him."

I had a fleeting thought to book plane reservations back to Florida.

I looked hard at her again thinking this *is* a lot of info and details, "How well do you know him?" I asked quietly.

She hesitated and looked away. "For a while, he would stop in at the Bureau regarding issues with his benefits, and there were moments when he would talk to me. I pieced some of his background from various conversations he shared briefly with me and others at the Bureau. His family was still known to several families on Wind River."

"Is that all?" My questioning look made her blush, but she didn't answer. We sat sipping coffee.

"Well Tess," she said as she stood to leave, "I don't know if this is him, I feel for him and how bad life has treated him, but I also believe that he is capable of great evil, dangerous." She furrowed her brow, "I don't know if there is any good left in him. There were moments when talking to him where I saw something, I don't know, like some desire in him for tenderness and it touched me, but I don't have any idea how to reach that.

I wanted you to know about him because I can't shake loose this idea that he's involved."

I could see that she struggled with this 'beyond redemption' possibility and her worry for me. She gave me a gentle hug and left. I watched her leave, still with this impression that there was more that she was not saying.

Chapter Seventeen

Three of Hearts

Patty returned about the same time as Jimmy and Dinah.

We made an evening of it, dinner, gun safety and target practice. I still had this concern that having the gun and minimal instruction might elevate my confidence level beyond my skill.

"Tess, you're a natural!" beamed Jimmy.

With raised eyebrows I responded, "Come on now." Jimmy chuckled.

The evening conversation rehashed the events over the last few days. The horror of the death of the officer was lessened with my company, but I also knew that that would end shortly.

Jimmy asked, "Are you going to be okay here alone? I can call Clint."

Patty responded, "I said the same thing, Jimmy. Tess, I am not sure you're appreciating the situation. Honey, at least stay with me a day or so until things calm down. By then they may have caught this guy. Okay? And you can bring the pups. No problem. Not sure I can sleep knowing you are out here alone with that guy loose."

Their words didn't help. Staying here terrified me, I realized. The idea had merit and I agreed.

I stayed at Patty's, but I traveled back to my home the next day. I was worried. I realized finally that this was my home, my life. I couldn't abandon it. As I pulled onto my property, I could see trash had been thrown about behind the house. The dogs immediately ran to the rear of the house. As we approached the back of my house, I could see all my trash had been emptied and strewn about. While picking up the trash, I looked around and watched as the dogs sniffed the bushes. Both dogs rushed through the bushes up to the trail. I followed. They disappeared into the underbrush, but I could hear them as they eagerly hunted. Following, I thought about where I had put the gun. They headed up trail towards the cabin. As I reached the cabin, I could tell that no one had been here in a while, no hot coals, no odors. I entered the cabin but was startled out of my skin by a voice behind me!

"What are you doing here?"

I quickly turned to the sound of Clint's voice. He was not happy. Both dogs bounded to him, and he rubbed them both friskily. Looking up, "Tess, what do you think you're doing?"

It was sobering. The weight of the situation hit me, and I felt foolish for being this careless. We stood looking at one another and I lamely explained the trash and dogs and … "I just followed …"

Frowning, he took a deep breath. But something played behind his eyes … softness. Feeling the same softness, I stood for a moment before speaking again.

"What are *you* doing here?" I managed.

"I was curious about the cabin." He said, not taking his eyes off me. "Jimmy told me about what's been happening and I wanted to have a look around and check things out."

I asked, "Did you find the cave?"

"Cave?" He stopped.

"Yes, it's supposed to be within view of the cabin. I haven't seen it," stammering nervously. "The police found items there that indicated that someone might have been living in the cave."

He was surprised at the news and checked our surroundings quickly. "Okay." I could see he was anxious for me to leave. I suspected he now had another mission, to find this cave. Moved by his care and concern for me and my safety, I felt the anxiety of the situation ebb. I knew I could trust him even though it presented deeper problems.

"Alright, I'm leaving. Will you let me know if you find anything?" I asked.

He didn't respond.

"Listen, this involves me. Please let me know. My life is upside down right now and I'm afraid to live in my own home. Would you at least let Chief Blackthorn know if you do find anything?"

Finally, he smiled. "Yes, Tess. I'd like a concession from you in return, don't check things out on your own and stay with Patty. Please? It's easier for me knowing you're safe," he softened. A deep sigh, "Do you understand?"

He knew where I was staying. My heart leapt at the thought. I stood near the cabin threshold staring at him, my breathing more rapid. This encounter was kindling a flame ... passion and fear ... such odd companions. "Alright … Are you keeping tabs on me?" I looked at him with a smile.

He didn't answer. But we had a moment where our past passed between us. We were both remembering. I could have run to him, but I checked myself.

Calming, it suddenly occurred to me to ask, "Do you know a guy named Sam Raven?" I said this as I left the cabin threshold and walked towards him.

"Why?"

"I don't know," I said as I walked towards him, watching him, feeling happier than I should. "It seems there's a possibility that he may be involved." I looked past him recalling each time I saw Sam. "I've seen him a few times," I said, my gaze turning back to Clint. "He appears to be watching me, and I don't get a good feeling. Not sure if it's significant. Rosa mentioned the possibility he could be involved based on his history. She gave me quite a backstory on him."

He was pondering this news and didn't answer as I got closer to him. As I started to pass, I turned to face him, there was the same dark intensity in his eyes I had come to know. He studied me for a moment, then leaned in, hovering over me, he put his hands on my waist, then his lips found mine. When he pulled back, he gently took my hand and led me down the trail to my parked car. Whistling for my dogs, he opened the door, and they jumped in. He opened my door, and as I moved to enter, he stood still, with one arm on the door frame and the other on the car, trapping me, studying my face. I could feel his heat; I leant in for one more kiss but found myself wrapped in his arms. Taking a breath, he stepped back, staring into my eyes, his hands moved a strand of hair behind my ear. Studying my face, "Tess …" he said lowering his head, gently kissing my forehead, "please leave this alone. I can't focus if I think you're in danger. Promise?" His eyes soft, almost vulnerable.

I nodded, smiling, I cupped his face in my hand, giving him a quick kiss as I turned to leave. I drove away, looking back in my rearview mirror, he was gone.

My care for him chased my shadows and on the drive back to Patty's, I felt happy. Seeing him involved in this made me feel safer. It occurred to me that Clint was alone hunting It's the unknown. Would he call if he found something? Would he be safe?

I drove around for a while before returning to Patty's. Finding a quiet place near the mountains, I parked my car. I sat staring at the scene outside my windshield. The mountains and the etched inlets with trees cascading down the mountains to meet rushing streams. The images are a dichotomy with recent events. I sat there thinking about Clint, remembering his touch, his kiss. I touched my lips. Warmth flooded my chest … explicably I felt calm. Lord, why do our paths keep intersecting? How do I heal? I have a request. If he isn't supposed to be in my life, end this without pain and Lord, keep him safe. Amen

Patty's two-bedroom home was tasteful. No surprise. It wasn't hard to be comfortable here. She made us tea as we sat and chatted about the day before heading for bed. I didn't mention Clint.

"I work tomorrow early; I'm showing homes to a few clients, but I'll stay in touch." She explained.

The following day I spent roaming around Lander. Found the public library and some novelty shops. I drove out to Wind River, stopping in to see Chief Blackthorn. "Sorry to pop in like this."

"No problem, Mrs. St. Michael, please have a seat. What's on your mind?"

"Just wondering about the status on the investigation?"

"There isn't any news. Sorry, I know how deeply involved you are in this, Tess, I *will* notify you if I hear anything, promise," he said. I tried to read his face, studying his eyes.

Finally, I started, "I'm staying with my friend in Lander. I was out at the house yesterday. I didn't spot anyone, although my trash had been dumped. I was interested … the other day at my house, I saw you and Detective Anderson talking over by the barn, and I was just curious, you're telling me everything, right?"

His demeanor softened, "Things are complicated, Mrs. St. Micheal. There are actually two investigations going on and right now, I don't know if they're related," he said. "We were discussing both but so far, there isn't any news or developments on either. Honest. I know this is disappointing, it's difficult for us. Missing children and an officer murdered. But there is a lot being done behind the scenes, trust me."

I could feel I wasn't getting all the intel and I'm not sure why, as the situation clearly concerned me, at least my property in some way. I pressed, "Do you know a guy named Sam Raven?"

"Yes, why?"

"Rosa mentioned him as a possibility in the death of the officer."

"She did? Hum." His gaze drifted. "He certainly could be a possibility; did she say anything more?"

"Just about his past. Sad but dangerous guy."

"Yeah, he's a bad seed. Why does she think it might be him?"

I mentioned the dance and festival and his demeanor around me.

"I'll look into that Mrs. St. Michael. Thanks for the info." He stood, ending our discussion.

With that I left. I had to believe that if they thought I was in danger, I'd hear more or there would be more precautions taken toward my personal safety. I told myself they were handling matters.

I spent the next few days at Patty's and Rosa kept Timmy with her. We stayed in touch.

Mid-week John called as promised, "Hey beautiful, how's your week been and are we still on for this weekend?"

John ... I hadn't deliberately pushed him into the back of my mind, but thoughts of him were not in the forefront. The events, investigation, Clint and now Timmy fully occupied my thoughts. If I'm honest with myself, I wanted both men. I didn't want to let go of John. He was the *normal* in my life, and I did care for him more than a little. On some level, I knew that a future life with John was possible; it was very appealing, and ... safe. I gave him a rundown of the past week.

"Tess are you okay? Why didn't you call me?!" His concern was tinged with anger. "I want you to come and stay with me. Bring the dogs. I won't accept no from you. I mean it, Tess. Pack up your things and I am headed over." Determined firmness in his voice sent a warmth down my spine.

I could tell he was upset that I hadn't contacted him about this. "John, I'm sorry. It's been a harrowing week, just trying to get a grip on this mysterious tragedy. I am staying with Patty, a friend of mine in town. Let's keep our date this weekend. I'll come to Jackson early Saturday, and we can spend the day. Okay?"

No response.

"John? Are you there?"

"Yes, just thinking this through. So, there's a disturbed person out there possibly stalking you and you live alone with no means of defense. I'm not getting the sense you appreciate the seriousness of this to you. I think you really need to put more distance between you and this guy. Do they know who it is? I'm happy you're staying with your friend, good move but I am still coming to get you. Where does she live?"

Now I was quiet thinking about this.

"Tess, I was serious about NOT taking no for an answer. I think you know that I care a great deal for you, and I need to not only know that you are safe, I need you to BE safe. Are you understanding me? How can I hang up and go about my day with you in danger? I know our relationship is new but let me protect you and take care of you. Where does she live?"

Like staying here with Patty, I didn't know how to say no to this, I had no good argument. It made sense to put more distance between this and be somewhere where my whereabouts were unknown, IF this was in some way connected to me. "Okay." I gave him her address.

"I'll be there shortly, honey."

I told Patty about the conversation.

"Dang, handsome and a knight in shining armor. Impressive, Tess. He's quite a guy. Take it from me, don't let this one get away. I'm glad he's involving himself. I hate that you stay there alone, I mean even once we get past this situation, I like the idea of you having someone that watches over you, and he may be the one. Obviously, he cares about you. Anything I can do to help you get ready?"

"I know. He's a great guy. No, I can manage but thanks for the offer," I said as I left to pack and think. These two keep colliding. I know I'm not handling this well and I feel bad. And Clint seems to know where I am, I was certain he would find out about this. My excuse, I couldn't manage the control necessary to handle one more thing, all I felt capable of doing was taking the next step, and that was John.

John arrived and immediately took control of the situation. Patty was introduced and then stood back and watched. I could see she was very moved by John's chivalry, and I could see she was comparing John and her last romance. My heart went out to her. I let John take charge; it was a relief. He gave her his contact information as he ushered me and my dogs to his SUV. I gave her a hug and we left. We drove to Jackson

Hole in silence. Both lost in our own thoughts. He moved me into his condo and got me settled in his spare bedroom. We took the dogs for a walk, fed them, and then decided to grab a bite to eat. Sitting across from this wonderful man, I felt safe, and I could see how much he cared. I wanted to return this. But the timing ...

"So, you now have a ward. And an enemy. And you managed all this in less than a week. Apparently, you can't be left alone for too long as things appear to be moving sideways." He looked at me like a father. A crooked smile on the corners of his lips.

"Are you saying that I need supervision?" I tried for this surprised look.

He reached his hands across the table and grabbed mine. "Unless you have a better word for it. Supervision may be putting it mildly, but it'll do. I'll take care of you, let me. I won't let anything happen to you, God as my witness." I stared into his eyes and felt myself start to tear up. This felt good. I could see the genuineness in his eyes, and I could see that he sees me. He deserves more from me.

"Thank you, I appreciate your help, but John, slow down for me right now. I'm smack in the middle of chaos." I went into more detail about Timmy, James and Jenny and the conversation turned to my ideas about a sanctuary. I gave him a full low down on the intruder, who it might be and where the investigation stood. Nowhere now.

"It's wild that no one has seen those two," I said. "Hard to fathom their ability to stay hidden and no one has caught them going through trash. Can't get my head around that. If they were spotted, we could start there, maybe they'd leave a trail?" I rattled, "The problem is, they've been surviving on their own for months. They are way ahead with this stealth ~ invisible behavior and it sounds like they are used to a hard life. This may be more of the same for them. Their norm, as hard as that is to comprehend. And we are playing catch up, but for them, this stealth, allusive behavior has kept them safe." I sat across from John, looking into his eyes as though they could provide clarity, answers. How am I in the middle of this?

"Alright my beautiful lady, I will take things slow with you, and I think that idea originated with me." He said with a look indicating he was already in the lead here. "They will find these kids. Somehow, they'll slip up and be spotted. I'm fairly certain of that." He paused, thoughtful, "But this guy, whatever he is up to and whatever he is after, the further you are from his grasp, and you may be his target by the sound of things, then this is the best place for you. I seriously doubt he will come looking for you here. Way out of his element, especially if it's the same guy you mentioned."

It made sense and felt safe but for how long? I felt sure Jackson Hole was not where I was meant to be.

Chapter Eighteen

Surrounded by Warmth

The weeks passed with no further news or developments.

John showed me Jackson Hole and introduced me to his life and friends. John keeps me busy. We explore Yellowstone and camp out, attend outdoor concerts, grocery shop and cook our favorite recipes. The world in Lander seems decades away. I've stayed in touch with the police, Patty, and Rosa. Still, mornings alone in the condo give me time to think … think about both men. The intensity of Clint is fading but not the foothold he has in my heart. Daily deliberately I close that door and day by day John gains a foothold. I keep Clint in a box, but he doesn't disappear.

The nights have turned romantic and as winter approaches, John is my summer. Surrounded by his warmth, I feel nurtured, I find myself falling for John. How could I not, there was nothing to sensor in this man. I visited him at work, attended hearings and helped with minor office work. I met his friend and partner, Stark Owens, and thought of Patty. Everything about life here was wonderful. It caused me to reassess why I was here and where I should be.

My days with John are filled with loving moments, warm touches, and tender kisses. Laughter and smiles are our constant, and I realize that I had never been this happy in a relationship. One evening after we made dinner John turned the music on and lowered the lights. "I recall you promised me a dance," as he leaned in to pull me towards him. Both smiling. "Okay, but you've been warned." It was a slow dance, and the moves were easy with John close. I loved the closeness, the movement of our bodies together and the atmosphere. Warm and romantic. The longer I stayed the more distant I felt towards Clint. I didn't think that that could have been possible. How was that possible? John was even accepting of my restraints on the level of our intimacy.

I was falling in love with him.

During my stay, I got to know Stark, he was a regular and I thought of Patty. I decided that they should meet. I called Patty and invited her to dinner with John and myself. She accepted. I also invited Stark. Of course, it was a small detail that I failed to mention this was a foursome to either of them.

"You don't have enough to do to add matchmaking?" John was smiling his crooked smile and shaking his head.

"It's in my genetics. But why not? They're both two of the nicest people, both single and come with resumes and personal testimonies. Right? If they don't hit it off, there's no harm done. If they do, I may have to take dance lessons."

"You already have them married? Really? Okay, well I'm staying clear of this. There may be an element of drama in your genes as well ..." he paused, "But I will say this, Stark's a great guy and in my opinion a good catch, but romance ... he hasn't been that successful with the ladies in finding the right one. Years ago, he was serious about this girl. High school sweethearts. You've heard this before, kind of a common story. They had been together for years but attended different colleges and she found someone else. I remember when he got the letter. I don't think he's recovered completely. And maybe it's just fear or trust. So, tread lightly sweetheart."

It hit me; I could apply his comments to us. Tread lightly Tess.

Happily, dinner was a fabulous success. By the end of the evening, they were both glowing and we didn't exist, so we exited, and headed for home. We didn't hear from either of them for a few days. Patty finally called. "I should be mad. Why didn't you tell me about dinner plans?"

"Well, the obvious. Didn't want either of you to stress, just wanted you to both come relaxed and if you didn't get along, it was just dinner." I added, "I deliberated on this meeting Patty; I did think about it for a while. You have both been hurt and I didn't want to contribute to that. Sooooo ... do you like him?"

"Yes." The animation in her tone picked up. "He's a great guy. Dark haired version of John," she said laughing. "How well do you know him?

Her comment 'dark haired version of John' oddly made me tingle, maybe some idea of hope for her and romance. "I don't know a lot. But I see him often. He's John's law partner and best friend. John loves him and I'll take that as an endorsement." Thinking about Stark I added, "I see him both socially and at work. He *is* a version of John, in my opinion also. Haven't seen him do or say anything that I didn't like. He is … normal. If I had seen anything I didn't like, I wouldn't have put the two of you together. I wouldn't have. John says he occasionally dates but nothing has connected. So, there's no ex's to stalk the relationship. But I'll add a disclaimer, I don't know Stark, and the caveat is to take it slow."

"Boy, John is rubbing off on you, talking like a lawyer!" We both laughed. That's probably true. She continued, "I like him. I do. Thank you for the bio. It eases my mind so I can relax. That night we shut down the restaurant and a lounge, and he got me a hotel room, no strings attached, a gentleman. He was concerned about how late it was and the drive home. The next morning, he came by and took me to breakfast. But once I got home, had some fears resurrect …" I could hear her concern in her voice.

Romance is dangerous territory.

"You've said this before to me about John, you can take this slow. Let it breathe and have its own momentum. In time, I think you'll have a pretty good idea if this is for you. I'm not going to push him on you. You're in control. Do you have plans?"

"Yes, he's coming here Saturday for dinner."

"So, you're hearing from him?"

"Yes, he calls me every day, sometimes twice." She giggled. I could almost hear her blushing. "I admit, I'm excited. And I'm not mad you introduced us." She chuckled. "I was just kidding. I want to continue this discussion but I gotta run. Have an appointment. But let's catch up at lunch, maybe next week? I'll call later to schedule. Love you."

"Okay, sounds good. Love you too."

That evening when John came home, I told him I had spoken with Patty. "Did Stark mention anything about Patty to you?"

"Can I have a kiss first?" After giving me a deep hug and a warm kiss, putting his things down and petting the dogs, he commented, "Stark and I had lunch today." He had this frank look on his face, noting a little attitude, then smiling, "And yes … he did talk about her. This may have been a good idea." I got a conciliatory smile. "He says they talk every day, and they have dinner plans in Lander this weekend. He was smiling all through lunch. Like a kid. I have to say it made me chuckle. He's happy. Are you happy, matchmaker?"

"Of course, like the A-Team says, love it when a plan comes together… She's happy too. Her last relationship didn't end well. She admits she likes him. I would love to see this work out for them."

"Me too. What's for dinner?"

"Oh, you're not taking me out?"

He stood for a moment wondering if this was the plan.

"… Okay, I'll let you off the hook. I made dinner. There were no plans," I said laughing.

John came over and started tickling me. I hate being tickled. He wrestled me to the floor, I was laughing and gasping, "Stop! Stop!" The dogs joined in, and it was a four-for-all. We laid on the floor for a while holding hands, relaxed and happy, with the dogs' heads propped on our chests.

"I love that guy." John said while lying next to me, eyes fixed on the ceiling. His head turned towards me, "He has been a brother to me. I've known him since second grade. We've been through a lot together. You know, growing up, I can't remember a day when we didn't see each other. I was at his house or he was at mine. Our families blended into one. His folks my folks and the same for him." He smiled, looking away, remembering. "We had a wild youth," his smile broadened. "In fact, not sure how we or our families survived!" He was still smiling as he looked over at me, "there were run-ins with the police, car races and all-night binges.... I was still recovering from one the day I got married. We both were and he was my best man," He laughed, "Not a good start," ... he got this faraway look in his eyes, "Maybe having been through those times gave me some insight into my clients and why that area of the law appealed to me. But Stark has been a brother soul mate and, ...you've heard the saying 'a brother from a different mother'," he looked in my eyes, "Tess, I don't want to see him hurt again. He's a strong guy but his heart still carries that scar ..." He was looking deep into my eyes.

My thoughts took me to my relationships with John and Clint. What am I doing? I sat up quickly, moving away from John and Kai and gaining my feet. John was startled.

"Tess! Are you okay? Was it something I said?"

I walked out of the room and stood looking out the front window. John came up behind me and put his arms around me, turning me to face him. I leaned into his chest, hiding the tears and guilt I felt and that I hadn't been open about things.

"Tess, I AM excited for Stark and Patty and please don't take my comments as a censor for bringing them together, I don't think that way and," he said, turning my face to look up at him, searching my eyes, "I am happy for them both ... I'll locate a good dance instructor," he said quietly as he gently kissed my lips. "We good?"

I looked into his eyes and tried for a smile, searching his face, "I love you, John." This was the first time this word was spoken by me, and I could see John was deeply moved. He leaned in for a long, lingering kiss and we stood lost to time, in a deep embrace. Hiding my tears ... happy and ashamed.

Still, I couldn't discuss Clint with him, there were no opening words that came to my mind ... Clint had ended things. I felt constrained about bringing this out into the open. What was there to discuss? In my heart, Clint belonged to another life and a different world, a ghost. John was here and now and all in, not running or hiding, no obstacles hindering my heart being wide open to let John in and in truth, John was chasing my ghost away, cleansing my heart and laying a new foundation that belonged to us. There didn't seem to be any point I told myself.

After dinner, we spent the evening wrapped in each other's arms, sitting in the dark ... together, just us, and nothing touched it. Bliss ...

I met Patty for lunch the following week. It was a long lunch consisting primarily of all things 'Stark' ... How cute and adorable he is … gushing's a good word. She was happy and I reported that Stark made similar statements to John about her. She seemed to melt at this ... this is a nice change to witness. Being in love is a good look, it's an 'everything's right with the world' look, it softens the face and puts light behind the eyes, and Patty wears it well.

I may *have* to take dance lessons.

Chapter Ninteen

Life turns on a dime

Being in Lander made me think of home. I decided to run by after lunch. Periodically, John and I would check on things at the homestead. As I drove up, I could see nothing had changed. I went inside. Needed a housekeeper ... dust everywhere. Went out back and stood on the deck, looked over at the barn, as is usual lately, I observed nothing to indicate anything was wrong. Standing on the deck and looking around, my prior life here was a blur. I felt removed from all of it. The love, the horror, the plans, Clint.

After months of being away, finally the need to return home started weighing on me. I needed to reconnect with my home, and I had taken on this responsibility for Timmy. Chief Blackthorn and Detective Anderson reported no new developments. There was no news regarding the missing children or the killer. But, if I can take anything good in this, things were quiet. No more missing children and no one murdered. Hoping my absence was not part of the reason for that.

There was a plan for my life, and I knew it was here. My time in Jackson was good in so many ways and my relationship with John had deepened. I didn't want to leave him.

The time came when I moved back to Lander. I discovered parenting and the responsibilities that came with that. The foster home situation did not work out, and Timmy came to live with me. Timmy needed to be packed up daily for school on the rez and motherhood started to define my life. John was a regular now. I was either in Jackson Hole or he was in Lander.

In the back of my mind, I knew Clint was an unresolved issue. But Clint was no longer a barrier to my relationship with John. In my heart there was still a corner that he owned, but it no longer diminished or held back my love for John. I was committed.

I started working with Pastor Allen and Stephanie Hunter and became licensed in the foster home program. As a result, more children were placed in my home. By now Timmy was speaking and connecting and became a friendly face to new visitors. It all worked somehow, and John didn't blink an eye about the activity or responsibilities.

As Christmas approached and winter deepened, I had started helping Pastor Allen and Rosa on the reservation. There were elderly individuals in remote locations that needed assistance and we brought food, medicine, hygiene products and hopefully hope. I had reconnected with Jimmy and Dinah. Jimmy was a big help and support, and Dinah became my right arm. She was over often and helped with the children and Jimmy assisted in navigating me around the Rez, locating individuals I had been asked to check in on with supplies and assistance.

Winter came with a vengeance, at least *I* thought so.

The week filled up with meetings with Child Protective Services, shopping for items for my new wards and dinner with Patty and on occasion, Stark. And this new life with John. The past events were becoming that, past events.

My John, faithful and patient with my Christian values on intimacy. I told him I knew if I slipped here, the guilt I would feel towards my other love could derail our relationship. Marriage was starting to enter my thoughts with John. Nothing said.

My Florida blood did not prepare me for Wyoming winters. I had considerable trepidation about the winters. I was comforted that I finally had a resource of people to help me and provide me with needed assistance and information. Dinah loved the children and stopped in to play and assist. She was thinking she wanted to be a teacher and so shouldered more responsibility than we asked, but we were grateful. I was also happy when I realized my thoughts and words no longer consisted of 'me' and 'I' but were now inclusive of 'we' and 'ours'.

Jimmy had done as he promised and occasionally when he found time we rode around on the reservation. I became acquainted with some of its remote residents, one in particular, an elderly woman named Wichapi Win. I found out from Rosa it meant star woman. I knew often with individuals in the Old Testament that their name described them, their character, and if their relationship with God changed their character, He gave them a new name. Names are important.

Wichapi lived literally in a box of sorts. Plywood and cardboard. Just one room and it contained all her worldly possessions. She had family nearby, I learned. I stopped in to see her as often as time allowed, bringing her anything my last visit revealed was some sort of need. What I thought she really needed was a better home, but she was not moving. She had lived like this her entire life, and she was rooted to the spot. Wasn't much of a spot. But she had planted a small garden, and it was hers.

I asked Pastor Allen about possibilities for putting in wells and ways of providing a heat source. The needs were overwhelming, and I couldn't meet them all, but I could start somewhere, and I picked Wichapi. It turns out there were ministries already in place that provided some of these needs. I contacted the Native American Christian Fellowship. They had their own radio station, orphanage, and schools. They were doing some of the same things but on a much larger scale. I found out that I could purchase a well and propane heating system from them and they would handle everything else.

One problem, Wichapi. She was a proud woman. She didn't ask for handouts, and I really had no idea how she would view my help. It was a fragile friendship. Jimmy and I started with trying to meet simple needs. We brought fuel, coffee, and staples. She had one cow; a gentle girl and it needed a better home. I asked Jimmy how he was able to help me with school and Clint's helper all at the same time. I needed his help and took what I got. I wanted to build a solid structure for the cow, so one day we threw wood and tools into the back of his pickup, headed out for her homestead, and went to work building this structure downwind of her house. It became apparent we needed more help than my small frame could provide putting in the supporting beams, so we laid a foundation but left early with Jimmy planning to get Duke to come out tomorrow to help. A few days later I returned with Jimmy to Wichapi's. I learned that Clint had stopped by after work and completed this for Jimmy. Clint here … Jimmy said he had mentioned it to Duke, but he couldn't take time off from his work. He had mentioned it to several other friends because he didn't want to involve Clint, but his friends had trouble with our timeline. Clint, all the way out here after work… It took us easily three quarters of an hour to reach her place.

He still has a power I found that could touch me. He had decided against the relationship, and I have found John. I wasn't going back.

Wichapi did not say much about the project, she stayed hidden and reclusive. Sometimes I would catch her peeking out to observe the construction. She didn't stop the construction, and she didn't ask any questions. Since the work was not officially *for* Wichapi, I felt that I had possibly circumnavigated some social faux pas that her mind could conjure. That remained to be seen.

Things went better than expected and we finished our project that day. She surveyed the work, and we watched as she brought her cow into its new home. That was it, pretty much. Nothing said and no real expression, but I had to wonder. God tells us to never tire of doing good, which I understood included random acts of kindness that weren't tied to any reciprocal issues. But deep down I prayed she liked it, and that this might help further our relationship.

Saturday morning Dinah called hysterical! A truck full of teenage boys had run off the road last night and all were dead! Tommy was one of them! He had been thrown from the truck bed, along with another boy. She couldn't stop crying. I could feel the pain of her loss. Sobbing she asked, "Can you come by?" I promised her that I would come immediately and got directions.

John was laid over in Jackson for a trial.

I pulled up to the Pierre farm. No sign of Clint's truck. It was a solid frame house situated in a valley and I could see that the family owned horses with a barn and corral. There was a barn and chicken coop in the back to the left of the house. The property was well maintained. I knocked and Joseph answered the door. The house was quiet. Dinah was in her room. Jimmy was out with Clint visiting the families. Mrs. Pierre came out of the kitchen. She gave me a tight hug and whispered thanks for coming. She took me to Dinah's room and gently knocked. Opening the door, Dinah ran to greet me, sobbing. We sat on her bed, hugging and rocking. There were no words for the tragedy. I stayed a few hours until Dinah fell asleep and left before Clint or Jimmy returned.

I learned more about the tragedy at the funeral. Sitting between Rosa and Dinah, Rosa whispered what she had learned of the tragedy. She told me that the boys had been returning home from a camping trip and were on a mountain road traveling too fast on the snow and icy roads. They lost control apparently at a switchback. They only found them on Saturday morning. A motorist saw smoke and called the police who investigated and found the charred vehicle. The boy driving had burned up in the truck and everyone else had been thrown clear. Three bodies were found near the broken railing just down the slope. All of them had died instantly.

I looked around at the community gathered to grieve corporately. The pitch of the women's trilling was painful to hear. It tore at the heart. The deep sobs and worst, the look of others numb with grief. Part of the soul of the community had been torn from it, and the essence and presence of these young men now gone forever leaving in their place empty space. It's hard when we lose our young, especially this senselessly.

As I sat there hurting for the people, Clint stood up. I was startled. He spoke to the crowd about the loss and said words that sounded like a prayer. As he spoke, his eyes found mine, and he halted for just a moment. When he had finished, we stood to leave. I didn't know most of these people and didn't want to intrude on their privacy. Turning to go to my car, I found Clint standing in the crowd nearby. Our eyes met for the second time today. To be this close and not touch. I looked at his face as he approached. He still cared for me. I managed to smile. He approached close and after a moment said, "Tess, thank you for supporting Dinah and the families. It means a lot… to all of us." I couldn't say anything at first, finally I managed, "Of course," in a whisper. The shock that he still had power I found deeply upsetting, My strength had evaporated, I hadn't been prepared for this. I nodded and turned to leave. Inexplicably, I found myself tearful. Managing to locate my car, Rosa shot me a look of confusion, then understanding, this was a place for tears. I had a vague memory of dropping Rosa at her house.

Pulling up to my house, needing time alone, I ran to my room and closed myself in my sanctuary. After a shower I camped on my bed, read, and prayed then fell asleep, my last thoughts were of his face.

John, Lord, help my love for him and not hurt him. I am committed. I won't leave.

Chapter Twenty

Wichapi

The holidays came and went filled with activity. John and I had fun with the children, filling their lives with Thanksgiving meals and Christmas wonder. We were busy with holiday preparations and activities. The population at the school was growing.

More than once I found myself a quiet observer of all He has done. It humbles me. Not even the love I have for John and, if I'm honest, Clint, not even the intense emotion I feel for them touches the depth of the joy and peace God brings in His intimacy with me. The long days allowed quiet moments to meditate. Meditating brings me closer to His presence, *into* His presence. It's profoundly holy.

My quiet observation also included myself. I was happy. I loved John ... completely. Well, I loved him as completely as I knew how. Love and intimacy were tricky for me. My history was to dip in and then run. Trust may have been at the root to this dip in and run behavior. My early years were marred by abuse ... molested ... it's a destroyer of innocence, of joyful childhood play but more importantly, trust. When you're molested, overnight the world takes on a dark adult color, an irrevocable change in the atmosphere, introduction into things that children should not know. No longer a child but not an adult. Finding no place to *be*, it left me feeling I was outside the camp of normal society, ungrounded, unprotected. Innocence in my childhood was replaced with fear and shame. It's hard to heal or get therapy because you must *name* the issue before it can be dealt with; I was a child and the event was hidden for many years. So, it has taken me years of painful honesty, facing myself, looking truthfully at tough situations that touched deep wounds, many causing breakdown moments, some cataclysmic; all the while God was orchestrating my 'get out of jail' card, my freedom.

I was finding this with John ... trust ... wholeness. I was happy. God was using John. John lets me know I am *seen*, he gives me a safe space to take down armor, confront demons; helps me see the best version of myself. Because he is authentic, he requires that in subtle ways with me; gently coaxing me out of hiding. Every part of me is welcome into his world, and I am learning about real intimacy in relationships; that honesty opens a path to intimacy.

The cold kept me indoors quite a bit. John made good on his other promises, beating me at board games and teaching me to ski. Patty and Stark were also involved in our activities with fun days skiing and warm evening dinners, fires and candlelight.

After the holidays, winter came in hard. I made trips out to see Wichapi to see about her needs. If Jimmy couldn't go, we would exchange vehicles. He was now in community college and doing well. I saw less of him, but he still made an effort to stop around. Patty, Dinah and Rosa were now my inner circle.

Wichapi somehow managed life. I couldn't fathom it. Survival at its most barebones. No amenities that I could see although I think she thought she had them. Her life consisted of small blessings that she took from the earth. Still, I could see etched in her face the harshness of a life canopied by the elements. I talked to Pastor Allen about locating a vehicle that was more practical. I needed a truck but preferably a van for transporting and for carrying supplies into remote regions on the reservation. He called one morning to tell me he had found a van in good condition. I added the van to my growing enterprise.

I had promised Wichapi I would bring her supplies, but the weather forecasted a huge storm front coming in today. I rushed to finish things at the house so that I could get on the road and get her the supplies. I loaded the van with blankets and fuel and food stables.

"Tess, you aren't going out in this?" I could see Rosa was not happy about this. I understood her concern.

This wasn't my element; I had little experience driving in snow and ice. But I felt there wasn't any way I could sit comfortably in my home knowing that Wichapi needed these supplies, especially in the face of this storm.

"I'm getting on the road now and I should be back before the storm hits. Promise." Not sure how I could make that statement, but it was the same one I told myself.

It was around noon when I headed out, leaving time to get there and back before the projected storm was expected. However, the weather turned bad about three quarters into the trip. I drove into low lying clouds, and I could see thick darkness ahead, bringing with it pelting rain and swirling snow. These were moving towards me like stampeding horses. Snow flurries and wind gusts became furious quickly, violently rolling across the road in front of my van. The conditions started to white-out. I slowed because I couldn't see the road, anything. I knew that proceeding was extremely dangerous, but so was turning around. I thought that I could do this if I just went slow. I crept along using my headlights now as my only guide, straining at the road and trying to recognize anything familiar, hoping the weather would pass quickly.

Finally, I spotted a familiar silhouette. There was just the faintest outline of a roof, it broke into the outline of the distant mountains providing some identifying features. The cow shed. When I arrived at Wichapi's there were no lights on, did she have lights? The storm had gotten fierce and when I opened my door the noise was deafening. The wind howled across the plains and snow was pelting me. To my surprise and horror, I stepped out into several feet of snow. The sky was depositing vast amounts as the fierce storm moved forward. I kept my headlights on to locate her home. When I got out, I tried calling her. Not sure she could hear me. The wind made it almost impossible to hear anything. The storm worsened and looked like swirling snow tornadoes. I realized I needed to make a decision in the event I couldn't make it back to the car, I grabbed as much of her supplies as I could hold in my arms, shut off the lights and closed the van.

Struggling and stumbling to her shack, I kept calling her. Nothing was stirring. I could no longer see the shelter where she kept her cow. I managed to get to her door and tried grabbing the corner of the door to pull it open with my boot. It would not move. I put the supplies down in the snow and threw my body into pulling the door open. The snow had collected on the ground and piled up against the door making it hard to open. I had to dig snow from the door to make any progress. The door finally gave, opening to complete blackness. Grabbing the supplies, I was able to get everything inside. I tried propping the door open, but the snow started piling up inside the shack. I forced the door closed.

The supplies included a flashlight. I found the flashlight button and turned it on. Squinting, looking around the room, I became alarmed, what if Wichapi wasn't even here. Was she safe with family and I was here alone? I searched frantically for her. Walking towards the location where I knew her bed was supposed to be, I found a mound of blankets. Something stirred. Wichapi peeked out from under her cocoon of blankets.

I was relieved. I was able to locate an oil lamp and got that lit. I put her supplies away and I added blankets to her collection.

Could I leave her here like this? No. She was watching me. I motioned that I wanted her to leave with me. Did a motion of driving a car. To my surprise she agreed. I knew that getting out and home was going to be challenging but felt we needed to try. Getting her unwrapped and moving was another matter. She was stiff and we had to find warm clothes and get her boots on. I had brought her new boots on my last trip along with a coat, hat, and gloves. We found them and put them on her. We both headed out toward the door. We couldn't get it open. We shoved and pushed, and I ran against it. The banked snow outside now made it impossible to budge the door. I looked for another exit, there was none. I was spending the night. We took the blankets and remade her bed.

We got the wood stove and warm drinks started. I had brought more coffee. This cheered us both as we sat on her floor and drank hot coffee. It was impossible to tell the time. There was no cell service out here and I hadn't worn a watch. The howling wind worsened. Sitting there in the quiet, I got a real sense of the life she lived here in this little room. My heart sank in despair for her. But if this was all she'd ever known ... I didn't know how to process her life against my own. We lived on different planets in life experiences. I remember a mission trip to India and the pastor telling us not to judge those living on corners with lean-tos for homes. He said the dynamics in that little space may be more precious, filled with more love and happiness than many affluent people know. The slums we passed through showed children in joyful glee running and playing, with their parents leaning comfortably out their door openings and chatting nonchalantly to friends across the narrow streets.

Happiness, I realized can be anywhere. It's more of a choice than happenstance, like choosing to love. She has a version of happiness here that I don't know a thing about.

Finally, we decided to turn in and I turned off the light. I looked for the flashlight and kept it close. Her wood supply was meager, and we were situated near enough that I could periodically feed the fire. Following Wichapi's example, I took wool blankets wrapping them around myself like a cocoon. I settled in next to her covering us both with the rest of the blankets. Neither Wichapi nor I were large women. I laid close to her to share body heat. Curling into a fetal position with my back towards Wichapi, I slipped my gloved hands inside my coat pockets after covering my head with blankets. It was going to get worse before it got better. Eventually, I could feel my toes and fingers starting to sting. I knew it to be one of the first signs of hyperthermia... As the night progressed, the fire died along with the wood supply.

How did she manage? My thin Florida blood wasn't helping. As the heat was consumed with the unremitting cold, fear crept in. I knew that the coldest hours were still to come. There would be a long night of this. My persistent thought was to fall asleep, to hurry in the morning. The cold ground was sucking my body heat, and penetrated my spine, running the length of it. I started to shake. As the shaking became more intense, I wondered if Wichapi knew what was happening. My fingers and toes were becoming numb. I had thought about having ID on us if we were found and remembered the van. My thoughts went to my family and friends, and how they would hear the news. Frozen to death. I started to tear up.

Father, is this my time? While lying there talking to God I fell asleep. I knew He knew where I was and that *nothing* happened outside His will.

Memories after that were vague and dark. I dreamt I was holding onto an iceberg, floating through a ravine surrounded by tall glaciers, while careening down a turbulent icy river.

Warmth. From a long way off I heard faint voices. "Clint, can you help me take her boots off…." Painful stabbing in my feet and toes as I tried to gain some level of consciousness. More warmth. The voices were louder, and I could feel activity around me. Light was filtering through my eyelids. They were heavy and I pushed to lift them. A woman was standing over me. Quietly she tells someone that I am awake. The other person leaves. Rousing my senses, this looks like a hospital room. What happened? I looked at the woman standing over me. She's in a nurse's uniform. Groggy, I think about my ex's medical uniforms at my home in Florida. I don't live in Florida. Do I?

She asks "Mrs. St. Michael, how are you feeling? The doctor will be in shortly. Just relax. I'm going to take your vitals." She puts a blood pressure cup on my arm and a thermometer under my tongue.

The doctor is in the room and John; Patty and Rosa have followed him. He checks my chart and tells me that the frostbite is minimal. Just a spot on two toes. I wiggle my toes. Ouch. He sees my grimace. "Your body is still recuperating. But you're doing great, and we can release you tomorrow. You need to stay hydrated and move slowly for a few days. You will find your feet sore to stand on but that will pass. Rest is always the best medicine. We will send you home with instructions and you will need to follow up with your doctor in a week or two."

Do I have a doctor, not completely coherent.

"What happened?" I asked him.

"Your body suffered from hypothermia, and we had to soak your hands and feet. We have you on an IV to push fluids and nourishment. Most of the treatment was to get your blood moving and your body temperature back to normal." He smiled, "Do you have any other questions?"

"How long have I been here?"

"Two days."

"What happened?"

"I will let your friends tell you the details. If you don't have any more questions, I'll leave you all alone for now." I couldn't think of any for him. The questions I needed answered would come from them. The doctor smiled as he and the nurse walked out together leaving us alone.

"Can you help me sit up?" John moved to lift me, fluffing up pillows and looking into my eyes, he kissed my forehead. "Hello sweetheart." They all found chairs and sat on either side of me. The story would come from Rosa.

"What *happened?* How did I get here? What happened to Wichapi?" I asked weakly.

Rosa started, "Tess, I was worried when you left. Really thought this was a bad idea. Then the storm escalated so quickly and became violent. I decided to call Jimmy. I knew he knew where Wichapi lived. Jimmy called Clint who called me for details. Clint and Jimmy drove out to Wichapi's place, and they rescued you. They found you unconscious."

"What happened to Wichapi?"

"Jimmy was able to start your van and he took Wichapi. Clint took you in his truck," Rosa added, "And today is the first time you've been awake. Thank the Lord."

"Where is she?"

"She's fine. The hospital kept her over-night and released her the next day and Jimmy took her home."

I marveled at her fortitude and strength. And I marveled at the selflessness and courage of the Pierre family.

Rosa continued, "Clint took you straight to the hospital in Lander. He assisted the staff the night you arrived getting your boots off, the hospital was short on staff that night due to the storm. It was a bad night. People are still digging out. Several deaths were reported." She looked at me, "Honey, you're lucky to be alive. If they hadn't rescued you both…"

I heard vocal agreement from everyone.

I looked at Patty. She had a hard stare.

"Yes, we're grateful to both. That was a treacherous trek and thank God for them." John added as he leaned in closer to look at me. "I met Clint here in the hospital. Jimmy's older brother? Those two are heroes. I'd like to have them over for dinner one night when you are up to it to thank them. Okay?"

I nodded. I didn't look at Patty.

"What happened at Wichapi's?" John asked. "I wish you had waited for me to help you. I know you care for her; I love that about you…" I could see he wanted to say more but stopped himself. The lecture would come later.

I was released the next day. John had slept on a cot provided by the hospital. He assisted in getting me ready and drove me home.

Patty and Stark dropped by the next day. John and Stark grabbed beers and went outside to chat on the deck.

Patty helped me to a chair, "I think John and Clint now know about one another," she said, as she found a chair, "if they didn't before. They bumped into one another in the hallway. I could see them both working out who each other was. John wondering why and how Clint was involved and Clint not wondering. Pretty sure he got the gist of your relationship at that encounter. John has been sleeping at the hospital. With you every minute. When John came, Clint left. It was pretty obvious to everyone that they both care for you."

"Where's Clint now?"

"When the doctor gave us encouraging news about your recovery he left. And we haven't seen him since. I don't know where he is now."

Neither of us spoke for a moment, looking at each other …

"He and Jimmy … he's right. They're heroes. That storm was something, I haven't seen anything like that before around here. Snow drifts in some places eight to twelve feet high. I know you care for Wichapi but Tess… You had John worried, you had us all worried."

"Was John stuck in Jackson?"

"Yeah, which I think made it worse for him, he was out of his mind with worry. Stark said he was pacing and calling in favors to find a way to get to you. He was right behind the snowplows getting here. His family seems to have some clout. Someone made clearing the road here a priority. Honey, I said this before, both amazing guys."

I stared at the floor for some time. Patty watched me.

I took a deep breath, "Let's change the subject." I said smiling, "Soooo, when are you and Stark getting married?"

"Whoa girl! Where did *that* come from?"

"Question has to do with my toes; I was worrying about dancing." I was having a hard time keeping a straight face. "You know I don't have any rhythm, I've made this commitment to dance at your wedding, so ... I need to know." I said, a smile breaking through, "John says I've had you two married almost from the first date. Of course, that isn't true. Well... I'm not confessing to anything."

Patty couldn't stop laughing.

"Um, my lack of rhythm isn't that funny."

Wiping the tears from her eyes, Patty squeaked, "I know but that came out of nowhere! I don't know anything about your dancing abilities but for the rest of that…it's a little soon." She said, eyes shining, laughing... I could see that she was happy with Stark.

"Seriously, how are things between you two? You look miserable, so thought I should ask as a friend." That started us both laughing again. John and Stark walked in …

What's all this cackling about? Did you two break into the wine?" John was smiling.

"We were discussing my grace and dancing abilities. But thanks for offering, yes, I'll take a glass. You Patty?"

He raised his eyebrows and looked at me then back at Stark, "If I'd known how demanding she was after recovery… she makes the most of it." He gave a wry smile to Patty, shook his head at Stark and went to open a bottle.

They stayed the afternoon and John helped me out onto the deck for an afternoon of laughter and good friends.

Chapter Twenty~One

Ancestral Bloodlines

Recovery was slow. The primary issue was ambulatory, shoes didn't fit. The swelling took time to resolve. John took time off to stay with me and was a patient and kind nurse. As I improved, we walked the property and visited with the families of the children. John is chicken soup for my soul. He never asked about Clint.

Safe Harbor was becoming part of the community, and I found I had my ministry. We were getting visitors interested in Safe Harbor but also commenting on the beauty of the place. Some were asking about retreat opportunities. We would need more space. There was an out-building next to the house I had left completely alone. I had a vision of a bottom floor for classrooms and a second floor as possible housing. I asked Jimmy what he thought, and he asked Clint about it. Clint, Jimmy says, has a lot of work, but he had names of reliable carpenters. Work started on the project.

Not a word on the intruder or the children. There were no further incidents on the property and no more children missing.

The investigations remained open. Neither the killer nor any of the children have been located.

"Good morning beautiful," John said as he joined me on the deck for morning coffee. Life with him was easy. He has enough drama with his work; he doesn't create any in his private life. Unless you count me.

"Tess, I need to head back to Jackson for a few days. I have some trials coming up shortly and I need to get back and prep. Now, we've discussed your need for supervision and the importance of making wise choices," trying for a stern expression, "so let's agree that, after your recent escapade, that you've gotten adventure out of your system, that is unless it's supervised. Is that understood?" giving one of his most disarming smiles.

"Well first off, I'm twenty-seven, not five and the only reason I'm agreeing with this is not because I need supervision, but to avoid a legal analysis and dissection of recent events, so, I'll simply agree, but only in concept." We sat looking at one another. I can feel the sweetness between us. "How long do you think you'll be gone?" I hate being separated from him.

"Not too sure. There have been some developments recently that impact one of my cases that could take some time to sort out the facts and I need to get ready for both trials." He paused, "Back-to-back trials, something I hate. It's harder to focus on each so I'll need time to concentrate. Would rather concentrate on you!" he says reaching for my hand, a warm smile clouding his face. He is beautiful inside and out. "What do you have planned for the day?"

Looking in his eyes, returning his warmth with a squeeze and a warm smile, "Not much. There's a Child Protective Services inspection today and a parent meeting this afternoon, going over their children's goals. Should be a productive day. Jimmy's planning on bringing horses. He would like to teach those interested in how to ride. Ms. Hunter thinks this could work into therapy but there are rules … so I need to get approval. Love the idea though." John nodded in agreement. "So, today he plans to introduce the kids to the horses. Maybe have them groom the horses to familiarize them with each other. He says it's a good place to start for both kids and animals. Therapeutic."

Looking at his watch, John says, "That sounds like a good idea, I like it. Well, I've got to get moving." He got up and moved towards me, lifting me from my chair and planting a warm kiss on my lips. "I love you beautiful," he says looking into my eyes.

"I love you too," returning his kiss and hugging him tight, feeling the strength and warmth of him. "Be careful on the road." I leaned back to look into his face, "I know you'll work out the snags in these cases, even if they are back-to-back. Let me know how things are going, call me and John … come back soon."

"Will do." He gave me a long hungry kiss, a tight hug, and left.

When he leaves, there's an emptiness, like warmth and joy go with him. Feels empty, like I'm passing time till he returns.

After John left, I started my day. Ms. Hunter arrived for the inspection. I appreciate her. She obviously cares about the families and works tirelessly to give them help and assistance. Never says no. The parents of four families meet. With each child we have an itinerary specifically suited to each child's needs and family dynamics. There're academics, athletics, and special help such as therapy and tutoring to discuss. Jimmy brought several horses which turned out to be a success.

The days pass and John finds more complications than anticipated. One of his clients was not entirely truthful and he will need to reschedule that trial. Hopefully, that means he will be home soon.

Plans for this week to meet Patty for dinner. Stark is in Jackson with John helping with trials. Something we share as friends.

More than ever, with the demands of Safe Harbor and volunteering on the rez, I needed my quiet walks. More familiar with my property and comfortable with my surroundings, I was no longer worried about getting lost. The dogs usually accompanied me but this morning I took off alone. I wanted to walk, to be alone with my Lord. There were things I needed to clear my head about, so I headed up a trail, one I knew by heart. It was my favorite, and it took me to a beautiful and isolated mountain meadow. The weather was warming and there was a hint in the air that spring was on the way. I reached the meadow and sat there meditating on the Lord. I felt at peace.

I decided to check out the cabin, to see if there were any new changes. As I started up the trail. I hadn't gone far when, again, I had a visceral sense something was different about the woods today. It wasn't anything specific I could put my finger on. It was as though the woods had suddenly become moody, dark, brooding. The sun was out but the yellow seemed muted, as though shining through a shadow or veil, unable to register its influence. As I stood looking around, Kai came running at me. Someone must have let him out accidentally and he was following me. Darn! He's hard to catch. It was upsetting because this was going to take some time. Already I saw the rest of my quiet time gone. I called him. He had become better about coming but that wasn't a certainty. It had been a very specific rule at the house about Kai. Everyone knew always, always keep an eye on this dog. There were not many rules, but for the safety of Kai, I expected everyone to comply.

"Kai!" I yelled. "Come Kai!" I repeated this constantly, he ignored this constantly. "Kai come!" He'd run around me and then romp off into the underbrush to re-emerge. It was a game. I tried walking back towards the road to get him to follow me home. He came bounding out onto the trail but then ran back up the trail. As I turned to watch him pull this last maneuver, I lost sight of him as he leaped into a thicket. I heard an ear-splitting yelp! I ran. Stepping off the trail to find him, I couldn't see him. Hacking through the shrubbery I saw that the ground had given away and he'd slipped and had fallen into a ravine that used to be an old stream bed, now littered with fallen logs strewn all along the bottom. One of the trees had a protruding branch and to my horror Kai was impaled on this branch, wriggling to free himself!

Kai is white but now he is covered in red and pink. Blood was oozing through the wound, and his wriggling was only making the wound bigger, I was afraid of doing more damage. "Kai!" I screamed. I rushed to him to try and get him to be still, to stop moving. I grabbed his face and tried to stroke him, trying to quiet him. Surveying his body, I couldn't see a way to extricate him. He started struggling violently. His violent movements snapped the branch and tore him out of my hands, knocking me back onto the bank as he ran off. Screaming hysterically for him, my hands grabbed at the dirt and roots of the bank to pull myself up. Frantically I searched for any sign of him, sobbing and calling his name. "Kai!" I kept screaming, stumbling through my tears and shrubs, running, trying to find him. Seeing the trail, I ran frantically towards the house. I knew I needed help!

As I ran screaming and sobbing, my eyes blind with tears, someone grabbed me! Immediately I thought someone had heard me and had come to help. I started babbling about my dog. When I looked up, it was the man at the community center, Sam. I felt confused. My mind could not register why he was here on my property in the middle of the woods. Instantly I understood he was not here to help! His look made that very clear. He had his own agenda, and help was not on it. My horror for my dog was now coupled with fear racing through my mind. My hysteria was now at a roar! My screaming became maniacal. I didn't have time for this. Concern for Kai, that he needed me and that he would die if I could not help him turned me into a mad woman. He struck me and knocked me to the ground. He hit me again. Hatred filled his face. My hands balled into fists, and I started beating on him, managing to scratch his face. He grabbed both my hands and held them over my head maneuvering to use one hand to hold them, freeing his other hand. The free hand started ripping my shirt and I could see that the image of my exposed body fueled his fury. I knew I had just moments to save my life. The only things I had free were my legs and with all my strength I brought one knee up into his groin. He had raised himself up for better access to my clothing and to free up his own. The knee connected and knocked him off me and, in that instant, my hand found a rock. Sam had let go of both my arms and with both hands now around the rock, with hysteria for my dog and now hatred for this man, I brought it down on his head. I heard a crack as it connected with his skull. I saw blood. He fell to the side, and this cleared a path for me to run.

Completely blind with emotion and fear, I grabbed at bushes to pull myself up and back to the trail. The road was just up ahead; I gathered all my strength to make a last dash to the road and help. A pickup truck blocked the road, and it looked familiar, but I thought it belonged to the man. Instantly I was caught up in arms again and I started screaming and flailing my arms wildly, scratching and hitting, screaming Kai's name.

"Tess!" I looked up into Clint's face. It isn't possible. Hysterical, I grabbed him and wrapped my arms around his neck clinging to him. He held me tight to him, calming me.

Sobbing wildly, I told him about Kai "We *have* to *find* him!" My hysteria abating a little, my head filled with images of Kai lying somewhere bleeding and dying. Grief tore at me. Pleading in my eyes for Clint to help me. He looked at my torn shirt trying to assess fully the situation. I saw him look up at the trail and squint. I didn't have time for that. I knew Kai did not have long if I didn't get to him and decided not to tell Clint what had happened. My only focus was on Kai. His hands reached to hold both my shoulders and his head lowered, his eyes intent on connecting with mine for comprehension, "Tess," He spoke deliberately and slowly, "Please calm down. We'll find him."

He picked me up and carried me to the cab of his truck and placed me on the passenger seat. He hurried into the driver's seat and proceeded toward my house, scanning the woods. He whistled for Kai. As we approached the house, we saw Kai bound out onto the road. I screamed! Bolting out of the truck, I ran towards him, stooping to grab him. Clint got to him a second behind me and gently restrained me. "Please Tess, you are not going to help him unless you calm down. Let me take him and get back into the truck. We'll take him to a vet." Trusting him, I returned to the truck, and he put Kai between us with his head on my lap and closed the door, limiting Kai's options to move. He climbed in on the other side and turned the truck around. I focused on stroking Kai's face and avoiding the gaping wound on his side. Clint took us to the animal hospital in Lander. Cradling Kai in his arms he took him inside. We were seen immediately.

The vet and employees looked at us alarmed. Kai had a gaping wound through his body; my shirt was covered in blood and half off. I was scratched and filthy from head to foot. As they looked at us, I was aware of how this must look. They were trying to make sense of my explanation that Kai had fallen, but I could tell that the explanation did not explain my appearance, especially not to Clint.

I offered no further explanation. I was afraid that Clint would go after Sam. I needed Clint with me now and pursuing Sam would separate us. I kept the matter hidden. Clint found an old work shirt in his truck and put it on, giving me his shirt. He waited against the wall while I stood near Kai's head and talked to the vet. Watching the vet as he assessed the wound on Kai didn't offer hope. He would need to run diagnostics to see how much internal damage there was. I asked if they could give him something for the pain. They had started an IV of fluids for shock and were already adding pain medication. There was nothing for us to do here. We would have to wait to hear from them. They took my home number and promised to call when they had any news.

As we walked out of the clinic, I was suddenly very aware of Clint's presence beside me. He walked me to the passenger side of his truck and closed the door. We drove back to my house in silence. I stole a glance at him as he was driving, he was staring ahead; one hand was resting on the steering wheel and the other on his door.

He startled me when he spoke. "Tess, what happened in the woods?"

Looking back over at him I was trying to gauge his thoughts. How will he handle this? It took me a moment before I responded, trying to think about what I should tell him. I was drained and needed to go home and get some sleep.

He looked over at me.

Exhausted, I sighed. "I was attacked."

He didn't say another word. Resting my head on the backrest, I closed my eyes. "Clint?" I rolled my head to look at him. He turned his head and looked at me. When I looked in his black eyes, there was a different kind of intensity. It left me unsettled. "Thank you."

When we arrived home, he opened my door, and I slid out. "Please, I need you right now. Don't do anything tonight. Stay here with me for a while? I'm afraid to be alone." I saw his eyes soften. He started to lean in to kiss my forehead, but instead he put his arms around me and helped me inside. We went in through the front to avoid the children. Rosa heard us come in and came through the kitchen. She gasped when she saw me. I motioned for her to be quiet, whispered that I would talk to her later. Her eyes raced from my appearance to Clint. She calmed.

Clint followed me into the library. There was a fire already lit. "Please stay here while I get a shower and get cleaned up." I desperately needed a shower but not wanting him to disappear, I called Rosa. Rosa came in and I asked her to fix something for us to eat. Clint didn't resist.

Upstairs in my room I grabbed clean clothes and headed for a hot shower. It was what I needed; the warm water eased my soreness. I started to inspect my wounds. The back of my head and back were sore as was my jaw and the side of my face. With the dirt and sweat removed it revealed swelling and bruising everywhere. After showering, I stood in my bedroom for a while. Clint downstairs, John away … honor.

Rosa had prepared a light meal, and they were sitting chatting quietly. He wasn't smiling. I walked toward his steady gaze, wondering where his thoughts were. He saw my face and his jaw tightened. There was smolder behind his eyes. As I drew close, Clint stood up and moved his hands to my face. "Tess." He pulled me to him and held me. Rosa excused herself.

There was a shift in his demeanor, his eyes softened. He was gentle, watching me intently. My heart reacted. I felt safe and warm with him here. We sat next to each other by the fireplace. "Tess, where else are you hurt?" He asked quietly.

"Just bruising and pain but no broken bones." His hands touched the back of my head.

"Clint" I asked quietly feeling peaceful, "How did you happen to be on the road today?"

Moments passed before he spoke. The soreness was nothing compared to the peace I felt. I wondered how I could distance myself from Kai and John so quickly when under his power. Betrayal? I can't think that could be possible because I know what all of them mean to me. I know that I love them deeply. He isn't replacing them, he just is. Somewhere in all this is God. There's room in my heart for all but two of them cannot co-exist, and I knew that. I desperately needed what Clint was giving me right now. Sam was still out there. The shelter of his strength and protection calmed me, I felt safe.

"Remember I told you when I was working at your house that I made it a point to know where you were?"

I nodded.

"I still do that," he said softly, "It's the only way I have of caring for you." I could see his pain. Leaning towards me, he pulled me into him. I rested my hands on his chest over his heart. Resting on his chest I could feel the elevation of my pulse in my fingertips matching the pulse I felt pumping in his heart. He put a gentle kiss on my forehead. "I know I ended things, but they haven't ended for me," he said quietly. "When I can see you, ... " struggling to explain himself. "I admit I can't stay away." He turned my face towards his, "I know about John ... believe me when I tell you I don't want to interfere with your relationship or your happiness. And I won't." I searched his eyes. He was firm and cleareyed. "Today I had work at the farm just up the road from your place and just happened to drive by. My window was down when I heard screaming. I slowed and the screaming got louder. So, I parked and stood listening trying to figure out what was going on. Shortly after that you ran right into my arms." His head tilted down, and his eyes fixed on mine, "What happened out there today?"

Having him here, I felt safe enough to tell him. "I'm not totally sure. Kai got out. I went to find him, he fell and as I was running to find him, that's when I was grabbed by this man."

"Do you know him?"

"I don't know him, but I know of him. Remember I mentioned him at the cabin, Sam Raven. I suspect he is the one that killed the officer and had been lurking near my property." I raised my head and looked at him. His eyes were fixed on me. I realized that I had not spoken with Clint about all the details surrounding Sam's involvement here. I gave him details of the man as best I could. "I saw him at the Community Center and again at the church picnic, both times I thought he was staring at me. I pointed him out to Rosa, she knew him, later she told me who he was and his name. I didn't see him again until today, but someone has been around watching, and I guess today makes it clear its Sam," I said. "When I ran into him today, Clint, there was such hatred in his face towards me. I don't know why he would hate me. Then he attacked me." I was still looking at him, gauging his reaction and how he was processing what I was telling him. His eyes were black.

"Do *you* know him?" I asked.

He didn't answer.

Since it didn't appear he was going to answer that question, I rested my head on his shoulder and asked, "Tell me about the winter rescue."

Gently I looked up at him, his eyes soft. "I think you know the details," he said, studying my face. "Rosa alerted us to the situation, and we drove to Wichapi's and found you both inside. We had to shovel snow to open the door." He looked at me, "When I found you, you were unconscious." The focus in his eyes shifted reliving the experience. He looked softly at my face, "I love you Tess," he whispered. Warmed by the fire, I fell asleep nuzzled next to him.

When I awoke, I found myself in my own bed. Clint was gone.

There was a soft knock at my bedroom door. "Tess…" Rosa opened. She was carrying a tray of food. "Thought you could use some breakfast. How are you feeling?"

I stretched, rediscovering painful areas and discovering new ones. "Fine, I guess. When did Clint leave?"

"I think sometime after midnight after he took you to your room." She sat down on the edge of the bed staring at me then looked at her lap. Looking up she started, "What do you know about Clint?"

I realized not much. "Jimmy gave me a basic rundown … school, college, Marines, wife died in childbirth and that he is a Tribal leader." I sat up watching her, not sure where this was going but I wanted to hear.

Looking at me, she started, "He comes from a significant lineage in our culture. He carries in his bloodline legends, war chiefs and medicine chiefs. Warriors and healers. His ancestors are strong in him. I know you and John are together," she said, searching my eyes. She looked out the window silent for a while.

I waited, curious …

She looked back at me. "I just thought you should know that I've never seen him behave this way around a woman. He shoulders much. He doesn't just carry his family; he is part of the backbone of the tribe. I see how he is with you." She stopped here for a moment. "I just thought you should know." She got up and left quietly.

I sat still, couldn't eat. I knew I loved Clint but couldn't say it out loud. Couldn't let myself …

The vet called shortly after and told me that Kai had passed during the night. I spent the day in my room crying … for all of us. A week later they delivered his ashes and collar. I keep his urn in my bedroom. The heart is an amazing organ – it can teeter on emotions of love while at the same time experiencing devastating loss.

John called every night. His work demanded he stay in Jackson Hole, but I could hear in his voice that this was taking a toll on him. I only told him about Kai, and other than Rosa and Clint, there was no one else to tell him the whole story. He had his own grief over Kai. He loved that dog. We all did.

Clint had disappeared.

Chapter Twenty-Two

My John

Weeks passed and my body healed. I told John I had injured myself trying to catch Kai. It was partly true.

If Clint was around, I didn't see him.

John came home and life went on… If I was going to have a life, a fleeting life with Clint I knew wouldn't work, yet the ache for him haunted me. That love would have to stay in another realm. Knowing he loved me I thought was enough. He separated us, not me and John, my John, was in it for life. He gave it all. It was a peculiar thing to love two men at the same time but odder still, to be fully each of theirs when in their presence. They were easy to love.

I told John about my stream. One day I took him to see where my other love often met me. It was quiet and spring was showing off, colors and scents and youth everywhere. John and I made it our spot and picnicked there often. On a particularly amazing day, we brought lunch and John a bottle of wine. We sat and ate, wadded in the stream, splashed each other, and laughed at ourselves. Happy? Without question. Back on the bank John broke open the wine and poured two glasses. We sat cross-legged facing each other.

"To us."

John sat for a few moments looking at his lap, the stream and then finally at me. I could see a peaceful countenance in John, "Thank you for bringing me here, where you meet the Lord. I can see and feel why this place is special. That you're sharing this with me, Tess. I know you cherish it here, sort of your secret. And you let me in." … seeing how this moved him, I realized our soul connection. We were meant to be together. I wasn't certain until now.

Looking at John, I see the orchestration in this ... He may be hidden but He is always involved. It's in these moments I get it, His plan.

"Tess," he said looking down, "I think you know how much I love you." He looked up into my eyes. "I've given this a great deal of thought for some time now," studying my face. "I can't imagine life where you aren't in it or life with anyone else. Even when I'm in Jackson, when you aren't there, life feels hollow." Warmth filled his face. "Tess, will you marry me? I promise I will always take care of you. No one has ever made me this happy. You touch places in me ..." His emotion was reaching his words, "You're with me every waking moment, shadowing my world. And sometimes it's a distraction that affects my concentration," he said smiling, "I don't want to lose you. Will you … marry me?" Then with a big grin he added, "I also think you need supervision and the only way I can manage that is to keep you close. Making you Mrs. Alesandra Lawrence."

"You know, I was really feeling it … give me a minute ……." I sat there studying him, his handsome face, that smile, but more than any of that, his heart, caring, kind and patient with me, and all of him, heart, body, and soul, belonged to me. I knew how blessed I was to have the love of this man. Mrs. John Allen Lawrence. I liked the sound of that. "Yes, I'll marry you, John. I love you too, you're *my* John," I said as I climbed into his lap, wrapping my arms around him. We fell backwards into the soft grass, spilling our wine and laughing, holding one another. Warm ardent kisses sealing the covenant we made. As I laid nestled in his chest, I looked up at John while he lay there, his eyes closed, smiling, I felt indescribable bliss.

We were both excited and set a date for September. Maddy and Patty took over the wedding plans. They were like a moving train, and I got out of their way. Every so often I was consulted about this detail or that. It was actually a relief letting someone else handle portions of my life. I never wanted a big wedding and was content to let them plan everything. *I* did, however, find my dress. It was beautiful. I chose a fitted gown sewn with miniature pearls, muted pink and white sequins. We decided to get married in the evening on the property. I liked their ideas, especially the idea of lights in the trees, magic in the air. Maddy was my maid of honor. John chose Stark as best man.

Life was perfect. I was looking forward to my wedding and my wedding night. We had stayed apart, and I had a sense that God would make this night magical. Nothing to taint or cloud our love. We weren't virgins, but it felt that way. Giddy kids. Laughter filled the house and it affected everyone. Joy punctuated life from sunup to sundown. John had cleared his calendar, and we were one day from our great adventure. The night before we had a rehearsal dinner, and everyone was there. Maddy, Rob, Anna and Chuck had arrived weeks earlier and the sanctuary had a festive celebratory feel in every corner. I hoped that these children from tough backgrounds would be able to see what love and joy looked like. We were so in love. The children decorated the horses and were included in the wedding plans.

After rehearsal dinner, and on our last night of freedom, John and I walked to our stream. "This is it," John said as we sat cross-legged by the stream. "You have less than twenty-four hours to run."

I sat there looking into his smiling, happy face, "I can't imagine being separated from you, ever. I never dreamed I'd have this. Have I told you today that I love you?"

John wrapped me in his arms, and pulled me to the ground, "Tess, I don't think you could love me more than I love you." We lay there filled with peaceful quiet joy.

"John?"

"Uh huh?"

"How many children do you want? I've been thinking about what they will look like. Little versions of John running around."

"Well, if they're like *you* maybe one," he said, tickling me. "At the least, a contained portion of Tess's adventuring spirit. Otherwise, I'm sure YOUR raising them will be a full-time job!" Laughing he looked in my eyes, "Hopefully they will look like you. My blonde beauty."

Listening to us talk about our children, I could immediately see images of them, us, and our life together. My images were filled with towheads running wild around the property, holiday rituals, and the day-to-day activities that came with a family; school, church, teenagers, weddings, old age and 50-60 years with this man … I saw it all in a moment. I was overwhelmed with joy.

I sat back up, "Let's start making them tomorrow," I winked.

John immediately pulled me back to the ground and rolled on top of me. "That's a promise," he said, as he piled passionate kisses on my hungry lips.

Looking into his beautiful face, "I can't wait," I whispered.

We kissed good night at my bedroom door.

"Hey guys," Patty was up, "It's bad luck for the groom to see the bride the night before the wedding."

John and I looked at one another and laughed. "I don't believe in luck." I said as I opened my door. "Night all."

I felt like a princess and floated to bed dreaming of John.

Chapter Twenty~Three

Hell & Heaven

I awoke sensing someone in my room, "John?"

But I wasn't in my room. I became aware of the sound of myself coughing, choking, and moaning; water dripping and a strong pungent aroma, the air thick, close, and sticky. I couldn't tell if my eyes were open or closed because I was staring into impenetrable blackness, weighty, dark, and musty … I don't know how, but I knew I was inside a mountain. I could feel the granite, the hard, dense, cold immovable rock beneath me. Other than the sound of dripping, the air was quiet, an eternal quiet, as though nothing had disturbed it for a very long time. Where was I?

I tried to sit up and found that any movement produced an immediate intense stabbing pain… there was excruciating pain *everywhere*, even the bottoms of my feet felt as though I had walked on glass. I realized to my horror that my arms were confined above my head, I heard chains rattling and from the cold damp on my skin I realized I was … naked! My legs were free. I was seized with terror! What had happened? The only thing I remember was sensing a presence in my bedroom. I tried calling out, but my jaw felt dislocated, and then more intense, stabbing pain! Tears, fear, and blackness …

I awoke with a sense that someone was nearby. A sharp searing light accosted my eyes. Squinting, I could make out a lantern to my left at ground level and someone stooping by the light. I couldn't speak. My senses were alert, and my mind was busy trying to work out what was going on. I watched my captor intensely. He stood and I found Sam staring back at me. He approached and stood over me. The lamp light flickered on his face, pulsating between light and darkness, intensifying his already hideous face, distorting it making it appear demonic. Sam was a sarcophagus and all I could see was a dark abyss in his black eyes. His rapacious appetite did not see me as human. There was nothing to appeal to.

He stooped beside me. Managing to scream, I tried to free myself. I felt a violent slap across my face as he forced himself on me. His hard, violent attack was tearing at me. Again, I screamed out into the darkness at the horror that was happening. "Someone help me!" I could feel his bites on my body and with every violent act, a fueled hatred. Guttural growls and animal noises emanated from his throat. I thought he would howl. I could smell the sweat produced from his heated animal intensity. He was a solid stone of fury. It felt as though all the evil Sam had experienced throughout his life was being poured out on me.

There are memories of bread and water being forced down my throat and violent choking. He never spoke to me; I was an object. But the failure of real nutrition and blood loss took my strength, and any consciousness now was a weak numbness, a vague and uncaring haze, a blessing. Even the horror railed often against my body I no longer felt… I had no hope … No possibility of rescue. No one knew where I was.

Once I awoke to find the cavern empty but for a lantern that had been left lit and I thought that meant that he was nearby. The flicker of the lamp illuminated the cavern, and this allowed me to look around the cavern for the first time. Oh, dear God … what I saw added to the horror I was experiencing. In front of me was horrific carnage, remnants of humans, skulls, ribs, and bones held in place by their bloody excrement; strewn about on the floor of the cavern. There were cages that contained ravaged lifeless bodies, still hanging by chains from their caged roofs and against the opposite wall more bodies pinned against the wall of the cavern, held upright by their chains. I tried to fathom the level of ruthless hatred necessary to commit this evil violence. It went beyond depraved; it went beyond any horror or description; I was in hell. There wasn't much left of their bodies, wasted, blood clotted carcasses, empty eye sockets and open jaws as though frozen in screams. The missing children? *Realizing their fate was mine*, I screamed hysterically until I fell into unconsciousness.

On and off I would awaken with no concept of time. I was living in horror and the torturous delight Sam found in destroying me. I remember thinking that I wished I had been frailer, weaker in constitution, because my hope was death. How long could my body endure this? Even if I lived, what would be left of me? Consciousness was now rare... No one knows where I am ... John ... the last undamaged part of me, my heart, broke and tears came in waves of sobbing despair.

In my delirium, my mind took my subconscious to safe memories where I found myself sitting on the deck of an oceanside café with the Gulf of Mexico framing the backdrop, enjoying a grouper lunch, a glass of wine and friends. Conversation loaded with girly chatter and humor while the warmth of the sun penetrated our souls with an invading sense of joyful freedom, and the sizzling glitter of the undulating waves flickering across sunglasses. Seagulls fished and floated and nearby docked boats creaked and rocked lazily adding a festive, vacation element to the moment.

But the waking horror always came back ... Finally, "Father God, heavenly Father and sweet Lord," I whispered. "Kai, I'm coming…"

Brilliant light surrounded me. I felt I had passed and a peace indescribable filled my soul which was now a light. I was standing in a meadow, and I saw mountains in the distance, capped with snow, while forests and meadows covered in wildflowers filled the landscape. Nearby was a crystal-clear stream and I bent, touching its sparkling flow. As my fingers touched the water, I found it was alive, and its invigorating sensation sent joy running through me. I stood breathing in the freshness surrounded by unspeakable peaceful beauty. There was a scent in the air, like lavender and honeysuckle, peaches and vanilla. I knew no earthly words, nothing in my vocabulary that could express in any meaningful terms a description of what I was seeing or feeling. Colors were deeper, richer, there were colors I had never seen before, and I could hear music and singing. I knew other souls were near. There were songs I heard in churches where I was elevated to holiness but those didn't touch this. This music and these voices were heavenly, higher than majestic, worship and love songs sung out to their Father. I was infused into love. Love was pulsating out of every living thing. Joy was everywhere. I was *in* GLORY.

I felt that the Lord was near. The light that I saw and felt was His light. Feeling surrounded by Him, I understood gentle words, unspoken but felt, relaying this message, "It is not your time, my child." I was called by a different name. "You must go back," I was told lovingly. "There are plans for you. Remember, you are never alone." I did not want to return but I saw the sanctuary that was to come and the good that will come to many from its sheltering walls.

Immediately I was back in my body in the mountain. But I felt more alive than I had ever felt before. My mind and soul nourished. I could see in the cavern. I heard a terrific clammer and could see that there was an intense, violent struggle going on between two men. It went on for some time. Finally, one overpowered the other as the defeated man fled the cavern. The victor stood and turned. Clint, standing there in an obvious struggle whether to pursue or rescue. He came to me and freed my arms. I remember being lifted into his arms … blackness enveloped me.

I woke up in a hospital bed. The memory of my horror was distant, vague, as though it had happened to someone else. I felt at peace and calm. I no longer felt any fear or horror. It had been erased. I felt an overwhelming sense of God's grace. I remembered what happened, but it had no attachment to my mind or my emotions.

"Tess's awake." Maddy whispered. I felt the presence of people and opened my eyes. Maddy and Anna stood by my bedside; relief erased the worry etched on their faces.

A doctor and nurse appeared.

They checked my vitals. "Welcome back Mrs. St. Michaels," said the doctor with a friendly smile. He looked into my eyes checking my alertness. Quietly he said, "You've been in a medically induced coma." He asked the others to leave while he examined me. "Just nod, don't try to talk. Your jaw is wired shut. You suffered fractures to your jaw and both wrists and your pelvis."

My hands went to my face, and I could see the casts. I winced in pain.

"This button here beside your bed is your pain meds. You can press it every 7 minutes. You can't overdose so don't hesitate to use the button. Okay?"

I nodded.

"Okay then, I will be back tomorrow to see you. Down the road, I am having a psychiatrist stop in to chat with you. You have been through quite an ordeal. The visit is just to determine if counseling is needed. Alright?" With that he left, and the nurse busied herself checking my monitor and fluid intake and updating my chart.

My friends stepped back into the room after they left. Maddy started, "Hi honey" she whispered as she approached my bed. "We know you can't talk but we want you to know we love you and we are here for you."

I slept...

I awoke one morning with no pain and bright sunlight in my room. I opened my eyes and saw Maddy asleep on a cot.

The nurse came in and excitedly said, "Well, welcome back Mrs. St. Michael."

A startled Maddy jumped up. She ran to my bedside as the nurse checked my vitals, tears running down her beautiful face brimming with a wide grin. I smiled back. "Can I have something to eat?" I croaked in a hoarse whisper.

"That's a good sign. I'll bring you a menu," the nurse said as she left the room.

Maddy hurriedly pulled up a chair, "How do you feel?" she said, concern on her face. "No, don't talk, I'm sorry I asked you a question."

I wanted to talk, "I want to talk." I winced at my dry throat. "Can I have some water?" My jaw was stiff, and I had limited range of motion. Maddy helped me sip water as the nurse and doctor came in.

He asked how I was feeling.

I croaked, "Okay, I think."

"What's your pain level?"

"No, pain," I squeaked.

The doctor and nurse busied themselves checking my vitals and assisted me in sitting up. I gave them my food choices. As the doctor turned to leave, he said, "Mrs. St. Micheal," he paused. "Honestly, when you first arrived, given the extent of your injuries … your recovery has been nothing short of a miracle." With that he turned towards the doorway, looking back at me, he winked.

He didn't know how right he was.

I looked at Maddy, "How long have I been here?"

"Months."

"How long have you been here?"

"Months."

I loved them.

My alert level was improving, I had questions. "What happened after I was found? How was I found?"

Maddy filled me in on the details of my rescue. "Clint had been hunting for you and Sam. He tracked Sam to the cave. He was alone when he found you both, there was a struggle and I understand that Sam escaped but barely. Based on what was later reported, when found Sam had gotten the worst of it. Clint didn't pursue Sam, instead he rescued you and brought you out of the cave. A huge manhunt was started, Tess. The FBI and all local and state law enforcement came together. They covered a large area on foot with dogs and helicopters. It was something. After he fled the cave, Sam was finally found in a remote cabin with the help of a canine squad. Sam was killed, they think it was suicide by cop. But in the end, it was Clint who found you. He never gave up." I could see she thought a lot of him.

It didn't surprise me that Sam wasn't taken alive. I felt calmer at the news.

"All that activity to locate me? Doesn't make any sense. Especially since so much time had passed since the officer's death and the missing kids. Why now?" Then the thought occurred to me, "Where *is* Clint? Is he okay? His injuries, how bad? He saved my life for the second time." I started to tear up. I needed a moment. Maddy could see I was having trouble controlling my emotions. There's a hero in Clint; his bravery and qualities saved my life. Both men created a great deal of conflict in my heart. I wanted to see Clint again, thank him for saving me. John.

"Where's John?"

She said quietly, "Heard Clint required some stitches but he's one tough guy. When you were rescued, they insisted on treating him, but he released himself against orders. Wouldn't stay for tests."

That didn't surprise me. Superman Clint. How do you thank someone who hunted for you, fought for you, and rescued you twice? I could not hurt John by going to Clint, but someday I hoped to let him know what his involvement in my life has meant. If it weren't for Clint… I don't know anyone like him. In fact, I don't know anyone who knows anyone like him. I loved Clint but I was marrying John, and I loved John. John had his own qualities. He was a hero in different ways. His superman qualities had a more gentile quality. I was happy that Clint wasn't the one to kill Sam. I loved them both.

"Where is John?"

I could see hesitation on her face, and she deliberated for an answer. "He's around. Tess today is your first day talking and I think there's time ahead for questions and answers. The most important thing is your recovery. I know you and you want to talk but now isn't the time. They are moving you tomorrow to a rehab facility which shouldn't be for too long and then home. Are you okay with going home?"

I couldn't understand her lack of response about John. It seemed off. I knew she was concerned about too much stimulation and wondering if my going home held bad memories. I couldn't answer that question myself. Kai, my abduction ... the shadows and the horror. Despite my out of body experience, which I couldn't share just yet, I knew there would be residual areas that I would have to deal with besides my physical recovery. Neither of us talked for a while. I didn't want to go to sleep but sleep was pulling me in.

I woke to find myself in a new room at the rehabilitation facility. Maddy and Anna sitting, quietly talking. When they saw I was awake, Anna left the room. She came back with the doctor. I was introduced to Dr. Waldron, a psychiatrist. Everyone grabbed chairs and Dr. Waldron grabbed a chair to sit by my bedside. A nurse came in and checked my vitals, and I was asked how I was feeling. Looking around the room, I had a sense of dread. Something was up.

My doctor started with, "Tess, I've asked Dr. Waldron to come here because we have some news to convey, and we are concerned that this could set you back into a relapse."

It was Maddy's turn. I could see she was emotional. She looked around at the others, I thought for support, she sighed and then started. "We haven't shared all the events around your abduction. It's bad, Tess." Everyone was staring at me, and my mind went wild wondering how anything could be worse than the horror in the cavern.

Taking a deep breath she began, "The night you were abducted Sam had entered your home through a front window." Here she stopped and her voice trembled, "Before abducting you he located the rooms where John and Rosa slept." Now tears were flowing down her face, "Tess," she sobbed, "he killed John and Rosa and the bodies in the cavern were the missing children, including James and Jenny. You mentioned why so much attention in the manhunt, this was why. It was clear Sam was a dangerous man and needed to be caught." She couldn't continue, by now her sobbing was uncontrollable. Anna came to support her. While Maddy sat crying I could see they were all paused waiting for my reaction.

I woke up a few days later. They had to sedate me.

Waking, the memory of Maddy's conversation sent me into hysterics, "Lord, I have no way of understanding this …. Why is grief upon grief piled on me? How can I survive this? John

murdered! Rosa murdered! I *don't* want to survive this. I don't …
I can't … I won't." My body started to shake, and overwhelming
grief shook my sobbing body. I tried getting up. I just wanted
to run, anywhere. Screaming, "Lord, I'm desperate for You,
help me!" Nurses came running into my room.

I woke up a few days later. They had to sedate me.

I woke up a few days later. They didn't sedate me.

Dr. Waldron entered my room and pulled up a chair. "Tess,"
he said, looking deeply into my eyes. "Can you talk, do you
want to talk?" There was gentle kindness in his face and voice.
I found it calming.

"Yes and no." I could feel his sincere concern. How do I talk
about this? "I don't understand what's happened to be able to
talk about it, what is there to say? I have nothing to compare
this to. I teeter between desperate grief, and numbness." It took
a few minutes for me to start again. "It feels like everything is
gone and I don't see any point in living. I don't think I want
to try for a life right now. I prefer sleeping. Being awake is one
continual nightmare. Being alive now feels like a sentence. The
only thing keeping me hanging on is my faith."

He sat for a few moments looking at me before he spoke.
Sighing he said, "I understand. You haven't had time to put
this into any kind of perspective. I'm not sure there is any way
to understand something like this. You weren't the cause; you
were the victim. Your recovery is more about you getting past

this and rebuilding. Because I don't know that there's anything to understand. The answerable equation lies in understanding Sam, and I don't think that is possible. Sam probably couldn't provide insight. I've heard something of his background, and I suspect Sam didn't know himself what drove him." He stopped, gauging how this was resonating with me. "Give it time. It's a slow process. Be kind to yourself and don't try for more than you are capable of. Everything *is* healing, your mind, body, and soul. It doesn't seem that way now because everything is so recent. Your severe trauma and now this horrific grief would take down an elephant. You're not expected to feel any differently, but time is a funny thing, and it will help. I will come and visit you every day, just to check in and chat if you're up to it."

I started sobbing uncontrollably. "I was getting married to the most wonderful person and hate and rage is all that's left of that. I keep hearing Mrs. St. Michael, but it was supposed to be Mrs. John Lawrence."

Dr. Waldron grabbed my hand. "Cry Tess. It's the best medicine."

Chapter Twenty~Four

Forged in Fire

I was regaining my strength and mobility. Daily I'd walk on crutches in the gardens at the center. My fractures were mended but muscles had atrophied, and rehab and walking helped regain my strength and mobility. Sitting under an Oak watching ducks diving, flapping, mating and grooming, their natural beauty and grace often made me smile. I decided I wanted to raise ducks. As I looked around at the grounds and took in the quiet grace before me, I saw Patty walking towards me. I struggled to my feet to greet her, and we gave each other a long and deep hug.

"How've you been?" she asked in a hushed tone, worried, as she found a chair.

"I think you said this before, it's a day at a time. How've you been? How's Stark?"

She looked down for a while, quiet. When she looked up, she was studying my face. "Tess, I'm sorry I haven't been around much. I saw you in the hospital when you first arrived, and it devastated me to see you in that condition. You look so much better, honey. In fact, you look great. How are you recovering? Do you know when you'll be released?"

"I'm better every day. Practicing patience and praying. They haven't said when I'll be released. I think it's soon. You haven't said how Stark is doing?"

"He's wonderful, Tess, but I don't know if you are ready to discuss some things, especially things that were close to John." At this she immediately fell apart, sobbing and grabbing her chair. I tried to get up to console her. Her whole body was shaking, and her sobbing became more intense. Nurses came to check on us. She took a deep breath and told them she was fine while she worked for composure, wiping her eyes. "Tess, I'm so sorry. You went through hell and I'm the one having a breakdown." She looked up at me, "I just can't get past how John and Rosa died…" Her sobbing started again, but she continued talking in gasps. "John bludgeoned to death and Rosa brutalized and beaten so severely that she was unrecognizable!" She looked at me, "I found them!" she wailed, sobbing in spurts as she tried to catch her breath. "I had gotten up early that morning and … Tess, there was blood everywhere. I can't stop seeing them! Our beautiful John almost …the hate and violence used on them! Who could do this?!" She stopped and looked up; she became perfectly still. "Oh my gosh Tess, I didn't mean to tell you this." Nurses came running.

I sat there staring, not at Patty, at nothing, my mind filling with images of them, my John.

I awoke in my room with no memory after I saw the nurses. Maddy was in the room and came to sit by me when she saw I was awake.

"Hi honey." She whispered. She sat there studying me with one of her endearing, sweet smiles.

"Hi," I looked in her face, "All I remember was the nurses running. What happened after that, what happened to Patty? Maddy, she found them!"

"I know."

"You knew this?"

"Yes, we all did. After everything you suffered, what would be the point in your knowing that?"

"I would want to know everything, now. What if I'd found this out later? Maddy, for me, getting all the ugly evil dealt with now is important for me to heal. It's the only way I can see to get this behind me, not have that horror revisit me. I need to know about what happened. I don't need pictures or photos; I have enough visions of carnage, and I don't want any more. But my John and sweet Rosa… I don't know how to understand that much hatred on people Sam didn't know." I sat quietly for a few minutes, thinking.

"Still, Patty shouldn't have shared this."

"No, she should have. She's carrying her own horror. She loved them and was close to both. It's bottled up and she needs to get it out. I totally understand that. I know she didn't mean to pour this out on me, and I don't think she came to do that, it was just that the subject touched on John…." I started to cry.

Maddy moved closer and held me.

The day came when they finally released me. Maddy and Anna had returned home but Maddy flew back when I was released to accompany me home and see to my mental and physical well-being.

We pulled up to the house. I just felt empty. All my hopes and plans seemed meaningless. Pointless. I remembered my death event and my Lord's comment about this place. That's the only thing that kept me glued here. Motivation and care are gone. No John. No Rosa. No Kai. I wanted to hate Sam but oddly I couldn't locate that emotion. Inexplicably, I didn't hate him. I knew he'd had a savage life, and I'll never know why he never found any redemption, why he was never able to put this behind him and find a better way to live. I'm sure chances happened. We all have free will, choices. Ecclesiastes says that God puts immortality in us, we *all* have an internal voice that knows God. God didn't just put eternity into man, He lovingly woes us throughout our lives. He's patient. He made a world that literally shouts His existence. You can't look anywhere in nature and not see an aspect of Him. He loved Sam. Sam made a choice. He allowed hatred to turn him into an animal, hatred consumed him. Does that mean that hate extinguished the essence of Sam? The persona of hate living in Sam killed them. I didn't want to give hate another victim.

Still, Rosa was a question mark when it came to Sam. Not only did he kill her, but she was the recipient of more violence on her than John. Was it women or something more with Rosa? Senseless. I could understand John in a way, the male threat, but Rosa, her room was on the top floor. How had he found her? Why did he look for her? It's like killing goodness. And John, I'm pretty sure Sam could have taken me without noise or discovery. I never heard him skulking around the property, just a sense something was off. But he found John and killed him too. I guessed he had been watching the house and the occupants. A witness to joy, fun, and happiness? Something he'd never known, ever? He wasn't just killing them; was he killing that? And those missing kids. Why? Thinking about them and their last days, I shivered, *knowing* their horror and their last moments, separated from family and protection, in a heartless, cold ancient cave; torture their only reality. So young to witness and experience such hellish evil. Thinking about this against my death experience, I realized that if the Lord had not taken my horror, I could not have survived. I sat in the car, all of this running through my mind as I stared at 'the house'. It was no longer my home. I had no home. I knew I needed time.

Maddy sat waiting. I turned, "I'm ready, let's get this over with." There were more questions. What was going on here while I was gone, and who was running the families? The answers came. Pastor Allen and Stephanie Hunter had stepped in and were in charge. Made sense if anything did.

"Maddy, I need a favor."

"Anything."

"Please make sure John and Rosa's room are closed up. That will take me some time."

"Already thought of that, honey."

I looked at her hard. "How are you so amazing? Can a non-Catholic be canonized? Saint Maddy." This made us both smile.

Inside we headed for the kitchen and coffee.

"Where's everyone?"

"Well, we asked everyone to stay out of sight for a few days, to respect your need for some privacy. Let you acclimate. They are out on a field trip today." She said, as she made coffee.

I looked around and could see that the large kitchen now made sense. Looked more like a cafeteria. Plenty of tables and chairs, and they had covered the walls with art made by the children. It had a lively, colorful feeling, happy.

As we sat and chatted, the conversation turned again to Patty.

Maddy said, "Patty took everything very hard. She had a breakdown of sorts and became something of a recluse for a time.

She stopped seeing Stark briefly but he's a charmer *and* what she needed. He'd lost his best friend as well. They needed each other and that support. Ya know, I think they're talking marriage!"

Suddenly I felt a tinge of joy. My eyes teared. Then I started to cry. That was supposed to happen to me ... my wedding. I started sobbing. "Sorry, that news reminded me of my own wedding." Maddy started to come over, I waved her off, "No, I'm fine and I'm happy for Patty. It's great news, finally something to celebrate."

"Me too. I agree. We all need to move forward, and I think that's the first positive not only for them but all of us. We all can dance at their wedding." I gave her a look, "You know, Anna and I didn't know John or Rosa. This was a triple whammy for her, you, John, and Rosa. She's a real sweetheart. Her love and emotions are transparent and deep. We both really like her."

"Me too."

For the first time Jimmy and Dinah were mentioned. "They stopped in at the hospital several times but same deal. They were very close to you and Rosa and the loss of James and Jenny, all that hit them hard as well. This has been more than a train wreck; this has been apocalyptic and being here, here and in town, there's a deep sadness. Everyone knows what's happened. Like it has sucked joy from the air itself."

I explained the losses that Maddy didn't know, "Maddy, Dinah lost her boyfriend, Tommy. He had been on a camping trip with friends when the truck they were riding in hit a guard rail. Plus, they were band members and friends of Jimmy, all four boys were killed. This happened not long ago." I realized that I wasn't alone with my hell and grief. Life stopped for all of us.

"I was wondering, and if this is hard don't answer, but do you remember anything about your rescue and Clint?"

"A little, I saw him fighting with Sam. And I remember he picked me up. But nothing else."

She nodded, "He was at the hospital every day. He was the one that had Pastor Allen call us about what happened. It's so weird because during that winter rescue and again this time, when you start recovering, he backs away. What's up with that? I never really got to know John and we never discussed how that romance developed, but I've met Clint, and I was, I guess sort of surprised about John. Guess I thought when romance happened, it would have been Clint. I can see how much he loves you, everyone can. Did you two ever have anything because it's hard to understand his closeness and involvement otherwise."

"Yes, and I'll tell you everything, promise. Honestly, now that I think about it, I don't know why I didn't. Since moving here, life has been a whirlwind. So much has gone through my heart and mind. Give me some time to grieve John. I know Clint's involvement has been huge but, in some way, I think talking about Clint would minimize John. My heart won't let me go there. John would have taken a bullet for me and taken Sam on, irrespective of consequences, he's a hero. There was a time when Clint would have been my first choice Maddy and I will tell you all about it. Can we talk about this later?" At that moment it struck me, funerals. "Were there funerals for John and Rosa?"

"Honey, when you feel it's the right time. Yes, there were two funerals. We did record them for you to see when you feel up to it. By the way, Johns' family knew how much he loved you. He's buried in Jackson Hole in the family plot. Rosa's funeral was at the Community Church, she's buried there."

"What happened to Rosa's children?"

"She has family here and they have taken them in."

"How was Maggie and JJ? Was his ex-there?"

"Yes, and her husband. Very nice lady, by the way."

"How were his kids taking this?"

"Bad, bad as can be expected. It was hard to witness the family's grief. Everyone is suffering. It's so senseless. Reminds me of stone hitting water and the ripple effect. So many are touched by this," she said, shaking her head.

Saint Maddy stayed a month and finally returned home. Bless Rob for his patience and kindness in sharing her. Thank you, Lord, for the gift that she is to so many.

Day-to-day I followed my old routine, coffee, Bible, and journal. Sprite and I sat together on the porch grieving our losses. I could tell she misses Kai. This is one of God's orchestrations, bringing Timmy into her life. He knew what was up ahead. They are inseparable. Ms. Hunter gave me a rundown on the status of Safe Harbor. I toured the new school and dormitory. Rooms accommodated twenty and three rooms we set up for visiting parents or families in crisis. I met the two horses that had established residency in the barn. Every day I moved away from the trauma to healing. I started back with my walks.

But the loss of John … this has been an avalanche threatening to bury me. Yet an indescribably intense warmth had accompanied news of his death. I experience this daily. Some days intermittent, but on other days this intense warmth lasts all day. I've heard grief described as an ache. I guess that could be it, its name but it seems like a hollow description because this feeling is so powerful it arrests me, stops any movement. It feels more like a tsunami than an ache. It feels as though his *essence* has invaded me, visiting my sorrow for comfort and it's a powerful reminder of John, of his presence. At these moments I stand still and let it surround me. They occur more often at moments whenever I think or bump into any plan, idea, event where John was an integral part of it, belonged to it, where it was an 'us'. I'm consumed with this intense warmth. Oddly, I love it. I stop and imagine he is standing next to me, holding me, remembering his kisses. I can still feel these caresses. Our intimacy. I don't want to let these moments go. I'm afraid for this to stop because I think it's what I have left of him, what keeps him here and it comforts me. If the feelings go, does the memory? I couldn't let that happen.

I've plastered his pictures all over my bedroom. I look at them every day, especially in the morning and before bed in the evenings, his beautiful smile, his intense, focused gaze looking straight at me. I kiss his pictures goodnight, put on one of his shirts, spray it with his cologne. He's the first thing my eyes see in the morning, and the last thing they see before turning out the lights. His goofy pictures, his serious pictures, his pictures blowing kisses, his pictures where his love for me fills his gaze … I miss him terribly, profoundly … Why can't I have him Lord!!!! Why?

I'm told there are five stages of grief … denial, anger, bargaining, depression, and acceptance. Not sure I recognize what my denial looked like, but I may be feeling some elements of anger. Senseless … God is in charge so how could He let this happen? Why ME?

Often, I go into John's room, where he was murdered. John's bed is gone but I stand looking into his closet full of clothes, go through his dresser drawers, touching things he put there, looking at the way he arranged things, the fact that they these items were chosen to be there indicate their importance to him. It's about as close as I can get to having him. These represent him, his personality. And I always feel his warmth here.

Outside, I look up past the sky and clouds, looking for the eternal, some sign to touch me, to speak to me.

My John and sweet Rosa. I was having a hard time with the image of them lying locked in cold caskets, buried in graves underneath six feet of dirt. So alive the last time I saw them. It reminded me of the time my friends flew back to Florida, but this was so much worse. It's the utter absence of them here and to think of where their bodies are now. Buried. They are permanently gone, forever. John. Everything, who he was, our life together that was just beginning, our hopes and plans, his laughter, playfulness, kindness, and happiness that he brought to everything. When he entered a room, light and joy followed. You couldn't be sad or upset around him. The physical beauty of him warmed my heart, but I'll miss more than anything the inside beauty of him. I desperately ached to see him one more time, to touch and kiss him. I know he's in glory, they're both there. But there's a hole in the universe and his absence is palpable. Like Clint, there isn't a place I can look anywhere in my life where he isn't imprinted. I love him.

Life here needed me, and I found I needed Safe Harbor. Its influence in the community grew and seeing the lives it touched was cathartic. We had horses, chickens, two cows and ... ducks. We made a pond with a water feature and as I looked around, I knew John would have loved it here.

Chapter Twenty~Five

Our Weapon ~ Choice

One day, months later, Jimmy and Dinah drove up. I hadn't seen since … Jimmy had a friend come by daily to take care of the horses. They both stepped out of Jimmy's truck looking quiet and reserved. I went to them and hugged them both deeply. I could feel Dinah sigh. She and I were both teary-eyed as we looked at one another. There was a change in Jimmy, and it saddened me to see it. His joyful exuberance was gone.

"Would you both like to come in?"

Both nodded. Inside we grabbed sodas, and I took them for a tour. This seemed to help them; seeing that life and goodness had returned to a place that had harbored hell. I was hoping this might be a restorative factor in helping them realize that we can move on. Jimmy stayed a while with the horses while Dinah and I walked through the classrooms and dormitories. I could see color returning to her face and interest in a new world outside death.

"How have you both been?"

"Dunno." She mentioned Rosa and started to cry. I held her and let her. She looked up staring at me. "I wanted to come see you so many times, but I just felt lost and I didn't know how you were doing."

"I'm better. Think we all felt lost. I completely understand, honey."

"I know you do and that made it harder because you'd had it so much worse." With tears streaming down her face she said, "I wanted so much to see you and talk to you." She fell into my arms sobbing. We just stood there letting her grief shed its energy. After several minutes, she quieted and stepped back rubbing her eyes. I found tissue and she blew her nose. She made me smile. I lost Rosa but she was here in front of me in a younger version.

"How's Jimmy?"

"Probably the same as the rest of us. He's changed," she said, clearing her throat.

"Yes, I can see that."

"I know. He loves you and … so do I. After all that happened, we were angry, it was so wrong. I loved Rosa, we loved them both and didn't know what to do. Then with what happened to you." She started crying again. "For a while I was afraid of everything, I didn't want to leave the house. After the truck accident and then you guys, I didn't feel safe anywhere. Those missing kids. Whenever I stepped outside, I'd look around, afraid of what might be out there. I knew Sam was dead, but are there more like him? I've just felt lost, terrified of life. I don't know if Jimmy feels the same about being afraid, but he's different now, losing his band & close friends gone, then …" She looked down.

"That all makes sense. Why don't we sit on the deck and talk?"

We moved to the deck. I wasn't sure what I wanted to say, but I felt she needed help.

The months had been cathartic for me. I was finally at the fifth stage. Acceptance.

"Dinah, there are bad people out there. I guess we both know that firsthand. But I'm not going to give my life to fear. Evil's out there but so is good. Humanity has an enemy. You know that, right? God is the author of love; our enemy is the author of hate. Do you know about Satan?"

"Yeah, my mom takes us to church."

"Well, I think understanding the dynamics between God and Satan helps me get a grip on why things like this happen. There is a war happening here continually between two forces, good and evil, and humanity sits right in the middle." I looked over at her, "Can I talk about this, will it bother you?"

"No, not at all."

"There is God and there is also Satan. Let me give you Satan's backstory. He was an archangel created by God. He was beautiful. At some point his vanity caused him to decide that he wanted to sit on God's throne. That, of course, couldn't happen, as he was a created being like the rest of us, not a god. He started a rebellion in heaven, acquiring the support of a third of the angels. Funny free choice. Having failed in the purpose of his rebellion, he hates God."

"Tess, are you okay?"

Turning to look at Dinah, "Yeah. Just thinking this through. Evil perpetrated against God in His own home by His own children; and the fact that there is now no redemption available for His sons in this choice ~ choosing Satan and evil against their own Father. They did this while living in the presence of Almighty God and residents in paradise and they choose evil … crazy." I sat there quietly for a long moment reflecting on this truth. Is there anything more painful than the loss of a child?

Choice, wonderful yet dangerous.

"Hard to fathom God not escaping evil. The only way I can think of this is His great mercy, and I think there must be some idea of justice in this that God allows Satan to continue. Is it a last chance scenario for Satan and mankind, tied to choice? Satan's end is certain but is there a justice in God that will answer every argument Satan can make against God? Such as 'If You had left me alone, *all* Your children would have chosen me…' God gives him a long rope, but that rope includes *time* for all of us to choose Him? To save us. If God doesn't escape evil, it's not surprising we don't."

"You know about what happened in the Garden?"

Dinah nodded, "Yeah, I think so, Adam and Eve?"

"It's another event about wrong choices. And what happened there determined humanity's fate. When Eve believed the snake and Adam followed, they turned their right, and all of humanity's right to rule the earth over to Satan. He is the lord of this planet. He has power here. When Satan tempted our Lord in the desert and offered Him ALL the kingdoms of the world, he could do that because he *owns* them."

I looked at Dinah to make sure she was following this. She was concentrating on the barn, "So, wait, two people made *that* happen? Maybe God should have started all over again."

I smiled. "Well good point, I guess He could have. There is mystery that surrounds God. The great mystery for me is where did evil come from? Maybe one day in heaven we'll have all the answers, or maybe the questions won't matter. Yeah…two people. But the point I'm trying to make is that the earth *is* Satan's. Knowing that he reigns here, it's not a hard jump to realize the why of what we experience here. We're living in enemy territory and our enemy is evil." I looked over at the barn as the horses were being taken out for a therapy session. "You know," I said, looking over at Dinah, "we're the only creature made in God's image, and because we resemble God, Satan hates us. We remind him of the battle he lost. So, the warfare here is about Satan's desire to get back at God by obliterating God's image in us. He can't harm God, but he can harm us. His biggest delight, I think, is when he makes us converts. I have this image of him, when the end comes, he's plummeting to hell with some of humanity following and shoving his middle finger at God. It's a small matter to him that vast numbers of humanity will be tormented forever with him in the lake of fire." I stopped here thinking about this fight and Sam. "It's a hellish thought that we can make evil happy. I wonder if God cries… did you know He sings and whistles?" The thought made us both smile.

My mind went to what I know about God, my years in a relationship with Him, how it's grown, and the history of answered prayer and lessons learned.

"God wants us to love; Satan wants us to hate." I looked at Dinah, "Hate takes all the good we can possess, morality, integrity, justice, kindness and replaces it with immorality, injustice, addiction, and anger that promotes violent rage. His main tool, hate, will consume us and it will take our future if we give into it. It took Sam's life. I don't want that; I don't think you do either." I looked into her eyes, "You're both so young, Dinah, to have had to go through this, I hate *that*. Joy, real joy is produced by love and love is the antithesis of hate. Hate's easy, finding how to forgive and love is what's hard. It's almost unnatural here, which makes sense since we live in an evil kingdom." I sat there for a long minute remembering, "Once I had a neighbor who disliked my family. On Christmas our tradition was to make cookies and put them on a festive paper plate with a card and distribute them to our neighbors. We gave one to them. I think that kindness was something they didn't expect. Hate expects retaliation not kindness. They became friends. Love changes things."

I saw Sam's face and shivered. "I tried to hate Sam," I continued, looking at the barn remembering my first encounter, "but I realized that would have been succumbing; would have meant that something wrong won which meant that John and Rosa's deaths were further defiled, and I would be replacing Sam with me, passing his hate on. I couldn't let that happen, honey. Don't you." I looked around the property, at the animals and the children playing, the landscape. "Capitulating, surrendering, giving into evil, makes us citizens of his kingdom and the loss to us is profound. We trade in every possibility of obtaining real joy, peace, goodness, and beauty here."

I sat there for a few minutes thinking about what I was saying, I wasn't just saying this to Dinah, guess I was reminding myself of these things. I looked at her. "Ya know, there's some measure of revenge in moving forward and choosing to work on being happy. There IS a life God intends for us. Both you and Jimmy are here for a purpose, you have a future planned. And it's good, not evil. We can't avoid evil, honey, because it resides here, but we can overcome it by making a good life, maybe that's our weapon."

We went for more drinks and walked around the property.

We stood watching the children in the classrooms playing games "These children and their families know evil and hardship. These last few months, I haven't wanted to live." I saw the surprised look on Dinah's face. "Looking around here and seeing that these children and their families gain hope and purpose, life has meaning again and not just for me, for all of us. It's a redemption of sorts for my losses, for my John and Rosa." I stood waiting to see how my sermon was resonating with her. "Is this all making sense?"

"Yes. I've been so mixed up. I love the way you talk about God; you make it personal." She was thoughtful for a moment. Looking out over the property she hesitated, "I don't have what you have with your faith, but it makes sense." She smiled. Turning to look at me, "I see how it has helped you." She took a deep breath. "I feel better being here." I could see peace in her face. I knew that was a lot to digest but I hoped some of it would stick and give her a better understanding and foundation to see things in a different light. Hope.

"Honey, it's hard to see how God could have allowed this. It's been hard for me. But give Him space in your heart." Changing the subject, "How's it going at school? Are you still planning on becoming a teacher?"

"Not sure. When I said I was lost, I'm lost with what to do next." She had tears in her eyes, "I really missed you." More hugs.

"Do you think it would help if you came back and helped around here?" I said as she pulled away.

Suddenly there was a broad smile. "Would that be okay with you?"

"Yes, of course, I've missed you guys. If you want, come any time."

"Tomorrow?"

Laughing, "Absolutely, Let's go see what Jimmy is up to."

Jimmy stayed distant. Friends and band are gone. I knew I needed to wait for a time when Jimmy was ready to talk. "When you can, and he's ready, bring Jimmy again."

———————————

Chapter Twenty~Six

———————————

Safe Harbor

During my absence a cook/housekeeper had been hired out of necessity. Her name is Clorinda, but everyone calls her Cloris. She is a tall woman in her early fifties and quite the character I'm hearing. She's organized, keeps everything clean and is an excellent cook. She orders food and keeps the pantry stocked. There was also a need for a bookkeeper to manage the finances. Her name is Gracey, she's quiet, in her mid-forties. Both ladies came with good reputations as both had worked for Child Protective Services previously, backgrounds vetted. It was a smooth transition, and they have kept Safe Harbor running.

Pastor Allen dropped by one day for a visit. "Good morning, Tess. How are you doing?"

"It's great to see you, glad you stopped by. Taking everything a day at a time. Would you like a cup of coffee?"

"Yes, thank you."

We settled in the small dining room with our coffee. We caught up on the recent events, including James and Jenny. I told him,

"I can see that Timmy is doing well and appears to be thriving, but I suppose I don't have anything to compare that to. He's become quite the leader on campus and that's encouraging. He's also grown pretty attached to Sprite and Butterfly, one of the horses. We were given two horses, and we use them as therapy horses. The other horse is named Rogerthat. Not sure how that came about." Pastor Allen laughed.

Butterfly was a beautiful chestnut mare and Rogerthat was an equally beautiful sorrel gelding.

"I think you're right about Timmy. It's been good to watch the changes, not only adapting, but maybe even flourishing. You look remarkably well after all you've been through."

"Thanks, and thanks for helping keep Safe Harbor afloat."

"It's mutual. Safe Harbor is good for all of us. It's needed and I'm grateful to you for your heart and willingness to open your home. It's a large responsibility so anything I can do to help, just ask."

"Thank you."

The conversation turned to Rosa. "There's something about Rosa that I've wondered about. Sam's violence was extreme on her in comparison with John, she was so sweet. She told me about Sam one day after the officer was murdered, she warned me about him, but during that conversation, I came away thinking there was more that she wasn't telling me about their relationship." I looked at Pastor Allen, "Seemed she knew a lot about him. She mentioned that when he would come into the Bureau, there were times when she saw a softness. I thought she was struggling with some idea of his redemption."

Pastor Allen sat for a minute, thinking, "Well, hum." He sighed. "I don't really know for sure, but I do know what you mean. I had a similar thought. She confided that Sam had asked her out and she went. It was just one date, dinner. She said there was a connection between them, but she knew his reputation and she was afraid, so she avoided him after that. That bothered her because I guess she thought she might be able to help him, influence him. She didn't say, but I got the feeling she really cared for him. At what level he cared for her, I don't know. But it's possible that his malice towards her was more personal, maybe he'd felt rejected. Dunno. I don't think he opened up to too many people and he let her in a little? Hard to really know." He looked away and I thought I saw sadness in him ... It occurred to me that Sam might not have been the only one to care for her. It took him a minute before he continued, sighing, "Well, I need to be going. It's really been good to see you Tess, you're a miracle. I've heard what you went through and seriously, it's a miracle." He stood to leave.

I walked him to his car and said our goodbyes. I thought about Rosa and Sam on a dinner date. Seemed impossible to place Sam in that setting. To put himself in that situation, polite company and table talk, he must have really cared for Rosa.

I can understand Rosa having some idea that she could have in some way at least helped him, maybe saved him. One can't know the possibility of that happening, but after my experience, it seemed remote. And I didn't see Pastor Allen caring for Rosa. Human beings are extremely complex creatures, maybe because their Creator is complex. After all, He made this unique planet and untold universes. One thing seems clear, Sam's devastating influence has larger boundaries than I knew. I sat for a few minutes thinking about the three. Rosa and Pastor Allen made sense.

There is truth to the workings of time. I was working through a lot of issues. I continued to see Dr. Waldron; he offered friendship and insight. Recurring nightmares started shortly after I got home. Walking out into the backyard after dark wasn't easy. It was a reminder but had been a favorite place in the evening to sit and think, peace down and pray. Maybe it's a good thing that it's occupied by animals. I hadn't realized the complexity of their behavior and language. Besides being entertaining, they were comforting. Their presence filled up the night air.

The transformed out-building now housed the children and families in crisis. It was rectangular in shape with classrooms on the bottom floor and the second story made up of bedrooms, bathrooms and a living area where the children stayed, and their sounds wafted across the evening air and that too was comforting.

My stream. I hadn't been able to venture there. Its last visits were shrouded in memories of John.

Patty and Stark were getting married. She planned a small wedding. She invited Maddy and Anna.

Patty and I drove to Jackson Hole and visited John's grave. I went back a few weeks later to visit him alone. Is it wrong to sit on a grave? John's grave felt like hallowed ground. I sat cross-legged, staring at his tombstone. *John Allen Lawrence – Taken too soon. Loved by all. Amazing son, father, and friend. Skiing with the angels…* "John," I thought about his face and his smile, finally, "John," I whispered, "I miss you terribly," leaning over his grave I started to sob. "I'm sorry. You didn't deserve this. It's hard going on without you." Straightening up, I looked at his tombstone, "It does help me knowing where you are and that there are no blemishes or scars, or pain, or horror, no memories. Just joy, forever young and whole." This thought helped me find some peace, "Knowing how you are and where you are is one of my few comforts. And knowing that we'll be together again gives me hope." I sat there remembering our last days, my time with him moved like a video in front of my eyes, "I wanted a long life with you. I love you, John. You have a place in me that you filled with all of you. You didn't hold anything back and I'll carry you always in my heart until I see you again." The peace I prayed for came and I sat there surrounded by John's essence.

"Hey lady, you alright?"

I had fallen asleep next to John's grave. Startled, I sat up, "Yes, yes, I'm fine. Thank you."

"Your husband?"

I shook my head, "My fiancé."

It was a sweet elderly man. I could see this touched him.

"Do you need any help?"

"No thanks, I'm fine, really." Looking up, I smiled at him as he walked away. It occurred to me, "think that's the first time we slept together, John." This thought made me smile.

Months passed. I started riding Rogerthat on the trails where I used to walk. He has filled the places Kai left. Rogerthat has this soft white blaze on his face where I nuzzle him. I love to stand and caress him. His eyes will close, and I can feel his warm breath on my face. Taking care of him is a gift. Our times grooming is a love affair, it's cathartic and we've bonded.

Still there were moments when I got alone with John. I've returned to my visits by the stream. Sitting there, I review my life with John and let the memories and their accompanying emotions fill me. John taught me about love. I learned a different understanding of love, a sweet selfless love that comes from a good heart that he didn't allow life to taint or deform. I think it's rare. Back in the house there is the quiet absence of him. His voice and face, his gentle eyes that gazed at me lovingly, taking me into his soul, his joyful smile, especially when he was walking towards me. I miss reaching for his hand and always finding it, his physique that towered over me sheltering me, his pet names for me and expressions that were totally John's … As I sit by the stream I can see him, and when I recall events, it plays again those movies. I'm back there, *in* that moment. I know that much of this will fade with time and I know there is health in that but I'm not ready for that just yet.

The home, children, families, and my friends filled my time, it helped me to heal.

Cloris ~ getting to know her has been challenging. I found I must interrupt her because at times she seems to get lost in her own words. She starts on one subject and then morphs into a full rundown of every single event that happened yesterday and today then moves on to her current television shows, mostly sci-fi or aliens. Nothing is too small to discuss, or too weird. If I don't control the conversation I could be stuck for hours. There are the unfortunate newcomers that get pinned before anyone has had a chance to intervene or rescue. To new employees we lovingly refer to this event as an initiation ... being 'Cloris'd". She has an incendiary approach to gardening. Her gardening technique consists of eviscerating practically anything living in the yard. She doesn't believe plants should touch. I asked her if she had ever visited any forests. She cuts everything down then starts on a plan of fertilizing dirt. Finally hired a gardener. She is also contemptuous of animal mating rituals. If left to her own, the animal kingdom could be decimated in one generation.

But no problem, she plans to beam up at a portal in Sedona, however getting a fixed date from her on this event is met with a cloud of cannabis smoke. I'm *assured* she's been vetted. Maybe the trip is a virtual concept, as the how's and logistics are vague, and she stares off to her left looking at the sky when discussing this. She is a walking encyclopedia on aliens and Tesla. We've had to keep a close eye on her every time she heads outdoors. Our gardener has an apoplectic event every time she gets close to stepping off the driveway. She *is* an interesting and colorful character, one of a kind and the kids love her. The softness in her heart is bottomless along with her kick-butt work ethic. She's tireless. Sometimes she comes across as querulous until you get to know her, and I think it's partly because she doesn't listen well to others, dominates conversations whether she understands them or not. I've noticed at times that she can be on a completely different topic with people, those are usually short lived, with people walking away perplexed. She doesn't have a learning/exchange of ideas style, rather it's more of a pedantic/teachy style. She takes time and there is never a dull moment with her.

Gracey ~ when she speaks, shows an introspective mind, a thinker. She is, well, different in many ways. She has a reticent personality that can come across as narrow and rigid in her perception of society and social behavior, might be termed old fashioned. But her prevailing and outstanding quality is her sweet disposition and endless kindness. She moves through the sanctuary like a quiet shadow but always leaves the room a little merrier than when she came in. She possesses a quiet sense of humor and is a subtle prankster, so the children watch her to see what she's up to. They brighten when they see her. She hides goodies on her person in unlikely places, like her pockets and sleeves and surreptitiously tucks them into unsuspecting little hands. Of course, now it is no longer surreptitious, it is expected. She doesn't always leave candy; she makes amazing animal origami figures. Some she dusts with glitter or sequins and those have a gossamer fairy quality that the girls cherish. I admit they're good enough, they could probably bring in money if she ever decided to sell them. Told her to investigate displaying them at local curio shops. She's not interested. Does this because it makes her happy. She's not alone.

I wouldn't say that Cloris and Gracey are friends. More than anything, they don't really understand one another.

Recently Cloris and I went to Lander. I'm not taking my own advice. On the drive I was a captive audience. I learned that vegans kill things, as she reports, thinking it's ironic because they don't think we should kill animals. She says, as though she knows this secret about them, she whispers, 'they kill plants'. And she looks at me as though she has found them out. I asked her if she recalled her gardening technique. She sat quietly for maybe 90 seconds. Throughout the trip she commented on practically every driver, their driving missteps, AND their thought processes for why they drove so poorly. She discussed the sequencing of the lights and the DOT ... I won't repeat this. In the store she vocally commented on prices and the rip-offs being perpetrated. I'm ashamed to admit I did ask her who she talks to when she's alone. No hesitation. She said she talks to the spirit in her. Not a bad response. By the time I was home I needed quiet and a glass of wine. In the future I may suggest she make a list.

Chapter Twenty~Seven

The White Mist

Stark called one day and asked to drop by. It was so good to see him. "Tess, do you have somewhere where we can be alone?"

Stark and I went into the library.

He sat for a few moments, studying the floor. When he looked up, I saw the moisture in his eyes. I remembered John's somber comments about his soul-mate brother, Stark, and the love between them. "How are you doing Stark?" I asked gently. "John told me how close the two of you were ... brothers," concern showing in my voice. I had forgotten about Stark and the pain and horror he must be going through.

Stark looked pained and I could see he was struggling for composure.

He didn't go there in his conversation, instead he started with, "Did you know that John left a will?"

Startled, I said, "To be honest, I hadn't thought about it."

He took a deep breath before beginning again. "He did," stumbling through his file of papers. "He redid this in preparation for his marriage. So sorry to mention anything hurtful, Tess. Are you ready to hear this?"

"Stark, I think this is hard on all of us. You haven't commented on how you are doing and I won't press you but don't worry about me, it's okay."

"Well, you're in it. He left a third of his estate to you."

I sat there for a few minutes processing this. Of course, John would do that. But this just made me miss him more. He has so many qualities and they don't stop after he's dead. Stark sat there watching me. "Sorry, I was just thinking about him, and this shouldn't surprise me knowing him. But truthfully, I wasn't aware of any will. It was never discussed."

"He also has given you half his partnership in the law firm. I don't have a cash value on the firm, but the rest of his estate's value is stated in the will. He set up trusts for both the children. I don't know if you knew this, but John came from old money. His family has deep roots in Wyoming." I remembered the snowplow incident. "All the siblings have old trusts set up and his trust has also been divided between the three of you. His trust is fixed and handled by a trustee. The distribution on the trust is a monthly event and would go directly to your bank account. We can discuss the best way to have the rest of his estate distributed, but I'm not a financial adviser, I can recommend several if you need that. The law firm, how do you want that handled?"

"I don't have a clue. What happened to John's cases?"

"Most understand the situation and want to be sympathetic, but this is not a civil practice, it's criminal and people are sitting in jail. Technically they are entitled to a speedy trial. I'm looking for a new partner. I have farmed out a few cases. There are a couple of excellent candidates. Actually, friends of John."

I remembered when we first met at the Stagecoach and friends standing at the bar.

"How is that normally handled?"

"I'm not sure. I could buy you out once we have a value assessed if you would prefer that."

"Is it necessary to talk about this right now? Don't you have better things to do, like plan a wedding? How's that coming, by the way?"

"I'm honestly not too sure." He bent his head as he smiled, and looking up with a sparkle shimmering in both eyes, he said, "Your friend Maddy and Patty work without any advice from me. I get running details ... This wedding has been good for Patty ... and me. She was a wreck after everything that happened. I was pretty worried." Suddenly cheerful, he continued, "Patty seems excited so I take that daily as a thermometer on how things are progressing," he gave me a thumbs up. Stark stayed and visited for a while. He walked the property and met everyone.

"I'll be in touch about the will. I didn't know about it so… let me get back with you on it?"

"No problem, Tess." Stark gave me a quick hug and left. He was meeting Patty for lunch.

I watched him leave. It occurred to me, John exited and Patty entered. God prepared for this.

More than a year had passed since John had died and I was healing, choosing to deliberately move forward. Safe Harbor had its own momentum. Guardian Ad Litem programs and the courts were now utilizing the sanctuary as a resource for placement of children on and off the reservation. It was turning into a farm. We had horses, cows, chickens, ducks, and goats and we're learning all sorts of animal husbandry.

One day while I was in Lander, I saw Clint's truck drive by. It was another area I had deliberately moved forward from, and it shook me to see him again. I had to pull over. I sat in my car, invaded by memories. This wasn't anything I had initiated but I let the images come. I hadn't grieved John fully. I decided that it was time to talk to Maddy about Clint and my death experience.

I called Maddy, and we talked at great length about both subjects.

"Wow Tess, heaven. Makes me want to leave now. Gave me the chills listening to your description."

Talking about it reminded me about the joy and peace that IS the air in heaven, I often feel the same way about it, chills. "Maddy, that experience helped me heal. When I came back to the cavern, the horror, terror, and fear were gone, completely. I still experienced the physical pain, the devastation of what happened to John and Rosa, my own physical healing." I stopped to think about where I was with everything. "But the horror that should have consumed me, that tried to destroy me, was gone. What was left was the physical pain and my grief. But even grief is cathartic really, it's therapeutic. Grief is a way of managing the loss and working through the pain." Thinking about John. "I think healing and grief are sisters."

I stopped here, looking off the front deck, out onto the lawn. "It's a hard concept for me and probably for most, that the bad we experience has a purpose. *I can only grow through bad events?* Seems mean and wrong. But … do we learn *anything*, character, discipline, selfless goodness when things are good, easy? I haven't personally observed that. Then realizing that I have learned things through these bad experiences ... In this horror, I learned, despite the hell I went through that God was there. He didn't miss a thing. I don't know why me, but this has deepened my faith. No matter how bad the hell, God had a purpose. He did deliver me." I took a breath. "So, my experience in the cave and in heaven, have given me clarity, an understanding of my purpose here and finally, that hope *is* ahead. I've passed through fire, Maddy."

Maddy was silent, digesting this.

"But why are we here at all? We're born with a sin nature, into the enemy's territory. Why? *Our 'start-up' is already coming from behind.* For me, what I have learned is that God wants something from us here. Maybe part of that is 'choice'. Every day we're faced with choices ~ temptations, decisions ~ good vs evil. As tantalizing as temptation is, will we stand and choose Him? Funny, reminds me of the childhood games during PE where teams are selected, each student hoping 'choose me, choose me'. Funny to think God is like that, 'choose Me'. Is this because God wants to spend eternity with souls that chose Him against all the beguiling, enticing temptations, souls that still stood with Him? But weirder, is that He desires to be close to us. Us. He is the Awesome God of the Universe, the Creator and He wants to talk to *me* every day. It does humble me. Often, I treat Him like He's a ghost, treat Him with indifference, wandering off into my own wisdom, *when* I've learned and have a history that real wisdom and power lie with Him."

I paused for a long moment thinking about Him.

"Tess, are you there?"

"Yes, just having a moment. There's a saying in other cultures, they say we cry at birth and rejoice at death, as a Christian, that concept makes a lot of sense."

"Yeah, I've heard that before." She paused, "Choices, I know, I wander away from my faith, get caught up in the day-today struggles. Reading about Moses, David, Abraham, Old Testament power houses, about their failures and that God still loved them, called them friend. I don't get discouraged anymore when I fail. I just keep going. I guess that's the nature of God's grace." She paused for a moment. "Tess, I see that God has taken that horror ... albeit not the pain." I heard her sigh. "Watching this with you has been, I can't think of a word bad enough to describe what I know happened ... I confess I was beyond angry and since this DID happen to you, I thought God was small and impotent. He didn't keep you from it. But here you are, standing ... I realize letting us experience this doesn't mean we aren't God's daughters, we are ... or that He doesn't love us, that's not the lesson. We're not the neighbor's kid, we are in His family, we're His kids. Jesus went to the Cross, He wasn't spared, but it changed everything. We don't get cocooned when we're saved, seems the opposite." Her voice firmer, yet soft, almost as much to herself as to me, "Our house stands for something in the neighborhood, we aren't elevated above life's troubles, in fact, because we are God's, we have a target on our backs because of where we live, *but when we still stand and still trust, our neighbors are witnesses to our truth.* Is our Dad real or a rumor? That's our truth, *He is real.* We prove Him every day we breath."

"Maddy ... such a deep truth. You're 'Iron sharpening iron' for me," I said softly.

She paused, "I was out and about in the community during your abduction. A lot of people were terribly affected by what happened. I witnessed it firsthand. I felt the shock of this in the air, saw fear on their faces with everything that Sam brought to this community, you, those kids. I'm sure they worried 'who's next'? Pretty sure everyone thought you were dead, and then after being rescued, that you were so badly injured ... Now, *I think you represent God's miraculous power, and there's hope somewhere in this for all of us.* You appear strong and show little of the horror we all know you experienced; here you are, standing. You are a walking testimony."

This wasn't a humorous moment. Neither of us spoke.

"Sooo... Clint..." Her voice elevated, "I hadn't realized the depth this relationship had reached. How did you manage to juggle two men?"

The timing on this was a bit off ... took me a moment to refocus. "I don't know, Maddy. It wasn't anything I felt I had control *over.* Something other than me was moving them in and out of my life. Clint's involvement in my life was always unexpected but at times when, obviously, I needed him. Reminds me of having a guardian angel. And John was my everyday angel. Yeah," I smiled, "I like that thought. There was so much going on that I often had to accept situations with each of them for what they were at each encounter. I hadn't made a commitment to either initially and then Clint disappeared, leaving time for John and

I." I was thinking about both men. I gave her an overview of both relationships and their timelines.

"One of the hardest areas for me is that if I hadn't met John, he would probably still be alive? I know we don't accidentally die; like we aren't an accident at birth. God's sovereign and death and life are in His hands. Still, I think about when we first met, if he'd known, maybe he wouldn't have approached my table. Kind of like I was his death sentence. That's a hard thought to get past. I do work at it, and I know this isn't a thought from God."

"That's a cruel torturous thought, you … John's death sentence. Life isn't serendipitous, that God doesn't have a plan. Let that thought go." She stopped.

I waited a few minutes for her to continue, I knew she had more to say.

"Tess, I know you're grieving John, but when you feel you've healed," She paused, "I'm going to interfere here since you called me," she waited a minute before beginning again, "I think you should go to Clint and talk to him. I don't think, from what I witnessed and now from what I've heard from you, maybe his thoughts about your relationship aren't the same any longer. You both love each other." I could hear her take a deep breath, "This may be the best medicine for everyone, to see you happy and in love again. Seeing that it's possible. I've always thought a lot of this guy. He's a good guy, that's probably a poor word, because there's more to him than simply saying he's good, he's pretty amazing. What I know about Clint from when he was remodeling your house, to his rescues. He took it upon himself to find you. When he rescued you, he went a step further to call Anna and I to come help you. He put his own life in danger twice *for you*. When I saw him at the hospital, I saw his care and concern. When he spoke, I noticed that everyone had stopped talking and listened to him. I think your future lies there if you both give this a chance. Remember your hesitation about your move there? I felt you would eventually come to regret not going. This is similar, I think your both not pursuing each other will be a big regret down the road. Think about it honey. This isn't an average relationship, like it happens to us all. Not so. Most don't ever find someone or love like this."

I didn't respond right away. I was listening and thinking.

"Okay, I'll definitely pray about this."

"Yes, but Tess be *open* to it also. We have control over our choices."

"Alright Saint Maddy!"

"I may be St. Maddy, but you're Joan of Arc! And keep me posted." I could feel a smile at the other end of the call.

I hung up and took Rogerthat for a ride. My mind went to thoughts of Clint, remembering our moments together. I hadn't thanked him for saving me, in fact, I hadn't seen him since then. Seeing him in his truck the other day made me think, at least it seemed that way, that he had moved on with his life. Was he dating, married? Was he still watching me? I looked around as I rode. I thought about Maddy's comments and her opinion on anything carries a lot of weight with me. She isn't one to jump in with both feet, she assesses. I knew what she meant about who Clint is, there's a power in him and people listen. I was remembering his confession on my deck that day. I started getting emotional. 'Lord, open this door or close it forever. You can heal our hearts and help us get over each other, if that's Your will. If You want us together, Lord I need something from You, a sign. Amen.'

My thoughts on Clint reminded me that I had not seen Jimmy in some time. I'd hired Dinah and she started assisting the teachers while taking night classes. We didn't talk about Jimmy, and Clint never came up in conversation. So, I had no news of either.

Seeing Dinah made me think about Jimmy. I wanted to talk to him about things. I asked Dinah if she could ask him to drop by for a visit. I hadn't come to a point where I felt I could chance seeing Clint, so I didn't want to go to their home. A few days later Jimmy showed up at Safe Harbor. He'd brought his horse and we went for a ride. He took us to the cabin; it was a secluded place. We sat outside and talked for hours about some of the same things I talked to Dinah about, his anger and hatred. He had a future and I wanted him to see that possibility. One day, a few weeks later, Jimmy came by to visit, and Timmy ran up to greet him. Timmy was six now and growing, as they say, like a weed. With all that that child had been through, he was a happy child and possibly a smaller version of Jimmy. They hung around the horses and somehow that started Jimmy coming by to teach Timmy guitar. They sit together in the afternoons, practicing, riding horses, and hanging out. I wondered if perhaps Jimmy and Dinah were replacing James and Jenny.

I don't always ride Rogerthat, sometimes I just walk beside him and chat. He's a good listener. We walk side by side, and it's probably corny, but I'm sure we're communicating. He always whinnies when he sees me. During grooming, he will nuzzle me.

One morning, early, I stood out on the back deck drinking my coffee, looking around. Warmer temperatures had been replaced with a cool breeze. I stood there feeling joy and happiness. I smiled, hearing the happy chatter of the children at breakfast. I left the deck and started walking. As I passed by the dormitory/ classrooms I mused how John's estate had helped provide many comfort items, furniture, additions, whatever the need we were able to accommodate. In a way, like Clint's imprint with the remodeling, this was John's lasting imprint here, I felt John would have approved.

Finally, there's peace in my life. I found myself beside the stream. The morning was spectacular, and I sat by the stream meditating on the beauty around me. The woods were full of deer this morning. They added to the serenity and tranquility I was feeling in their whispered silent movement through the trees. I closed my eyes and sat listening. Our senses are a gift. I opened my eyes and looking up, a white mist was moving quietly on the other side of the stream, through the trees. It moved closer and seemed to hesitate, then turning, it started moving towards me. In the hushed quiet, a deer calmly looked up from grazing to watch as it passed. It crossed the stream, and came to rest in front of me, then finally encompassing me. I could feel the cool mist as it touched my skin. 'Tess'… I looked around. 'Tess'…tears started flowing. 'John, are you here?' I whispered. 'I love you.' Within moments the mist dissipated but in its place was left a transcendent peacefulness. I looked over at the place where John proposed, and I could finally smile about John and not grieve.

Chapter Twenty-Eight

Life Lived ~ The Land's Legacy

I felt Cloris shaking me, "Miss Tess, Miss Tess, wake up! We've been looking everywhere for you!" Startled, I roused myself and sat up. "Oh, I'm sorry Cloris. What is it? What time is it?"

"It's 10:00 and you have a visitor."

"Okay, give me a minute and I'll be right there. Thanks."

Cloris hustled off but I couldn't quite make myself move. Regaining alertness, I sat in the stillness. I knew that something wonderful had happened. I believed that John had visited and released me. This too is hallowed ground. Meditating on this, I got up and headed back towards the house.

When I came around the barn, I saw Clint's truck. I stayed hidden for a moment, collecting my suddenly racing heartbeat, trying to understand why he would be here. I looked back towards the stream. Tears welled, Lord was that my sign … rubbing my eyes and taking a deep breath I turned and headed towards the house. The children were on recess and noisily playing in the yard. After greeting them, I walked towards the deck. I saw Clint standing there, watching me. He possesses power, I could feel it as I was walking, his proud straight posture and self-assurance, and that face ... handsome chiseled facial bones and clear dark eyes, raven black hair ... He takes my breath. It was all I could manage to keep walking towards him. Still, I felt peace and managed a smile. As he watched me walk towards him; I saw something flicker in his eyes, his face soften.

"Good morning, Clint," I said as I walked up the steps.

"Good morning, Tess," he said, with a focused look. He stood for a moment, not speaking, staring into my face. "I was wondering if we could talk?"

"Yes, here?" There were a lot of eyes on us. "How about inside in the small dining room?"

"I was hoping you'd have time for a drive?"

"Okay ... Let me get a jacket." I realized that my whole body was tingling, on high alert. Having to work keeping myself in control, my insides suddenly in turmoil.

He nodded as I went inside. Dinah was smiling watching me. I gave her a quizzical side glance and headed to retrieve my coat. My heart was thumping wildly ... why *is* he here?

Outside he helped me into his truck. He got behind the wheel, his face immobile. Pulling into a public park, he parked his truck. We sat for a few minutes in silence. He pivoted in his seat to face me with his left arm resting on the steering wheel, his right arm over the seat back. "Tess, first," he said as he looked at me, "I wanted to thank you for helping Dinah and Jimmy. After everything, especially Jimmy, it changed them, we weren't sure how to help them." His eyes softened as he looked at me, "Each of them told me about their visit and conversation with you. There's a difference in them; we could see the impact you've made. And now Jimmy, getting out of the house, and playing guitar again," he shook his head, "it was a relief. Mom wanted to come by and say thank you too, but I wanted a moment with you first," he said warmly.

"Let me stop you here," I interrupted. "I'm the one who needs to thank you," I was getting emotional and it took me a moment to proceed. I realized I had a lot of pent-up emotions regarding this man, the rescues, my heart, my gratitude. Clint watched me as I tried for control ... I studied the park outside the windshield, looking at him was rattling my composure and stealing my thoughts. Taking a few calming breaths, I turned to him, studying his face. "I thought about coming to you several times but ..." His attention was fully focused on me. "You saved my life, Clint; all I did was have conversations with them. There's no comparison. Everyone, especially me, Clint, thinks you're a hero..." I stalled, "You're my hero." I said this quietly, as my eyes filled with tears and my heart filled with deep warmth for him; I could see it moved him.

We both sat there looking at one another. Just staring.

He sat there for a long moment before finally speaking. "There was a second thing I wanted to talk to you about." His face was open. He looked out the windshield, then started, a half-smile on his face, looking again at me, "I keep you close, Tess; I suppose it could be termed stalking," he smiled, "but my way of thinking about my behavior is I'm making sure you're safe ... I still check on you." He turned again to stare out the windshield before speaking. He sighed, turning towards me, "I suppose Tess, it's a way I can love you." He searched my eyes. I suspected conversations in this area might not come easily. He started again, refocusing on my face, "Up until now…" there was a long pause. "I know all about John ... and your loss," he said, there was no hint of jealousy or negative emotion in him, he sighed and said softly, "I'm sorry about what happened Tess. I know it tore you up. I wanted to do something to help, but there wasn't anything *I* could do. I knew you needed to be alone with your loss, and I wasn't a part of that. I guess why I'm saying this, I saw you the other day in town. It made me wonder if you'd had enough time and if you might be ready to start a new relationship ... Maybe ready for us?"

A powerful surge went through my body ... this caught my breath. Us ... Was I hearing this?

Looking deep into my eyes he continued, "You're on my mind all the time, you're in my head and in my heart ... still." Emotion flickering deep in his eyes. He looked away, staring out the windshield. "I have a few close friends on the rez, and I've talked to them about you, our relationship and our different cultures. They helped me gain ... maybe ... I came to see us differently," he said as he turned towards me. "Our culture believes that there exist soulmates, souls destined to be together, that transcend skin and cultures." Looking deeply into my eyes, "Tess, you complete me. Nothing has diminished for me, instead, my feelings have deepened. You're everything to me, and you are the only woman for me. I know this. I love you and if you still feel the way you felt on the deck that day, and you feel ready, I would like to see you. Like you said that day, 'see where this goes'."

I sat there for several minutes overwhelmed by his words, moved speechless, just sat looking at him, all of him. Is this happening? His eyes were intense, deep as though there was an open portal in them for me directly to his heart, clear-eyed, no barriers. He was mine. I moved over to him; he put his arms around me and pulled me close. He studied my face and his eyes found my lips. He leant in, his soft lips on mine. It was a gentle kiss that grew intense as he pulled me tight.

Tears started flowing and he felt its wetness and pulled away to look into my eyes. He was confused and concerned. I started crying uncontrollably. Clint held me and let me weep, for John. He held me for a long time it seemed. This felt right grieving the love I still have for John with Clint. We three were a composite, linked together spiritually, inexplicably connected with one other. After some time, I pulled away and we stared at one another. Clint was looking deeply into my face, and I was studying his and I began to smile. I knew viscerally that the grief I felt for John was gone now, and only his goodness remained, the best part of him. The heart that had learned to love through John was now open and ready to embrace this new love.

"The last time I saw you after Kai's injury, you said you loved me. I've never told you, but I feel the same way, Clint, I do love you, I always have." I found myself unable to continue.

Clint's face softened and he pulled me back into him, tightening his grip for a deep hug while kissing my hair. I realized at this moment, this freedom was a long time coming, the freedom to finally submit to his love, to openly express this love we shared. The freedom to enjoy his kisses, his touch, to be near enough to feel his heat, smell his scent. I had longed for this, thought about, wondered about … and he was sitting here now holding me, loving me and it felt as natural as breathing. I don't think either of us thought this day would come. I put my arms around him and looked up into his face searching for his lips. As our lips met, he pulled me down onto the seat, his body resting on mine, his lips on my neck, his face in my hair, his hands circling my waist. I wrapped my arms around him and pulled him tight to me. It felt right. I could feel our passion growing and I pulled apart slightly. He was smiling as he studied my face.

"My little bird, my beautiful blue-eyed Tess," he said, eyes shining as his eyes roamed my face.

I felt warm and small beneath him. Healed and whole.

As I lay under him, I whispered, "I think you have my answer." Emotion flickered behind his eyes as he rested his forehead against mine.

He takes my power. He is fire.

We stayed together the entire day. Every time he went in somewhere, I watched to see if he would disappear. He brought me home late, and we sat in the truck until after midnight. It wasn't so much that we talked, but more that we wanted to be near each other. I just felt that I wanted to absorb him into me. This must be part of the oneness God talks about. I know part of this is sexual, but I think this is another element of that. Trying to explain what I felt to myself, the best way I found to describe it is, in his words, he completes me.

I woke up very early; it was still dark outside. Clint was my first thought. Warmth consumed my body, I was giddy, awake, alive. Was he awake, I wondered? Was he thinking about me? Is he the desire of my heart You promise that only You will fulfill? It feels that way Lord. John, I was finding it hard to express to myself my honest feelings about Clint because I had trouble shaking this lingering thought that it seemed like it *should* feel like a betrayal of that love. With yesterday's visit from John, I knew God knew I needed to be able to love Clint, love him with a free and unhindered heart, the way I can see Clint loves me. How many times have I looked at both men? Assessed their differences. I could have spent my life with John and been deliriously happy. He was nurturing, he gave all, he was more than words. I will always love him. I had asked God for a sign … I smiled.

I made a pot of coffee and sat outside on the front porch with my Bible and journal. I needed to process yesterday and record my thoughts.

Words… Trying to journal, my journals had always been my way of expressing my private thoughts, but it also contained my history. Finding the right words that nail the event or emotion was important to me. I can reread them and relive events, relationships, so I wanted to get this down, get it right. Losing John, he's there in my journals. My thoughts, for me, needed to be honest, and accurate so I guess I can keep the good forever, maybe keep memories alive. It's *my* requirement, otherwise, why do I journal? Journaling helps me understand things because I pull things out when I write about them, I guess that helps them breathe and helps me get clarity. But, if I get it right, it also contains the emotions that I can revisit … the good, the bad and the ugly.

I'd had relationships but always had this idea of what real romance and love looked like, the knight, the perfect prince, rescuer, nurturer, and devoted lover. Over the years I came to see this image as a mirage, an unattainable dream. I knew few who'd had that *one* love in their relationships. It always seemed to me that most settled, like a calculated decision that took into consideration concepts outside true love. In the past in accepting less, the argument to myself was that the perfect prince was a fabrication, a fairytale, a myth. Things like 'we're compatible', 'he's safe', finances and status, 'this is the best I can get', 'I *do* love him on some level … I know their stories, I've lived a few. I knew this with Clint was the real thing. It's along the lines of an intuitive sense... like 'I know like I know', I just know. I was meant to be Clint's. I knew, as I wrote, that I was now free to love Clint, nothing held back.

So, with this new exhilarated sensation, fear was also lurking, wanting to create doubt, a constant companion in my storyline, this idea that I don't deserve this, and Clint's prior disappearing act didn't help this old fear. Did yesterday happen? Of course. My mind rewound all of yesterday, the conversations and the 'us' in everything we did. We were a couple. He held my hand all day as though it was always us. Confident as he moved through the day. I belonged to him, and he had adjusted to that thought already. It felt as though, with his constant touch in town, that he was claiming me publicly.

I looked up at the lawn as the sun was rising, the birds were waking, and our roosters were crowing. Life has routine, day in and day out movement. Nature responds to man, but … irrespective of lives lived, nature stays the same. The same sun, forests, mountains, oceans, animal instincts were here from the dawn of humanity. The thought makes me feel small, but I'm part of its hum, its song, its story. I may be a footnote, but I'm here, I'm alive and I'm happy. Seems a queer thought. It made me smile. I remember hiking in the Smoky's and the constant reminder that humanity had a legacy there, maybe someone someday will think about my legacy in much the same way. My history will also be part of this land's story, its legacy.

I could hear the sounds of activity, clatter in the kitchen, the smell of breakfast, the noise of slow-moving adults waking to the day and the noisy chatter of little people. I went inside to help.

"Well, Miss Tess, did you just come in?" said Cloris.

I smiled. "No Cloris, I woke early and was having coffee on the porch." Not sure why I felt I needed to explain.

She looked at me and I could tell she had questions about yesterday and my disappearance. But I just smiled. I went outside to take care of the animals and prepared to take Rogerthat for a ride.

"Tess," Cloris yelled, "You have a phone call."

"Coming," I turned to Rogerthat, "I'll be right back."

It was Clint, "Good morning," he said quietly, warmly. I was smiling ear to ear as my body filled with warmth for him, my heart racing.

"Good morning, you've been on my mind all morning." Returning the warmth.

"Me too, do you have plans? I'd like to come by."

I was assailed by an intense flutter in my abdomen, smiling I said, "There are parent conferences this morning. If you don't mind hanging around while I meet with them." Quietly I said, "I would love to have you here." I managed, "I was going to take Rogerthat for a ride. Let's go horseback riding. What do you think?"

"Sounds like a plan. Let me get one trailered, and I'll be over shortly." Then whispered, "Tess, … I love you."

"I love you too, if you were here, I'd say it with a warm kiss." I whispered.

"I had the same idea, see you in a few."

I went out to finish grooming Rogerthat and Butterfly. I whispered in Rogerthat's ear, "Clint is joining us today. I can't wait to introduce you two." He nickered and turned his nose to nuzzle me.

When I went back inside to change, Dinah ran up to me with a big smile. "You and Clint!" She kept hugging me, drawing the attention of everyone.

"Ssshh," I whispered, laughing, and pulling her aside.

"Clint is … I don't know, I've never seen him like this before. You're getting married!"

This caught my breath. It wasn't a question, to which everyone stopped moving. I looked around and told everyone, "Whoa, whoa, she's kidding, really." I gave her a look that communicated, quiet! in facial sign language. I could see Cloris eyeing me suspiciously. I took her upstairs with me while I got dressed.

"Dinah, it's a little premature."

She said, "Is it?"

How much did she know about us? I gave her a questioning look.

"We've known about you and Clint now for a while. He and Jimmy have talked about it."

I looked at her surprised.

"I've never seen my brother act this way around a woman. He loves you Tess," she said warmly, looking into my eyes. "We all know it. And since we all love you, it just makes sense. My sister! I'm so happy!"

Moved almost to speechlessness, "Okay, Dinah, really ..." a love for this young woman filling my heart, I said quietly, "I appreciate the exuberance, but it's a bit early. Let's just table this for now, okay?" I started laughing.

"Oh sure, ... okay, but can I be in the wedding?"

"Don't you have something to do? Like help a teacher or something?"

"Oops, gotta run. Love you!" She yelled as she ran downstairs.

I couldn't move… married? Maddy, I AM open.

Clint arrived and busied himself in the barn. I met with parents and their children. My joy was evident everywhere. I could see that they warmed to my expressions. In all the blessings I was feeling at this moment, I prayed that Safe Harbor offered similar blessings for these families, it seemed that maybe, there was hope for them and their children's futures at Safe Harbor. We had that in mind; it was our stated goal. It occurred to me that we probably should have a mission statement.

"Your future's complete success is our goal"? Cheesy…

The parents left and I found Clint. He was busy in the corral giving the children training on horse psychology. I stood and watched him show them how to get the horses' attention, how to use a crop to get them moving and how to handle horses that were easily spooked. I watched transfixed, I didn't know any of this myself. He saw me and shortly ended the lesson. The horses were saddled and ready for us to go.

Finding my meadow, we rested the horses. We sat down underneath my Bur oak. I remembered when I had sat here alone after the dance, eyes closed, thoughts fixed on his face, on the evening, mind confused and heart aching. And now he sits next to me, arms wrapped around me, holding me close, my head resting on his shoulder. Almost feels surreal.

I looked around at the quiet beauty and up at Clint. He seemed deep in thought.

"What are you thinking?" I asked.

He smiled. His face turned to look down at me, "Hum … I was remembering the first time I saw you and our conversation on the deck." He looked to the meadow ahead. "Honestly," looking again at my face, "I never thought we would get here." His eyes took on a deeper black, the golden flecks shining. "I want a lifetime of this Tess," he said tightening his hold.

A smile crossed my face. "I know. Me too."

Suddenly, our lips met, passionate and ardent. Finally, both breathless, we separated, smiling at one another. We both rested there quietly, my head resting on his chest, absorbing being together.

"Clint," I started, crinkling my brow. There was an area in our past that had bothered me because I didn't have answers. I sat up, "Clint," he raised himself up next to me, looking into my face. I started, "That night when … can you tell me what happened? It's the last piece I need for me to close the book on this and a part of our history I don't know." I watched his reaction. "How did you find me in the cave?"

I could see he wasn't anticipating a conversation along these lines. He looked past me to the tree line, remembering. It took him a long time before he started to talk, not looking at me and sighing heavily.

Turning to me he started, "Patty called hysterical. She was incoherent. I went over immediately, not sure ... " He shook his head, and looked at me with something like pain, "I was aware that this was the night before your wedding, Tess ... " he said as he looked deep into my eyes and back toward the trees ... he paused, then turned to look at me, studying my face. "When I arrived, I found Patty hysterical, unable to talk. I took her outside and made her sit in my truck. I waited until she could calm down. It took some time before I was able to learn what had happened. She told me that you were gone, didn't know where you were and that she thought John and Rosa were dead. I went upstairs to your room first and found you gone, then I checked their rooms and could see that they were dead. I called the police. Immediately I started to search your house, and I discovered Sam had come in through a front window." He stopped for a minute, searching my eyes, not sure how I was taking this news. I could see revisiting this was hard for him, but I didn't stop him. "I did a peripheral check of the grounds then went to stay with Patty. Waiting for the police was hard but I didn't feel I could leave her alone. When they arrived and someone arrived that could assist Patty and check on the children, I left to try and find you." He looked again at me gauging how I was handling this.

I sat quietly, listening, composed.

"I checked the surrounding grounds but didn't find any human tracks, front or back or any tire marks. I left to head up the mountain, thinking the absence of tracks meant that that was where you were taken. I got as far as the side trail that exited to the cabin when I ran into a horse caravan." He looked at me, "There's a company that owns the land next to yours and apparently they've started using the property for employees, team building." He stopped, thinking, "Anyway, the horses tore up the trail. I spoke with the riders and asked if they'd seen anyone. They hadn't. I went to the cave, the one the police had found, but that wasn't the cave where I found you." He stopped for a moment, remembering, "If he'd carried you up this trail, there would have been some sign of disturbance in the foliage. I didn't have a timeline from when this happened to when Patty found them," he continued. "During the days that followed I kept searching for you. It took time hunting the mountains near your house." He looked at me, "I felt that the location of your house was somehow involved, it seemed clear that he was watching your home, which led me to believe he was probably staying somewhere nearby." He looked back at the surrounding trees, "Eventually I found the cave where you were held and Sam was there. There was a fight, and he ran." He looked back at me; I could see the struggle behind his eyes as he studied my face. He sighed deeply, "I took you to the hospital and alerted Lander Police and Chief Blackthorn. I also explained to both about the other bodies I found in the cave, probably the missing teenagers. They initiated a search and finally the canines located the shack where Sam had been living." He looked in my eyes, "That's pretty much everything, Tess." There was a distant look in his eyes.

I leaned closer him and grabbed his hand. I looked in his eyes, "You saved my life, Clint." He put his arms around me and pulled me close. We sat there for some time holding each other and thinking. Neither of us spoke. I thought about what he went through for the first time. My thoughts hadn't gone to Clint after the rescue, I suppose because of John, but this… I looked at him. He had been alone with his love for me and his need to find me, risking everything. Looking at his face, his words that he knew about my wedding plans the night he came, just now struck me, his loss of us, and that he experienced everything all alone. I had had to compartmentalize my feelings for Clint to love John. I put him on a shelf I couldn't allow myself to revisit. Grief struck me. Realizing, he also saw my broken body in the cave, he released my arms from the chains, saw the horror, the teenagers and that he had picked me up and carried me to safety … he had experienced his own horror there in that cave, and then, how long had he been searching to then find he had to stay away, not knowing my situation. Would I heal? Who would tell him? I looked deeper into his face, studying it, my eyes taking in everything, the set of his eyes, his high cheekbones, his proud brow and full lips … realizing how much he had suffered. What were his thoughts when came in answer to Patty's call, knowing it was the night before I was to marry John, still, he came, not knowing the situation. I laid my head on his chest and he kissed my hair. We held each other tighter.

I don't know that the word love reaches the depth of what I feel for him.

Clint and I saw each other as often as we could. He keeps his horse, Reno, stabled here.

I have scheduled time with the children twice a week, a sit down, where we sit and chat about life stuff. I wanted to give them a new foundation. I recalled, when I got older and I would run into problems, I would search for the answers based on what I had been taught. I wanted to give that to them. I also wanted to give them something higher to believe in and trust, grounding. Instill qualities of integrity, justice, and kindness. I introduced Christian concepts and discussed my faith. We would take walks and discover God's world outside. During these times the children would ask questions, and I encouraged them to talk about themselves. Their ages ranged from 4yr olds to 18yr olds and these times, I hoped, would help foster a sense of family, community. It wasn't unusual to see Cloris and Gracey standing nearby, listening. Some of the children live on campus and some are dropped off during the day. We had suites set up for families in crisis. We hired three teachers and Dinah as their helper. Everyone pitches in with the animals.

Chapter Twenty~Nine

One Soul ~ Two Bodies

Finally, the day arrived for Patty and Starks' wedding. I was her maid of honor and Maddy was her bridesmaid. It was a small affair outside at a botanical garden underneath a trellised canopy. Pastor Allen officiated. Stark's groomsman consisted of one of the guys I had first met standing at the bar that evening, so long ago. Several times I caught a look at Clint, who was seated beside Rob and Jimmy. I wanted to see his reaction to the wedding ceremony. I didn't know his customs. I found him deep in thought, intently watching the proceeding. Once he turned to look at me with a warm smile that melted my heart.

The reception was at the new home Stark and Patty had purchased. Before the wedding, her family had been busy decorating the house and yard. White linen, lilies, hors d'oeuvres, champagne, and a fiddler started the festivities, later, a DJ finished the evening, helping all dance into the night. Dancing… It wasn't funny that people kept asking me to dance. During a break in dancing, when I managed to escape to the bathroom, Patty pulled me aside, laughing. She mentioned that some of the ladies that were keeping Clint busy at the champagne table and dancing, were the same ones she knew hadn't been able to turn his head. It didn't help that he was now a celebrity of sorts, everyone talked about him as the local hero. I remember her earlier comments to me about his being the local heartthrob. That comment seemed like a lifetime away. Finally, Clint came to my rescue, or maybe his. He pulled me onto the floor for a slow dance. We danced close, he lowered his head, bending down to kiss my neck. It felt good to have this freedom to love each other publicly. His arrival at my side kept further dancing partners away, for both of us.

Maddy joined me at the champagne table, "I love seeing you finally happy." She searched my eyes. "You look whole Tess. Amazing … could not have seen this after last year's hell. But here you are …" She started to tear up and I grabbed her hands. She has been a sister to me my whole life I realized.

"I am happy Maddy. I know." My eyes found Clint standing talking to Rob. "To publicly love each other, not hiding, him not disappearing. So much has passed between he and I, forged in fire." I looked back at Maddy, "I'm truly happy. Are you going to take credit for this?"

"I know, I think we can all see that, it's pretty obvious how you two feel about each other." Her smile turned thoughtful. "I think I love him too but for obviously different reasons. I know you're safe with him. There's something, I don't quite know the right word, he has a commanding presence, exudes confidence, and looking at the ladies tonight maybe something else." She was a little giddy, "Of course, I'm taking credit for this." She gave me a conspiratorial look and whispered, "I'm already planning your wedding."

"How much champagne have you had!" We were both laughing, definitely champagne. "Do you and Dinah know something? *She* already has us married."

"Well, I'm not giving anything away and I'm not going to jinx this," she said lowering her voice, "but it's going to be beautiful." I was quiet, tears filling my eyes. The idea of this took my breath. My eyes searched the crowd; I found him standing surrounded by admiring ladies. A new look for him. Not the warrior but a celebrity. He was taking it in stride. We both broke out laughing, our laughter was getting attention. Rob and Clint came up in time.

Rob said, looking at Clint, "These two need chaperones?"

Clint smiled and moved towards me.

Rob continued, "So ladies, this is the last dance. How about it?" As he gave Maddy his arm.

Clint's tall frame hovering over mine, as he put his hand in mine and I followed.

"You look happy," he said as he pulled me close, nuzzling my neck.

"I am happy, are you?" I asked warmly.

"There aren't words Tess," he said as he bent down, his lips touching my forehead.

The magic in this wedding was contagious. Champagne and music were fueling festive and joyful emotions. There was laughter and people having fun wherever I looked. It was a beautiful wedding.

I hadn't seen much of Jimmy that evening. Clint pointed him out, sitting at a table in a far corner with a lovely young lady. Smiling.

Dinah caught the bouquet. Jimmy wasn't the only one smiling. Pastor Allen and the young men kept her busy dancing all night.

Patty and Stark rejoined the crowd, said their goodbyes, and headed off to a honeymoon in Maui.

A year passed and Patty was pregnant. Safe Harbor was growing, and we were able to purchase the hundred acres owned by Wellers, Inc. They left their team-building ropes course and their wooden-canvas structures. Readymade for campers and retreats. It felt as though God was opening doors and the forward progress had its own momentum. It seemed to me that things just landed in our lap. There were now five teachers, one of them Dinah, an extension to the classrooms and living quarters, a cook and assistant manager. Cloris first objected to the cook until she found she enjoyed the food and the lessening of responsibilities. She was a storyteller and often she was found with a captive audience, both the children and the parents. She was changing, blossoming.

Another interesting development occurred when several students asked if they could prepare a native meal for a special dinner they were planning for their parents. They asked for cooking assistance from Cloris, which developed into a weekly shared cooking class. The children share native recipes, and Cloris teaches them her favorite recipes along with cooking basics. The once-a-week activity morphed into Gracey joining with art classes and Jimmy, seeing this while visiting one day, offered to contribute music lessons and animal husbandry, including horseback riding lessons. None of it planned.

In the year that passed, my relationship with Clint deepened. Clint continued the awakening John had started. Our private moments were filled with conversations learning about each other, shared quiet moments and warm touches. Any vulnerabilities or shadows remaining, Clint cracked open, often when situations arose where my past stepped out of the shadows. It was the same for Clint. Trust was growing between us. He shared his childhood, his hurt when his father left and his deep love for the one that replaced him. I learned about his marriage and single parenting trials. We were finding a shared purpose, shared space like our souls converging. He doesn't create restrictions, make demands or set up barriers to my forward growth nor I him.

He has come alongside Safe Harbor, stepping in when needed and adding assistance with the children. They follow him when he is around and he has set up a workshop, teaching anyone interested carpentry, mechanics, … tools needed to be self-reliant.

Lord, I know You've done all this. I could not have imagined this a year ago. I don't have words to express how much I love You. I know Safe Harbor; its growth was Your design. Amen

Clint had made arrangements at a favorite restaurant of ours in Lander to celebrate our one-year anniversary. So impressed he remembered. I realized sitting at a table lit by candlelight and wine, Clint is romantic. His eyes shimmered as he looked across the table at me. He wasn't a drinker; the wine was for me. After dinner we went for a drive out onto the reservation to a secluded waterfall. We walked to the waterfall and sat under the stars. Listening to the water tumble and the night sounds, I felt that everything in my life was perfect. Lord, I had this same thought with John, please don't let this disappear.

Clint pulled me onto his lap, both facing the waterwall and he wrapped his arms around me and kissed my hair, his chin resting over me, my head on his chest. The moment was peaceful.

Finally, Clint turned me around to face him. "Tess," he said, looking deep into my eyes, "you know I have loved you, I think since the first time I saw you, your golden hair and blue eyes … later, sitting across the fire that night, watching your contentment and peace." Studying my face he said, "And the dance ... " He took a breath, "When I held you, touching you for the first time, feeling your power, the scent of you and then your embrace when you moved close," his eyes were shining. "I have been yours, maybe even before we met, my soul waiting for you. Tess, I think it's time we were married." I looked in his face at the warmth he felt towards me and the deep love I saw reflected in his eyes, "Tess, *will* you marry me, be my partner in this life?" Looking deep into my eyes, "You are my soul, my heart, my joy. I feel complete, something that is new to me. I promise you that all I have, all I am, belongs to you." His eyes dark, searching mine, moving across my face, waiting ...

His handsome face, transformed with a softness that he reserved only for me ... his proposal made with surprising poetry ... my heart was so full, it rendered me speechless. Looking into this face so full of love for me, sitting there I couldn't imagine life without him. I put my hands on his face, "Yes," I said breathless ... "Yes, Clint I'll marry you. I love you with every part of my being."

His eyes fixed on mine, joy evident, shining; he reached in his pocket for a small box. He handed it to me. Inside was a ring, a diamond surrounded by small sapphire gems. It sparkled in the moonlight, reflecting the stars overhead. Clint put it on my finger. He looked up into my eyes and said, "Tess, this is the beginning of my promise to you, to love you to eternity and to stand before you as your partner and protector. I give you my life, you have my heart."

I was tearfully breathless with the beauty of his poetry and his love, speechless in the overwhelming warmth that flooded inside me. I sat on his lap locked in an embrace that melted us into what I can only describe as a spiritual oneness.

I had long forgotten Sam, but he had left a permanent mark on my body. Doctors told me I wouldn't be able to bear children. I pulled away from his embrace and turned to look into his eyes. "There's something I haven't told you." I wanted him to know this before he committed himself to me. I paused to collect my thoughts. A concerned expression crossing his face. I looked deeply into his eyes, "After what happened, Clint, I won't be able to have children," searching his face for his reaction.

There was sadness in his eyes, I thought sorrow for that loss. He searched my eyes, "Tess, I am sorry, more than words ... that that happened to you. Sorry and angry but you're all I've ever wanted. To tell you the truth, I haven't thought about us having children. I have Oliver, *we* have Oliver," he stopped and looked at me, and I felt warm at this thought, "and that's enough. It doesn't change a thing for me." He leaned down touching his forehead to mine and staring into my eyes. "You're all I want."

Chapter Thirty

A Future with Hope

We told everyone about our commitment. While everyone seemed happy at the news, no one seemed surprised.

Maddy, Patty and Dinah had been at work for months on this, I learned. I asked if they would permit me to choose the invitations, flowers, and dress. "I don't want to put a damper on your wedding plans; would that be too much of an inconvenience?" We were on a conference call. They needed some advice and wanted to update me on my wedding. At least they were calling it my wedding.

Maddy said, "Now there's no reason to get ugly, Tess. Ladies, she doesn't mean anything by this remark, she just gets testy like this sometimes. She just needs chocolate."

Patty chimed in, "Of course honey, you can pick out your dress."

I said, "What about the flowers and invitations?"

There was silence. Maddy spoke, "Well, I think we can all agree to this provided you run your choices through the wedding committee."

I hear three voices giggling and assenting to this. "Maybe I need a new set of friends." By now everyone was laughing.

"Okay, Tess, Dinah and I will meet you in Lander and run by a few shops. Everyone agreed?"

"Well, I already have a dress, flowers and invitations in mind. Let me email my selections to the committee to view them. Do you have your own webpage?" being facetious. "Seriously, I would like to hear what you all think. So how about lunch in Lander? And we can catch up on how the plans are going. Okay? And ladies, I do appreciate what you are doing for me, I do. Thank you. Love you guys."

"Ah, we actually do have a webpage and a following. Maybe we could arrange to take a vote on your selections, you know, community involvement. And ... you're welcome. Love you bunches. I'll have to attend via video!"

"I'll set the phone next to me ... Maddy is turning into a comedian. Very funny about the webpage ... It is just funny, right? Oh, by the way, you did get my guest list?"

Patty answered, "Yes, we have them. And we love you too honey. I'll send you the webpage link." They all laughed. "We are very excited about your wedding."

"I wouldn't have guessed."

Jimmy was one of Clints groomsman, along with Nahali, his best friend, and Chuck. Oliver would carry the rings. Maddy was my maid of honor, and Patty, Anna and Dinah rounded out my entourage.

The *day* was fast approaching. One day Clint and I sat in the barn to get away from the noisy clammer. I wanted to talk to him about our vows.

I waited until I had his full attention as we sat on the barn floor, near Rogerthat and Clint's stallion, Reno. Clint was leaning against a pillar, and I was seated next to him.

"So," I started, "there's a romance book in the Bible, the Song of Solomon, and I took a verse or two from that along with scripture about marriage. Can I run these by you?" I pulled out a sheet I had made notes on.

Clint smiled looking at the pages, "Yes, of course. I'd like to hear them."

"It's a three-part vow." Was that a wince?

I began ...

Pastor

Lord put a seal upon each other's heart so that nothing can harm their love for each other.

Love is as strong as death; let their love be strong until death separates them.

Jealousy is cruel and destructive; keep them from this.

A man would give all he has for a great love.

Lord, thank You for being their matchmaker and for the provision of this great love.

You alone have put a wall of love around them, give them peace and bless them all the days of their lives.

You

Tess, I promise to love you, as Christ loved the church and gave her His life. I will love you as my own body. I promise to nourish, protect and cherish you always.

Tess:

Clint, I submit myself to you as my husband. I acknowledge that you are the head of me and our home, even as Christ is the head of the church. I will trust your wisdom and will honor you in everything.

Pastor

In joining yourselves together you both become one flesh, one mind, one heart and one soul.

Since God has joined you together, let no one interfere in your marriage.

"And you took this out of the Bible?"

"Yes, a lot of it's paraphrased. Does it sound corny? I can update or change anything."

I love these scriptures and the meaning behind the words, but he may not, I realized.

I studied his face for disapproval then looked outside the doors of the barn.

Looking back at Clint, his lips were curved in a half smile. "Tess, I think it's perfect, especially the submit part," his eyes smiling.

"Okay ... " giving him a look. I studied the ground for a moment, "There's a concept behind these promises, to promote harmony in marriage." Taking a deep breath, I looked back at Clint explaining, "If you think about an army, there's one general that has the responsibility of making the final call, otherwise there's chaos, and that is the responsibility God gives to the husband, you." I looked at him and winked. "But, before you get the wrong idea, the husband is *required* to love his wife more than himself, he puts her interests first, he doesn't diminish her by not consulting with her, her opinions carry a lot of weight."

He was listening. "Tess, in our culture, we have always respected our wives as our partners. We know they are the backbone of our community."

I always marvel at his wisdom and sat quietly watching him, admiring him.

I continued, "Oddly, God doesn't require the woman to love her husband, God asks her to respect and honor him." I watched Clint's reaction. I could see he was taking this idea in. Will my deep faith scare him away? This discussion was resonating with me also; I realized that I wanted there to be understanding between us. "There's a reason for this, there is an elemental need in the male for respect, admiration while the woman needs to be loved. When the woman respects and admires her husband, it grows his love for her. It's like a harmonious circle. He loves her, she believes in him, this promotes oneness."

His hand touched my face, and I got the smile he reserves for me, the one that arrests my heart.

I looked down, "There's something we haven't talked much about," I said studying him "... my faith. I need to tell you what happened to me in the cave. If, after you hear this, and you digest this mini sermon, if you want to run, I'll get it." I was sincere. So, I told Clint about my death experience.

Neither of us spoke for a while. Things had turned heavy.

"I guess it's my turn." Clint had a serious look on his face. It took him awhile before speaking. "Your recovery…" He searched my eyes. "It surprised me that there was little residual that showed of the horror I know you experienced. I know that horror, Tess, and what happened to you, I was there, I saw it." He paused studying me. "I know about horror and PTSD firsthand and I'm grateful for your spiritual experience. And I believe you when you tell me this because, listening to this, I realize that *some kind* of internal healing had to have occurred, you were broken, I could see that, and whatever that was, it helped us to be together. Supernatural ... I have no quarrel with that. That event would have destroyed most and here you sit, from what I can see, a whole woman." He said, his eyes shining, warm and gentle. "Tess, I'm not scared away."

A faint smile crossed his lips. "When my mother met you at the festival," he said looking at me, "she said she knew then who you would be to me. The other part of my soul. They call her Hono Cebisee which means Walks in the Sky. She sees things. When she told me this, I was reminded of the first time I saw you, something in me had changed. I couldn't not love you. But there was a war in me. I was a leader in the tribe and had been a strong voice to keep marriage within the tribe. My mother called it pride ... " He looked away. "Maybe it was, an example to others that I would sacrifice my happiness ... but," he turned to look at me. "Those issues are resolved in me. I know who you are *to* me. And I think I know you. I know that your faith is part of what makes you amazing. It isn't a reason to run." He looked out the barn door into the yard and back at my face, "I've had time to get to know you, you Tess, *and* your faith. What I see makes me love you more, not less. I don't need to be *required* to love you, that's easy. And I have no intention of running. I've lost you twice, once because I pushed you away and the second, because of John. There won't be a third."

Then it occurred to me, "Do you have an Arapaho name?"

He smiled, "Nee Cee Nii Scih, it means lone chief," chuckling.

"Meaning, you are *my* lone chief …" I said with a warm smile.

He looked down at the paper. "Let me reread it," he said gently. I watched his response. He looked up and stared again at the open door. "Funny, I hadn't thought about marriage in these terms. I like it," he said turning to look at me. "I think that explains how I feel about you, I want to take care of you. I don't know if what we have is supernatural, but I know it's deep and I know that you are the other part of me. I like the message in the vows. I don't think it's corny and don't change a thing." He leaned over and pulled me to him. "I love you Tess, every bit of you." I felt his warm lips on mine.

The time came when I felt I needed to share the stream with Clint. It was the one thing I had held back and if our marriage was a complete union, no secrets, no hidden chambers in my heart then Clint needed entrance and access to all of it. It felt comfortable, this decision. I wasn't replacing or removing John, I was adding Clint.

I took Clint's hand as I led him to the stream.

"So, this is the stream." Clint looked around and stood still, quiet. I watched him. After several minutes he turned to look over at me. He took my hands in his. As he looked at our hands, I could tell he was thinking about something. Finally, he looked up at me, staring into my eyes, "Tess, I love you with all my heart. There was a time when I didn't think it was possible that we'd be together. Many nights I laid in bed and wondered what life with you would be like. And here we are. There never was a time when you weren't close to my thoughts." He looked gently at me, "We haven't talked about John, and I don't want to. But I knew he was in your life and honestly, because he seemed right for you, I knew we would never be together." He pulled me into a tight hug and held me for a long while. I could tell he needed to share this.

When he released me, he walked around the stream, grabbing my hand as he helped me across the stream. When we crossed back over, he stood quiet. Kneeling, he reached into the stream, cupping water into each hand; then raising them above his head, he closed his eyes, quiet, as if in prayer. After several minutes he let the water spill back into the stream. His mood was reverent. Native Americans have a connection to the earth that is deep. He stood and turned to me, "I love it here, Tess."

We sat by the stream, peaceful, taking in the surrounding beauty.

Clint sat quietly, lost in thought. Turning to me he shared, "Our tribes' ancient ceremonies and customs are rooted in our spiritual and reverential connection to the earth," he said as he turned, staring into the woods. "We honor many stages and events in our lives in our ceremonies, births, rites of passage, weddings, celebrations of life itself." He looked over at me, his eyes shining. I could see a deep well of pride and emotion, love for his people in his black eyes. "Our dances express cohesion, identity and are living prayers. We have the Ghost Dance which embodies not only deep spiritual aspects but was also a prayer for a return to our old ways; the Sun Dance is a dance of endurance for renewal, sacrifice and prayer." He paused, "Our dances connect the tribe, strengthening a tribal communal bond. The word animal is not in our vocabulary," he said, "we have always seen them as sisters and brothers, family."

He sat quietly for a time. I studied his profile, his straight posture, his masculine command and power softened by his love of his tribe and the land. I sat listening to his deep voice, sharing his reverence with me for his connection to the land. He spoke of their belief that their ancestors are alive in the stars, watchful of the tribe, the rich beauty and honor in their tribal customs, a collective communion and custodial commitment as stewards of nature. My Christianity shares so much in common with his spiritual understanding.

We headed back to the house, hand in hand, both with a sense of hushed reverence. His respect for the land added reverence to the atmosphere around the stream. He stopped me before we passed the barn. "Something else I wanted to tell you." He stood standing in front of me. "I have been to see Pastor Allen. This coming Sunday he will baptize me." He looked deep into my startled eyes. "We cannot be in step if we live with different values and beliefs. So, I decided to speak with Pastor Allen, just to understand things. I have decided on the path of Christ as the one true path." There was truth in his eyes and a gentle smile on his lips as I studied him. Tears flowed in a joyful embrace.

Lord, thank you' I whispered.

Maddy and Rob, Anna and Chuck flew in. The night before our wedding we all shared an intimate dinner in the small dining room. Clint's family, Mrs. Pierre, Oliver, Joseph and Tamara and her husband, Jackson, Jimmy and Dinah, Patty and Stark, and Timmy, all joined us.

As the joyful festivities wound down and Clint's family left, I turned to go upstairs. I froze. I had been here before. Clint came up behind me and pulled my back into his strong frame, wrapping me in his arms. "You are safe. I won't let anything happen to you," he whispered.

The others stood nearby, understanding the moment.

"We have prepared for this." Maddy said quietly, "We're having a sleepover of sorts and ... " she looked at me, "everyone is staying on premises, with the promise, eh hem ... no one will peek at the ladies." She said this softly. She winked at Clint and turned to me, "You won't be alone tonight, honey."

I heard Patty sobbing. Stark grabbed her comforting her. She looked up, looking at Clint, "I have never thanked you for ... really everything. Your strength and support after ..."

Clint nodded, helping her.

The ceremony was set for six o'clock. It was at Safe Harbor, on the property. We wanted the children to attend before it got too late. The girls had arranged for a make-up artist to come and assist us. Patty, Maddy, Anna and Dinah were excitedly chatting as they busied themselves with helping me. I wasn't allowed out of my room. Breakfast and mimosas were brought in, and we spent the morning hours sitting cross-legged on the floor eating and laughing. Later we took short naps and around midafternoon the busyness resumed. During my time alone I thought about many things. I was beyond grateful and happy. I knew Who to thank. I love You Lord. I want to honor You in my marriage. When the girls came in, they were fully dressed. Their glow added to their beauty. They helped me get dressed. The five of us stood next to the full-length mirror. There wasn't a dry eye amongst us. As time for the ceremony approached, they all left.

There was a quiet knock on my door.

"It's open."

Mrs. Pierre, Clint's mother, entered. Her eyes took in my appearance; I could see her repressing tears. She quietly walked over to me, looking into my face. "Tess, there is much I have wished to say to you," she paused. Studying me, "You've healed my son's heart after losing Nina. It changed him, he shut down." She searched my eyes. "And then Jimmy and Dinah … the car crash and Sam." Her eyes showed pain, and there was distance in them, remembering. A mother's pain. She took a deep breath,

"When I saw you at the festival, I had a vision of who you would be, not only to my son, but my family." Her smile was warm and she approached me, giving me a deep hug. She stepped back, her hands still holding my arms, looking into my face.

We were both teary-eyed.

When she stepped back, I noticed she held a package, and she handed it to me.

I opened it. It was an ornate box covered in leather with intricate beading, symbols I knew represented their culture. I opened the box. Inside was a necklace. It was a polished oval turquoise stone embedded in silver, ringed by small turquoise and silver beads. The stone pendant was held by a string of while shells, miniature pearls and silver beads. It was beautiful.

"This necklace is ancient, passed down generations. It is intended for the firstborn son's wife. Nina had it until she passed. It is yours now." She clasped my hands, her eyes misty, "Wear it as a symbol of hope and protection daughter."

She put the necklace on me and together we stared at my reflection in the mirror. Remembering 'something old, something new, something borrowed, something blue … the turquoise.

I started to cry.

"Now now, you'll spoil your make-up," she said laughing and then leaned in for a tight hug.

"Thank you, Mrs. Pierre," I said, moved by this gift, understanding the importance of what it represented, the magnitude of the gesture.

"I'll see you downstairs," she said warmly as she left.

Lord … so many reasons to be grateful, and I am.

Shortly after she left, Cloris came in, "Oh My! Tess, you are beautiful!"

"Yeah?" I looked back in the mirror. Was that me?

"I won't spoil things, but you should know those ladies were up late and decorated the yard. I can't wait for you to see what they've done. Everything is ready. The children are so excited, everyone is. Rob is waiting in the hallway to escort you."

"Thank you, Cloris. Tell him I'll be right out." I stood still, I needed to find some peace, my heart was beating so hard, I thought everyone would hear it. I collected my senses and met Rob in the hallway.

"Tess! Holy cow. Wait till Clint sees you. You look beautiful."

That helped, "Thank you, Rob. I'm pretty nervous so I may lean on you pretty heavily. Don't let me trip or fall down!"

"Honey, you look like an angel. I think you will float across the yard so no worry on that end."

When I stepped into the backyard, I didn't recognize it. Everywhere there was magic. They had transformed the yard into a spring garden. It was impressive! How had they managed this? Trellis' were everywhere, covered in roses and calla lilies, silk curtains and ribbons were draped and flowing on a gentle breeze that carried the scent of the flowers. White lights were in all the trees. It reminded me of Lothlorien in Lord of the Rings. The caterers were in the reception area, which was covered by a tall canopy, and tables draped with linen and my favorite flowers, canna lilies and orchids. Candles decorated the tables. The fiddler from Patty's wedding was playing softly in the background. Then I saw him, Clint standing in front, under a canopy, Pastor Allen standing to his right, his best friend Nahali, Jimmy, Joseph, Jackson and Chuck to his left. My knees buckled.

Rob sensing this whispered, "You'll be fine, Tess," taking a firmer grip on my arm.

The girls and Oliver led the procession. Rob and I followed. I couldn't look at Clint, I was busy concentrating on staying upright.

As I neared Pastor Allen, my eyes finally caught Clint's. He was dressed in a white tux, his tall, proud posture, his copper skin and raven hair, the beautiful strong features in his face, so handsome. His black eyes were shining as he watched me. Rob kissed me on the cheek and put my hand in his. The look in his eyes as he took my hand … Before Pastor Allen started, he allowed us a moment to face each other before we turned to him.

"I think we are all here for an occasion we have *all* been hoping and waiting for, Clint and Tess's wedding. And all I can say is 'it's about time!'" I heard cheering. Pastor Allen continued, "They have prepared their own vows."

With that introduction, Pastor Allen started the vows as Clint, and I turned to face one another. He noticed the necklace and looked into my eyes, the gold flecks in his shining. We recited our vows slowly with eyes locked on one another. Pastor Allen concluded the ceremonial vows, saying, "I now pronounce you husband and wife. Clint, you may kiss Tess." 'Sealed with a kiss' meant something new to me.

We turned to face everyone, and Pastor Allen announced, "I present to you Mr. and Mrs. Clint Pierre."

The reception was a fun blur. Happy chatter, music, good food, laughter and yes, dancing. There was a local band playing and Jimmy and Timmy had prepared a solo. The reception went on well past midnight. And Dinah caught the bouquet …

During our slow dance Clint whispered, "Tess… you are incredibly beautiful." I looked up into his face, into his eyes, and warmth flooded my entire being. As the evening waned, Clint took my hand and led me into the house. Everyone stopped and clapped. We heard loud expressions of their joy for us as we turned to them and waved our goodbyes. I was too emotional to speak.

We planned to honeymoon in Scotland~Ireland, I wanted to see castles and the roaring North Atlantic, but our first marital night was going to be here. I went inside to change as the crowd started to leave. Clint knocked on the door. Laughing, I opened the door. "You realize you live here now, right!" Clint stepped inside, he had changed. Closing the door, he picked me up and carried me to our bed. Our kisses were sweet and passionate. Suddenly, Clint stopped and propped himself up on his elbows. "I have something I want to show you." With that he got up, pulled me up and took my hand leading me downstairs. The house was quiet now and quietly he led me out the back door, past the barn, to our stream.

He had set up a bedroom with down blankets, pillows, lights, and candles, covered by another canopy. He opened a bottle of champagne, staring into my eyes, "To my Tess, my little bird, I will love you forever, that's a promise," he said as he stood looking down at me and studying my face ... my body.

"In my culture we also have a wedding ceremony, and I want to honor that and blend our cultures. We speak words to each other from our heart, alone, in private." Clint stood me in front of him grabbing both my hands.

"Tess," he started, taking in my face and speaking into my eyes.

"I pledge my strength to your protection,

My knowledge to your growth,

My heart to your happiness,

Where you walk, I will walk beside you,

What you face, we will face together,

Until the last sunset of my life, I am yours."

I looked down at our hands and then up into his face. I composed myself, reflecting on his pledge. I thought about his words and what they meant.

"Clint, I promise to love you, always.

I promise my strength to your support,

My knowledge to our shared wisdom,

My heart to your keeping,

Your people are my people, as mine are yours,

Your path is my path,

Until the last sunset of my life, I am yours."

Clint produced a circlet of twined horsehair from Reno and Rogerthat. He placed this circlet binding both our wrists and said an invocation over us as he looked toward heaven, "From this moment, our path is a shared journey, we are one spirit in two bodies. Lord, we ask a lifetime of blessings on our coupling."

I said "Amen."

He sealed this with a deep kiss.

He untied our wrists and took my hand, leading me to the stream where he had placed cloths, and towels. He turned to gaze at my face, then my body. With a touch so gentle, it felt like a breeze, he removed my clothes and stood me in front of him, surveying my body, "You are beautiful Tess," he breathed. At his words, standing naked before him, a tingle enveloped my entire body. While watching me intently, he undressed himself. He was magnificent, emanating power and beauty that took my breath. Taking my hand, he led me into the stream. Dipping the cloths into the water, he bathed my entire body, his gaze often returning to my face. He then bathed himself. When he had finished, he dried us both with soft towels. Picking me up, he carried me to the down bedding, under the canopy.

Laying down beside me, he moved hovering over my body. I saw in his eyes his love, his hunger, as he moved, his whole body touching mine. Shivering under the heat of him, smelling his scent; we were face to face. Our eyes met, and he kissed them, his eyes moving to my lips. His kisses were tender at first, our passion growing as he pressed harder into my lips, tasting each other. His hands caressing me. My body responding, awed by his passionate yet gentle touches, his lips and touches exploring my entire body. Finally able to surrender to him completely; my body was experiencing a revelation of emotions and responses I had never felt before. In our interludes, we laid beside one another, caressing and watching each other, smiling, naked before God. The night air was cool and there was a hushed silence in the woods tonight as though all things shared in our joy. My word, *sublime.*

I woke up in my bed. Immediately I sat up, looking for Clint. Sensing my thoughts, Clint reached his arm over to me and pulled me to him. "Good morning, my little bird, I'm still here," he smiled warmly. I climbed into his arms. No one disturbed us.

We left that day for our honeymoon in Scotland/Ireland. It was filled with love making and fun. We toured castles, ancient sites, walked through cobblestone villages, enjoying the local pubs and cuisine. We sat on stone walls watching romantic sunsets.

On our last day we climbed to the top of the cliffs overlooking the raging North Atlantic. A storm was threatening and we stood gazing at the ocean, watching as turbulent waves pounded violently, pummeling the cliffs with powerful waves. Spray assaulted the rocks and cliffs below us causing a heavy salty mist to race up the cliffs, assailing our skin like sprayed pellets.

Days earlier we had made this same climb on a calm sunny day, where rippling white caps moved along the tops of gentle waves, the sun shining a path towards the cliffs, completely opposite to the raging view before us.

Clint wrapped me in his arms as we stood watching the turbulence in the darkening sky, the whipped fury of the ocean. It seemed like a fitting expression ending our honeymoon, a fitting reminder and description of the last two years. I knew there would be future seasons of rest and peace and seasons of great turmoil. It's the cycle of life.

We returned home prepared to face it together.

Sometimes it's hard to see God in every detail of my life. He doesn't promise bad, or even horrific things won't happen; He promises to be with me through them. With all that *had* happened, I knew that God had been with me throughout every single moment. I was never alone, and He fulfilled His words; "For I know the plans I think towards you, says the Lord, thoughts of peace and not of evil, to give you a future and a hope."

About the Author

Kari DuMouchel Parker writes from the "trenches of life," where faith meets the reality of survival and redemption. Her own life experiences come alive in the voice of Tess who answers a "compelling calling" that has led her to the rugged beauty of the West where she builds a safe harbor for others. Her avid outdoorswoman brings emotional texture to the quiet of the wilderness where Tess finds the presence of God. She uses her story to prove that no matter how deep the fire, hope is always ahead.